The Fighting Essex Soldier

Brass of Sir John de la Pole and his wife Joan de Cobham. The couple are portrayed holding hands, a feature found between *c*.1380 and *c*.1430; most of the marginal inscription has been lost. John was descended from the elder branch of the de la Pole family and was an active soldier in the Hundred Years War after 1369, serving in Aquitaine under the earl of Pembroke and in Brittany under Thomas of Woodstock and John of Gaunt. He died in 1380 and Joan about 1385. They were buried in Chrishall church, which Margaret Peverel, John's mother, and John himself rebuilt in the early Perpendicular Gothic style.

The Fighting Essex Soldier

Recruitment, war and society
in the fourteenth century

Edited by
Christopher Thornton, Jennifer Ward and Neil Wiffen

Essex Publications
an imprint of
University of Hertfordshire Press

First published in Great Britain in 2017 by
Essex Publications
an imprint of
University of Hertfordshire Press
College Lane
Hatfield
Hertfordshire
AL10 9AB

British Library Cataloguing in Publication Data
A catalogue record for this book is available from the British Library

ISBN 978-1-909291-88-1

Design by Arthouse Publishing Solutions Ltd
Printed in Great Britain by Hobbs The Printers Ltd., Totton, UK

Publication Grants

Publication has been made possible by generous grants from
The Friends of Historic Essex and *Essex Journal*

The conference from which this publication originates was generously
supported by the Essex Record Office

ESSEX RECORD OFFICE

Contents

Figures

Tables

Abbreviations

BL   British Library
CCR   *Calendar of Close Rolls*
CFR   *Calendar of Fine Rolls*
CIPM   *Calendar of Inquisitions post Mortem*
CPR   *Calendar of Patent Rolls*
ERO   Essex Record Office
PROME C. Given-Wilson (ed.), *The Parliament Rolls of Medieval England,*
     1275–1504, 16 vols (Woodbridge, 2005)
TNA   The National Archives
VCH   *Victoria County History*

Preface and acknowledgements

This book is the result of the successful Essex Record Office (ERO) conference, *The Fighting Essex Soldier: War Recruitment and Remembrance in the Fourteenth Century*, which was held on 8 March 2014 in Chelmsford. That conference was inspired by Anne Curry and Michael Hughes' *Arms, Armies and Fortifications in the Hundred Years War* (Boydell, 1994). Discussing with Gloria Harris various aspects of her research on Hugh de Badewe kept my interest in the Hundred Years War alive and this was furthered when in 2010, as Hon. Editor of the *Essex Journal*, I was in a position to commission an article from David Simpkin on his research (2011, reproduced in this volume). Following on from this and talking to Jennifer Ward about possible fourteenth-century-related projects, I then suggested to Chris Thornton (Essex *VCH*) and Hannah Salisbury (ERO), with Jenny's backing, the possibility of the ERO hosting a conference similar in style to that which culminated in *Arms, Armies and Fortifications*. With their support, initial approaches were made to various historians in 2012-13 and once a draft list of speakers and papers were confirmed detailed planning for the day of the conference could begin. Without the generous support of ERO in general, the conference would not have proceeded. The enthusiasm and dedication of Hannah Salisbury, in particular, to ensuring a well-received and successful conference cannot be overstated and those of us who attended the conference were well rewarded. To echo Curry and Hughes' introduction, *The Fighting Essex Soldier* was 'aimed … at pursuing a wide range of topics in a lively yet informative way'. I think all who attended the conference would agree that this was successfully achieved. This book, then, is a wonderful record of the papers that were given at the conference as well as a valuable addition to the historiography of Essex and one of which I am immensely proud to have played some small part in bringing about.

The publisher, editors and authors are grateful to the following for their kind permission to reproduce illustrations: H. Martin Stuchfield for the Frontispiece and Figures 2.1 and 2.3; the Essex Record Office for the Cover, Figures 1.2(a), 1.3 and 4.1; the National Archives for Figures 3.2 and 6.2; the British Library for Figure 1.4; *Essex Journal* for Figure 6.3; J. Ward & Saffron Walden Historical Society for Figure 3.1; H. Eiden for Figures 7.1, 7.2, 7.3 and 7.4; H. Salisbury for the Preface photograph; and N. Wiffen for Figure 1.2(b).

Presenters at the Essex Record Office conference, *The Fighting Essex Soldier:
War Recruitment and Remembrance in the Fourteenth Century, 2014*
(l–r) Chris Thornton, Herbert Eiden, Craig Lambert, Gloria Harris, David Simpkin,
Jennifer Ward, Sam Gibbs, Martin Stuchfield, Neil Wiffen

Figure 2.2 is taken from J. Foster, *Some Feudal Coats of Arms and Others*
(London, 1902). Figures 1.1 and 6.1 were drawn by Cath D'alton and Figures
7.1, 7.2, 7.3 and 7.4 by M. Grün, T. Jarmer and Cath D'alton. We are grateful to
them for their cartographic expertise.

Neil Wiffen
November 2016

Chapter 1

Introduction: crown, county and locality

Christopher Thornton and Jennifer Ward

Crown and nobility

The successes of Edward III in France stand in strong contrast to the royal failures and baronial reluctance to serve overseas characteristic of the thirteenth century. John's loss of Normandy in 1204 followed by his failure to hold Anjou, Maine and Poitou resulted not only in the decline of his prestige but in the confiscation by Philip Augustus of France of the Norman estates of a number of Anglo-Norman barons. At a time when wealth was derived from land, this entailed a drop in income in a period when England was suffering from high inflation. Although John attempted to recover his continental lands, Philip Augustus' victory at Bouvines in 1214 sealed their loss and led directly to baronial rebellion and Magna Carta.[1] Henry III's expeditions to France – to Brittany in 1230 and to Poitou in 1242 – achieved nothing. Moreover, his great council of barons and churchmen refused to consent to the levying of a tax to finance either expedition. In 1259 Henry III concluded the Treaty of Paris with Louis IX of France, giving up his claims to Normandy, Anjou and Maine and to Poitou. He retained Gascony as Louis IX's vassal, performing homage and fealty to him, and in the years that followed the problems inherent in this relationship multiplied, resulting in 1337 in the Hundred Years War.

At the same time, however, significant developments were taking place in England which were to be crucial for Edward III's victories. England was one of the few kingdoms of western Europe which had a national system of taxation, based from the late twelfth century on the levy of a fraction of the value of a man's movable goods. John had raised a tax of one-thirteenth in 1207, which yielded the immense sum of nearly £60,000; this was said to have been granted by the common counsel and consent of the king's council, whose members, however, may have been forced to agree to the king's demand. The king's right to levy such taxes was regulated in 1215 by Magna Carta, c. 12 and 14.[2] No aid was to be levied unless by the common counsel of the kingdom, except for the aids to ransom the king's person, knight his eldest son and marry his eldest daughter once. To obtain common counsel, the archbishops, bishops, abbots, earls and barons were to be summoned to a definite place on a specific date; 40 days' notice was to be given and the business to be discussed was to be stated in the summons. The aid, once it had received the great council's consent, took the form of a tax on movable goods, a specific fraction being agreed to. The great council under Henry III did not always give its consent, as in 1242, when it wanted the king to wait until his truce with the king of France had expired.[3] The council gave its consent on behalf of the community of the realm, binding the lower social groups as well as themselves. The basis of consent was broadened when knights and burgesses were summoned to parliament by Simon de Montfort in 1265 and by Edward I.

After the Norman Conquest both barons and churchmen, as tenants-in-chief of the crown, owed military service to the king; they were expected to produce their *servitium debitum* (service due), namely a fixed number of knights to fight in the royal army for 40 days. By the early thirteenth century there is evidence of reluctance to fight overseas. The 'Unknown Charter' of Liberties, probably drawn up early in 1215, limited military service to Normandy and Brittany, but Magna Carta c. 16 was very vague: 'No one shall be forced to do more service for a knight's fee … than is due from it.'[4] This was not the only problem; inflation made military service more expensive and, from the king's point of view, 40 days was too short a time to conduct a successful overseas campaign. Barons accompanied Henry III on his French expeditions, but took a smaller contingent of knights, described as their quotas, and this continued under Edward I and Edward II. However, although Edward I conquered Wales and was partially successful in Scotland, he encountered resistance to his call for a French expedition in 1297. Churchmen and barons protested about excessive taxation and infringements of Magna Carta, and pointed out that they did not owe service in Flanders, where the king was planning to campaign.[5] This obstacle was overcome only by Edward III after 1340.

In the long run thirteenth-century social change helped to solve the problems over military service. The Norman settlement had seen William the Conqueror granting lands to his followers in return for their military service. The Norman lords had similarly granted lands to their knights in return for service in his military contingent. Over time, as these knights were succeeded by their sons and grandsons and holdings were divided and passed to other families, the personal bond between lord and vassal disappeared. By the thirteenth century some lords were having difficulty in keeping track of their tenants and knights were increasingly used by the king in local government.[6] Bastard feudalism, where the relationship between lord and retainer was based on a money-fee

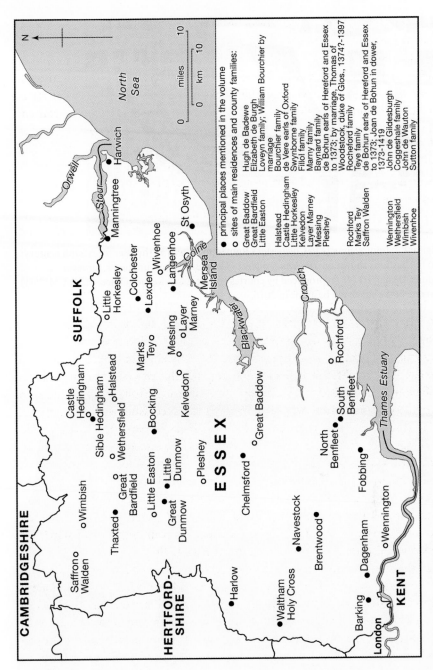

Figure 1.1. Fourteenth-century Essex.

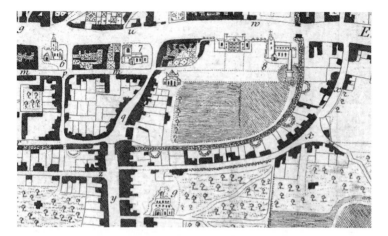

Figure 1.2. Improvements to Colchester's Roman town wall in the later fourteenth century: (a) the bastions shown on *The Ichnography of Colchester*, by an unknown surveyor [James Deane] *c.*1748 (reproduced by courtesy of the Essex Record Office, MAP/CM/25/1); (b) one of the surviving bastions in 2016.

rather than on land, ensured that the lord still had a personal following; such relationships were often short-term and obviated the problems of a permanent tie. The use of retainers, which was growing in the mid-thirteenth century and was used to advantage in Edward I's armies, was to be developed much further during the Hundred Years War.

The physical defences of Essex also largely relied on a partnership between the crown and the nobility. The county had about 25 early medieval castles, built to provide the Norman nobility with security against internal and external threats (Figure 1.1). Some of them, such as Pleshey and Saffron Walden, played a role during the events of the Anarchy in the mid-twelfth century, and others in the tumultuous reign of King John, when, during 1215–16, Colchester, Hedingham and Pleshey castles were all besieged or seized by either royalist forces, the barons' party or their French allies under Prince Louis (later Louis VIII).[7] However, by the Hundred Years War most of the greater Essex castles, such as Castle Hedingham, belonging to the de Vere family, earls of Oxford, and Pleshey, belonging to the de Bohun family, earls of Hereford and Essex, were perhaps less strategically important because of their inland location (albeit still significant as residences and centres of estate management and local government). Increasingly, the possibility of French seaborne raids, like the ones that were to cause devastation along the south coast, influenced a shift in emphasis that saw new royal fortifications on the Thames estuary and collaboration with urban centres and settlements under more direct threat.[8]

The Norman castle at Colchester, sited within the town walls and overlooking the river Colne, had originally been built to defend the strategically important town against Danish attack in the late eleventh century. It changed hands several times in the troubled reign of John, experiencing occupation by French forces in 1215–16, and was probably still regarded as militarily significant. It was certainly still being maintained by the crown in the early fourteenth century, and was fortified and garrisoned in 1307–08 and again in 1321–4, but by the second half of that century appears to have been paid less attention.[9] Colchester's town walls, Roman in origin but repeatedly repaired, were also maintained, for in 1312 the borough levied a 'tallage' on the whole community to repair the walls and gates. North Gate, Head Gate and South Gate were perhaps rebuilt about this time. However, in parallel with the castle the defences were apparently allowed to lapse later in the century, perhaps as the result of overconfidence after English victories; parts of the town ditch were built upon and additional problems were caused by properties adjoining the wall or parts of the wall being robbed for the stonework.[10]

Changing circumstances towards the end of the century, however, stimulated the Colchester borough authorities to carry out extensive repairs between 1381 and c.1413, including the rebuilding of part of a collapsed section of the south

Figure 1.3. Hadleigh Castle, rebuilt by Edward III c.1359–70, occupies a commanding position overlooking the Thames estuary (The north view of Hadleigh Castle …, drawn engraved and published by Samuel and Nathaniel Buck, 1738; reproduced by courtesy of the Essex Record Office, I/Mp 90/3/1/28).

wall and the addition of round towers or bastions to the south-east corner of the wall between East Gate and the Scheregate postern, of which four survive today (Figure 1.2).[11] The location of these bastions, strengthening the defences facing east and south, suggests that the main threats were perceived to be from enemies disembarking from the Colne at East Mill and advancing towards East Gate; or coming from the Hythe and advancing past St Mary Magdalen's Hospital to assault the south-east walls or South Gate; or coming from Mersea Island up the Mersea Road to attack the southern walls near South Gate. Although the timing of the repairs to Colchester's urban defences may suggest a reaction to the Peasants' Revolt,[12] they may also be seen as a direct response to the decline in English military fortunes in the later fourteenth century and in particular to fears of Franco-Castilian fleets penetrating the Colne estuary.

The change of initiative in the Hundred Years War also highlighted the need to defend the Thames. Hadleigh Castle, located on a naturally defensible spur overlooking the Thames (Figure 1.3), was built by the justiciar Hubert de Burgh in the 1230s at a time when the loss of Normandy meant that the English no longer controlled both sides of the Channel. It had soon after been forfeited to the crown and suffered neglect, as well as damage from landslips, although some further work was undertaken by Edward II. However, the castle was to gain a new lease of life when it was refurbished by Edward III *c.*1359–70 after its strategic value for defending the Thames estuary against French raids was again recognised, although it was also developed as an important royal residence. This work took place in conjunction with the construction of Queenborough Castle and town in the Isle of Sheppey, on the Kent shore opposite. The king spent over £2,000 at Hadleigh, building a new gateway, a high tower and a barbican, other additional towers, a strengthened curtain wall and enhanced residential quarters.[13] However, it is probable that Hadleigh's defences were never tested and they do not appear to have acted as much of a deterrent to the Franco-Castilian fleet in August 1380, when it entered the Thames estuary, pillaged shipping and caused havoc on both the Essex and Kent shores.[14]

In the far north of the county, but still part of the outer Thames estuary, the rapidly developing port of Harwich, at the mouth of the Stour, was also a vulnerable location.[15] Harwich was important to the English naval war effort not only because of its safe harbour, shipping and mariners but also because its position facilitated English naval action in the important theatre of war in Flanders. The pool of Orwell, where English fleets assembled, lay close to Harwich and armies probably embarked for the continent from the town on a number of occasions, one of which may have been when the English invasion fleet sailed for Flanders from the Orwell in June 1340.[16] However, before the great naval victory at Sluys on the Zwin estuary on 24 June 1340 gave the English a mid-century dominance at sea, French naval forces had been raiding

Figure 1.4. Harwich's town walls, initially built sometime after 1338, as depicted on a map dated 1543 (BL, Cotton Augustus I.i).

settlements and shipping on the vulnerable English coastline. The port of Southampton (Hampshire) was sacked on 5 October 1338 and on 24 March in the following year a similar attempt was made on Harwich. Although the town was unwalled the townsmen were able to beat their attackers off, thus avoiding the fate of Hastings, on the Sussex coast, which was looted and burnt on 24 May that year.[17]

The Harwich raid had perhaps been expected for, in the previous year (1338), a grant of murage for five years had been obtained, which gave the town the right to levy tolls on goods coming by land or water 'to their town or to the port of Orwell pertaining to the town' and to spend the proceeds on the construction of town walls. The extent to which the town authorities were able to collect the tolls and for how long remains uncertain, for the grant over the Orwell was revoked after complaints by the Suffolk port of Ipswich. However, in 1352 the townsmen obtained a licence to strengthen and crenellate a stone wall, perhaps suggesting that one had been successfully erected.[18]

By the late 1370s matters would have been even more urgent, as the maritime community would have been fearful of Franco-Castilian raids like the ones that burnt Rye, Hastings and Lewes in the summer of 1377 and devastated much of the Isle of Wight.[19] Harwich obtained further grants of murage in 1378 and 1405 and the walls were apparently accompanied by a 'castle' (a large tower) at the north-east corner of the town, although the second grant seems to indicate that it was not built until the early fifteenth century.[20] Sixteenth-century depictions suggest that this was a substantial tower, rather than what we might think of as a castle, appearing to be similar to the Cow Tower in Norwich. The illustration of 1539 depicts a gun within an embrasure, just as the Cow Tower was designed for artillery. Harwich remained an important naval base in later centuries and its defences were repeatedly upgraded, so that little physical evidence of these medieval fortifications survives; however, depictions from 1539 and 1543 do show, in perspective from the east, Harwich protected by a wall with mural towers and three gates. A plan from the later sixteenth century confirms the presence of several eastern entrances, a defended gate to the south and a combination of common D-shaped and round mural towers on a wall extending around only part of the town. Extensive earthworks were by then protecting the southern entrance, but there was possibly only a ditch on the western side (Figure 1.4).[21]

These physical defences and their garrisons were augmented by the traditional warning system of beacons on higher ground and the raising of local defensive levies organised under keepers of maritime lands and commissioners of array.[22] In emergencies additional forces could also be employed under royal direction. For example, on 1 July 1377, with the Franco-Castilian raids underway, a commission to the constable of Hadleigh Castle ordered him to select Essex men-at-arms and archers for safekeeping the fortress against hostile invasion, and five days later another commission was issued to install a royal garrison at Harwich comprising men-at-arms, hobelars and archers, and to ensure that the local populace was 'suitably armed and arrayed' to resist the king's enemies.[23] On 7 July an ordinance was issued for the safeguard of counties of Kent and Essex, commanding beacons to be set up in pairs along the Thames estuary. The watchmen at the outer beacons of Sheppey (Kent) and Shoebury (Essex) were to light their fires as soon as the enemy's ships were spotted, and to warn the country, by use of horns and shouting, to muster in arms at the river to guard settlements and shipping from harm.[24] It is interesting to note that among the Essex beacons recorded in 1377 was one at Fobbing, a coastal village on the Thames whose inhabitants, accompanied by those of other neighbouring communities, such as Corringham and Stanford-le-Hope, were soon afterwards to play a significant role in the outbreak of the Peasants' Revolt in 1381.[25]

Essex and the Hundred Years War

Demands for men, money and supplies for the war, together with the need for the realm of England to remain well ordered in the absence of the king, led to the development of strong administration by central government and by the leading men of the counties. The importance of the 'home front' is discussed below by Jennifer Ward in 'Essex and the Hundred Years War: taxation, justice and county families'. The policies adopted to secure the war effort were the result of considerable experiment, with parliament providing the forum where the king and his officials could discuss the affairs of the realm with the nobility, leading churchmen and knights and burgesses from the counties.

During the early fourteenth century taxes on movable goods continued to be levied. Each tax was separately assessed by a commission of two or three of the leading men of the county, who appointed four or six local men to assess the tax in each place. This method was abandoned in 1334, when a quota based on the fifteenth and tenth of 1332 was imposed on each village and borough. It was up to each place to decide how to levy the quota, either on landholding or on goods, and whether the poor should contribute to the tax. The amount collected fell during the fourteenth century, particularly after the Black Death, and, with the intensification of the war after 1369, new methods of taxation were tried. The most notorious were the poll taxes of 1377, 1379 and 1380–81, which sparked off the Peasants' Revolt. After 1381 poll taxes were entirely abandoned until the 1980s.

Changes took place in the way military forces were raised. During the first half of the fourteenth century retinue leaders were responsible for raising their force of knights and men-at-arms in accordance with their contract with the king, while county gentry were appointed as commissioners of array to survey able-bodied men of the county aged between 16 and 60 and to choose the best to serve as archers or foot soldiers at the king's wages. By the later fourteenth century these men were chosen by retinue leaders along with the knights and men-at-arms; often mounted archers were employed.

Considerable experimentation took place in the first half of the fourteenth century in terms of the best way to keep law and order and bring criminals to justice. No permanent solution was found until after the Black Death. According to the statute of 1361, county gentry, appointed by the crown and afforced by professional lawyers, were given power as justices of the peace to hear and determine felonies and trespasses, and, apart from a few short periods, they retained this power until the nineteenth century. The justices of the peace were also responsible for enforcing the labour legislation imposed after the Black Death to keep wages at their pre-plague level.[26]

Justices of the peace were chosen from the leading county gentry and often ranked as knights or esquires. They also often served as knights of the shire in parliament; as sheriffs and escheators; and on a variety of commissions. Escheators were responsible for taking lands into the king's hands on the death or forfeiture of a tenant who held directly of the crown. They were men of considerable experience, not only as county justices and administrators but also as landowners well aware of the problems posed by the drastic drop in population as a result of the Black Death. Many enjoyed close relations with the nobility and had fought in France and elsewhere. They often also had contacts with the royal court. The Essex gentry constituted a fluid group in the fourteenth century, with great differences in landholding and wealth. Some families died out in the male line, and daughters took their inheritance by marriage to new, ambitious, upwardly mobile families, often lawyers or London merchants. Despite their responsibilities as justices, they were not necessarily law-abiding, as is shown by the career of Hugh de Badewe.

David Simpkin, in his chapter 'The contribution of the Essex gentry to the wars of Edward I and Edward II', shows how Essex was affected by the changing composition of late thirteenth- and early fourteenth-century armies. With wars in Wales, Scotland and France, there was a marked increase in the number of military campaigns under Edward I. Although the king made some use of the earlier obligations of knight service from the tenants-in-chief of the realm in the Welsh wars of 1277 and 1282, it became more usual for knights and men-at-arms to belong to retinues under the leadership of the nobility, while foot soldiers and archers were recruited on a county basis. Payment of wages by the crown became the usual practice. The need for more knights was met by the royal policy of distraint of knighthood, under which men with £20 or £40 worth of land a year were expected to become knights – a policy which met with varying levels of success.[27]

Simpkin argues that these policies marked a militarisation of English society. The principal noble families in Essex were the de Bohun earls of Hereford and Essex, the de Vere earls of Oxford and the Fitzwalter barons of Woodham Walter and Little Dunmow. All took part in the wars of Edward I and Edward II with their retinues, recruited from their families and estates, together with men attracted to their service by their reputation. The retinue of Earl Humphrey de Bohun (d. 1322) that fought at Bannockburn against the Scots in 1314 included his nephew Henry, who played a dramatic role in the battle, and men from his Welsh lands and his estates in Essex and Middlesex. Essex men included Nicholas d'Engaine and William de Goldingham. Such service may well have broadened the experience and horizons of members of the retinue and brought them into contact with men they would not otherwise have met. The de Bohun retinue remained popular with Essex men in the Hundred Years War. Some men made other choices; according to the government's Gascon rolls, 27 men in 1294 and 1295 were getting ready to serve in Gascony with Sir Robert Fitzwalter. The extent of militarisation in Essex can be seen by the number of campaigns in which individual Essex knights were engaged: Nicholas d'Engaine fought in Gascony in 1294–5 and in Scotland in 1300 and 1303, as well as at Bannockburn in 1314. The Rocheford family can be traced in campaigns between 1296 and 1328.

The militarisation of Essex continued into the reign of Edward III, as Gloria Harris makes clear in her chapter 'Organised crime in fourteenth-century Essex: Hugh de Badewe, Essex soldier and gang member'. Hugh was lord of a small estate in Great Baddow, where the principal landholders were the de Bohun family, earls of Hereford and Essex. As a young man Hugh fought in the Hundred Years War in the retinue of William de Bohun, earl of Northampton, in 1337, 1338 and 1340; he was knighted about 1339. There is no evidence of his fighting in France after 1340; instead, he participated in gang warfare alongside men whom he had presumably met in France, such as John de Vere, earl of Oxford, Bartholomew Burghersh the younger, John Fitzwalter – who became notorious as an Essex criminal – and Robert de Marny, also well known for crime and sharp practice. Hugh was involved in three gang raids: in 1340, when John de Segrave's park at Great Chesterford was attacked; in 1342, when several parks of Earl Humphrey de Bohun were raided; and in 1348, when an attack was mounted on the manor of Wakes Colne, belonging to Thomas Wake of Liddel. Lawlessness was certainly a problem during the king's absences in France during the 1340s, and there may well be a link between violent behaviour on the battlefield and organised crime in England. Other factors possibly included local feuds and family conflicts, rivalries over status and landholding, and the love of hunting and poaching. After the Black Death Hugh settled down to play his part as a local justice, serving, for instance, as a justice of the peace and a knight of the shire in parliament in 1361.

Nobles and knights were better documented under Edward III than were ordinary soldiers, but the availability of the muster rolls of 1369–1453 online has made it possible to discover far more about the archers in a magnate's retinue, as Sam Gibbs reveals in his chapter 'The fighting men of Essex: service relationships and the poll tax in Essex'.[28] The names of the archers were recorded in the muster rolls, and Gibbs focuses on their backgrounds, military careers, peacetime occupations and networks. To do this he makes use of the poll tax returns of 1377 and 1381 alongside the evidence of the muster rolls – the occupational data for Chelmsford, Dunmow and Hinckford hundreds in 1381 being particularly useful.[29] The poll taxes and muster rolls have been combined in a relational database and information taken for archers serving between 1367 and 1391, within ten years of the levy of the poll taxes.[30] Few archers were recruited from their captains' landholdings, and it is likely that they offered their services to captains outside Essex. Some archers probably made military service their career, fighting in Scotland and Ireland as well as France and serving at sea or in garrison duty as well as on campaign. John Maldon of Navestock, for instance, was involved in six campaigns at sea. Archers were recruited from the ranks of the wage labourers and artisans; some have been linked to smiths and to the cloth industry, then rapidly expanding. For a man wanting to see the wider world, desiring higher wages than he could earn at home and seeing visions of plunder and loot, service as an archer must have been attractive.

In order to transport troops, horses and supplies or to bring them home, to defend the ports on the west coast of France, where there were English garrisons, and to fight battles at sea, ships and mariners were essential, and these needs are addressed by Andrew Ayton and Craig Lambert in their chapter 'Shipping the troops and fighting at sea: Essex ports and mariners in England's wars, 1337–89'. It is estimated that transport and naval operations called on over 40,000 mariners and 27,000 'marines' (soldiers at sea). In addition, ships and mariners were needed for coastal defence against French raids and threats of invasion. Since no royal navy existed, the burden of supplying these fell on coastal and estuarine communities.[31] The analysis of the Essex mariner survey of 1372 brings out the pressure that coastal communities were under. It is not clear why Essex was the only county surveyed; possibly it was regarded as a pilot study, never taken further because the fleet under the earl of Pembroke was destroyed by Castilian galleys at the battle of La Rochelle on 22 June 1372.[32]

The Essex survey is incomplete, but provides a valuable picture of coastal communities. It was conducted by the sheriff and constables of the hundreds in two separate inquiries; the king asked for the names of all mariners living in 20 coastal and estuarine vills, mostly in Essex, and in the hundred of Dengie.[33] A total of 452 mariners was returned in the two surveys. The return for Harwich shows that over half of its mariners were at sea at the time of the survey, ten of them serving in the earl of Pembroke's fleet. Ayton and Lambert stress the large number of Essex mariners, many of them in small places. Possibly the government intended to make greater use of the smaller ports in the war effort at a time when the merchants had become a stronger group in the realm, able to exert pressure on the king not to impress shipping in the larger ports, a practice liable to damage a port's trade. Naval operations increased in frequency between 1370 and 1389 and greater numbers of mariners, 'marines', knights and men-at-arms were needed to fight at sea. In the fourteenth century as a whole Colchester and Harwich supplied nearly two-thirds of the Essex ships before 1354, but from 1355 emphasis was put on the smaller ports, especially Fobbing.

Research into the mariners is hampered by problems of documentation, although comparisons are drawn between the mariner survey and the 1377 poll tax. Ayton and Lambert argue that the mariners were recruited from the coastal zone and that some mariners probably belonged to family groups. The intense demand for manpower after 1370, coupled with naval pressure from France and losses of life at sea, put great pressure on coastal communities, and at least some mariners who were also farmers already had grievances over servile obligations. The dangers inherent in royal service may well have added to existing discontent and contributed to the outbreak of revolt in 1381, in which Fobbing was heavily involved. The crown underestimated the effects of its plethora of demands in the wake of the Black Death and subsequent plagues, and restiveness grew as a result of the disabilities stemming from serfdom and the labour legislation. The defeats in the war after 1369 and the imposition of the poll taxes were to these men simply the last straw.

The mounting discontent is emphasised by Herbert Eiden in 'Military aspects of the Peasants' Revolt of 1381'. His analysis also shows the probable effects of the war on the military tactics adopted by both the rebels and the royal army suppressing the revolt. As is well known, the revolt spread rapidly in Essex after its initial outbreak at Brentwood on 30 May. While some rebels continued their destruction in the county, three groups moved to London, the capital of the realm, from the Manningtree area – picking up Chelmsford rebels on the way – from the district around Harlow and from the Thaxted region, joining up with rebels from Hertfordshire. They arrived at Mile End on 12 June, the same day as the Kent rebels reached Blackheath. All this suggests careful advance planning by the rebels of the sort expected from military commanders. It is significant that the archers discussed by Sam Gibbs had experience of military discipline and tactics and came from the same social groups as the rebellious peasants, labourers and artisans. The same would apply to the mariners discussed by Ayton and Lambert, and, as they point out, places such as Fobbing had grievances over the burdens of the war and made their protest at Brentwood on 30 May. In suppressing the revolt Thomas of Woodstock may have had soldiers with him who had fought on his Brittany campaign.[34] Eiden argues for the victory over the rebels being won at Rettendon, rather than Billericay; this was followed by the judicial prosecution of the rebels.

The war's impact upon localities: St Osyth, Barking, Great Bardfield

In the fourteenth century all social groups were involved with the wars, either as fighters or on the 'home front'. This involvement has to be set against the drastic fall in the population of Essex by as much as a half owing to the Black Death and subsequent outbreaks of plague. All towns and villages were affected by the royal demands for money and men, but it is only when we look at particular communities that we can see whether the crown was making extra demands on lords, peasants and townsmen. Further questions arise. Did towns and villages largely continue with their normal routines? Were there other problems that seemed more pressing to the local community than the demands of war? What was the effect of French raids on the coast or the passage of an English army through the county? Did plague and the revolt of 1381 cause more disruption than the war? How much did peasants and townsmen know about the war?

Much more research is needed to assess the impact that the war had on individual towns and villages, in the form of a trawl through royal and local records both online and in the National Archives, major repositories and local record offices. Royal letters had occasion to mention many places, and their calendars (summaries) are available in English.[35] Taxation rolls, lists of retinues and ship returns for England are available in the National Archives and some can be accessed online. Many of these records comprise lists of names, so their compilation in Latin poses few problems to the researcher. Local records include manorial deeds, accounts, court rolls and surveys which survive for the fourteenth century to a greater or lesser extent. They are usually written in Latin or Norman French, but guides are available to help with the format, language and technical terms. Fourteenth-century handwriting, once mastered, is often more legible than the hands of the twentieth and twenty-first centuries. Three places are examined here to try to illustrate the impact of the war on the local community and to find the answers to some of the questions: St Osyth, Barking and Great Bardfield.

St Osyth

St Osyth, in Tendring Hundred, in the north-east of the county, was a large rural parish (over 8,000 acres) with a long coastline partly against the open sea and partly against the Colne estuary and subsidiary creeks. The parish was dominated by a large and wealthy Augustinian abbey outside of whose precinct stood a small town. The abbey, founded as a priory by a bishop of London in the early twelfth century, had substantial landed endowments, making it one of the wealthiest in Essex.[36] In 1327 St Osyth had the highest tax assessment of any parish in Tendring Hundred and the second highest number of taxpayers (42), although Harwich, Brightlingsea and Manningtree were probably already more 'urban' in character and ultimately became more significant ports.[37] Half a century later, in 1377, after the advent of plague, some 362 lay people over the age of 14 paid the poll tax, suggesting a total population of perhaps 500 to 650 inhabitants. Although the balance between the rural inhabitants and the urban community cannot be easily estimated, it had clearly remained a significant place.[38]

Although the abbey's fourteenth-century administrative archives have not survived, slightly later material reveals that the monastery held about three-quarters of the parish. Its wealth came from arable production, the managed timber in the heavily wooded north of the parish and the abbey's 'wick' farms, facing the extensive coastal marshes. The latter were home to both dairy and fattening cattle, kept for meat, milk, butter and cheese, and to thousands of sheep producing meat, wool and cheese.[39] Local produce was traded through the town's market, first recorded in the late twelfth century,[40] and through the quays on St Osyth creek and at other landing places. The abbey's wool clip was bought by Italian merchants in 1293–4 and a wool fair was recorded in 1310.[41] The market was evidently thriving in the early fourteenth century, when the larger town and port of Colchester complained of its competition.[42] A customs account, covering September 1387 to January 1388, indicates that St Osyth's quay was then used to export cloth, wheat, cheese and butter.[43] Fishing, using nets, trawls and fish traps, was probably important too: in 1377 three men from St Osyth were among local fishermen accused of using damaging nets called 'wundyethonns' to trawl for fish along the coast between Walton and 'Seyntositheweres' (i.e. St Osyth's weirs or fish traps).[44]

Fourteenth-century warfare against the Scots and the French, together with the threat of civil war or disorder, created a wide range of burdens on this coastal community. Significant demands were for manpower and shipping, with small Essex ports such as St Osyth being a likely source of fishermen and other mariners suitable for impressment. For example, in 1311, when Edward II and Piers Gaveston were campaigning against the Scots, Henry Canon was sent by Richard Consedieu, master of the ship 'La Marie' of Westminster, to find men in St Osyth to go to Scotland 'on the king's business'. Three of the men he chose, Richard de Dalt, Henry Hanekot and Richard le Heyward, refused to go. Canon claimed that they then had him falsely indicted before the sheriff of Essex (perhaps out of revenge or just to avoid service) for an alleged trespass against Richard de Riveres and John de Riveshale, which led to his outlawry.[45]

Edward II's precautions against invasion by Queen Isabella in 1326 also led to mobilisation orders in east coast communities. In August 1326 St Osyth was among ten Essex ports and coastal towns required to join John de Sturmy, admiral of the fleet in the north, presumably by sending men and ships.[46] In the following month the bailiffs and commonalty of St Osyth were ordered, along with equivalent officers from 37 other ports along the East coast, to arrange for all the owners and masters of ships of 30 tons and upwards to assemble at Orwell with their ships, arms and victuals, and other necessaries for a month at least, under double-manning.[47] These arrangements ultimately failed either because of treachery by the higher commanders or because the mobilised seafarers refused to fight, perhaps in either case (or both) because of their hatred of Edward's favourite Hugh le Despenser the younger. Isabella and her forces were therefore able to sail unhindered into the port of Orwell and apparently made landfall at Walton-on-the-Naze, a little further north on the Tendring coast.[48]

The number of St Osyth men who served against the French was probably low in absolute terms. In 1339 the St Osyth mariner Richard le Wrigh[t] (perhaps a shipwright) received a pardon for the death of Robert Gros of Stonham, 'barber', in consideration of his service 'beyond the seas in the king's company and staying there in his service until now …'.[49] Possibly he had served since the time Edward III had been assembling a fleet from the spring of 1337.[50] Later in the war, William Smart and his son John Smart, both 'parkers' by occupation (perhaps of the abbey's Great or Little Park in St Osyth), appear to have served the king in the Crécy campaign in 1346 as part of the retinue of Lord Robert de Morley. It is not stated whether they had served in a military or a maritime capacity; perhaps they had contributed to the mass of stores that were landed in Normandy with the English army.[51] In June 1372 the returns of mariners for Essex indicate that the smaller ports usually contributed fewer than ten men, and in St Osyth's case just five were recorded: John Yernemouthe (i.e. Yarmouth), John Harry, Roger Mayde, Roger atte Noke and William Cut.[52] Roger atte Noke was probably related to Robert atte Noke, one of the local fishermen recorded in 1377.[53] Nonetheless, even a trickle of mariners from each small coastal community could make an important contribution, as a great many ships were needed. In the absence of a permanent naval organisation, Edward III's English fleet depended on many requisitioned mercantile ships, which were typically small, in the range of 30 to 60 tons, each conveying relatively few fighting men.[54]

Not all St Osyth men covered themselves with glory, and local interests did not disappear in time of war. John Sumpter was apparently a local merchant who had loaded broadcloth into the Gabriel of St Osyth in September 1387,[55] but six years later in 1393 protections granted by Richard II to John and William Sumpter, in the belief that they were serving the king with Sir Thomas Swynborne, keeper of the important castle of Guînes in Picardy, were revoked because they tarried in Essex on their own affairs.[56] Their activities appear to have involved St Osyth abbey, for in 1390 and 1393 John Sumpter stood as mainpernor for men in law suits relating to that house, in one case where a man had illegally left the abbot's service.[57] In 1394 a mainprise of £200 was made by Thomas Swynborne and Robert Bulloigne for John Sumpter, and an undertaking by him of equal value that he would do or procure no harm to the abbot, his canons, steward, men and servants. Possibly Sumpter was acting for the Swynborne family, as their acquisition of the manor of East Mersea in 1386 had led to a dispute with the abbey.[58] Later, in 1404, John Sumpter the elder and John Sumpter the younger were among St Osyth inhabitants implicated in a plot against Henry IV led by Maud de Vere, Countess of Oxford, and the three abbots of St Osyth, St John's (Colchester) and Beeleigh (Maldon).[59]

As well as men and ships, St Osyth was called upon to provide many other sinews of war. The most immediate and costly were demands for cash. At the start of December 1347 the abbey was among many religious houses that lent the king money towards his expedition to France. The abbot's £12 was to be repaid at Christmas 1348.[60] A similar loan in 1379 was larger, at £40, and in

1397 another was 40 marks.[61] Victuals were also demanded from the abbey; in 1310, for example, it was one of the monasteries in Essex that was asked to loan victuals to Edward II for his Scottish campaign.[62] However, the crown paid for many goods and services demanded, and this may have provided some compensation. The abbey's woodlands were a significant resource, and in June 1348 the sheriff of Essex was ordered to pay the abbot of St Osyth for timber that had been taken for repairing and amending the port and 'bretaches' (breaches) of Calais, and to cause the timber to be sent there with all possible speed.[63] Local merchants and shipmasters were diverted from their normal mercantile activities to supply royal forces, but presumably still to their profit. In 1375 Richard Wodehewer of St Osyth had a licence to load 20 quarters of wheat, 100 quarters of malt and 60 quarters of flour in the port of Dunwich and bring them to London to sustain the king's lieges.[64]

Perhaps greater difficulties derived from the disorders that plagued Essex in the mid- and later fourteenth century. In 1362 the inhabitants of St Osyth were among those from 13 ports that petitioned the crown against the actions of Lionel de Bradenham, who had claimed that the common coastal fisheries in 'Le Suyn' (the major coastal channel now known as The Swin), 'Gende' and 'Le Parrok' were in his lordship and had illegally annexed them. He let them to men who blocked the entrances to the fisheries by driving piles into the seabed and, in his role as a justice of labourers, he had levied ransoms against 'all the boats of that country' and made other illegal levies.[65] Bradenham was a lawyer, land agent and businessman employed on both private and crown business who held a manor at Langenhoe, near Colchester, from Robert Lord Fitzwalter. In 1350 Bradenham had besieged Colchester, possibly over disputed fisheries in the river Colne, for which that port claimed jurisdiction and a court of Admiralty.[66]

St Osyth also appears to have been affected by the Peasants' Revolt of 1381, although the sequence of events and their cause remains obscure. On 12 or 13 June 1381 Nicholas Davenant, chief chamberlain of Aubrey de Vere, whose family had a close relationship with the abbey, was taken from there and beheaded at Brentwood. The rebels forcibly entered the house of Adam Dyer and compelled him to make a fine with them, probably to secure the safety of his person or property. The abbey was entered on 16 June, the abbot was assaulted, imprisoned for three days and made to pay a fine for his release, his rent collectors were assaulted and charters were burnt; the abbot was threatened again on 27 June, the day before the Essex rebels were defeated near Rettendon.[67] John Preston, who was a wealthy tenant of the abbey from Hadleigh in Suffolk, appeared before the commission headed by Thomas of Woodstock after the rising and presented his demands, which echoed those of the rebels at Mile End; he was beheaded.[68] In addition to the 1381 revolt, St Osyth faced the threat of natural disaster. In 1383 the abbey secured the advowson of the church of Elmstead from Aubrey de Vere to compensate it for losses sustained when tides breached three miles of marsh walls and extensive flooding seriously affected the abbey's pastures. The abbey's tide mill on St Osyth creek had also been wrecked.[69] Flooding was a serious problem faced by many coastal and river communities at this time, as is also found at Barking.

Barking

Barking was a large parish covering the modern areas of Barking, Ilford and Dagenham, situated at the point where the river Roding joins the Thames and stretching northwards for about seven miles. The parish was divided into several manors. According to the account of Westbury and Dagenham of 1321–2, mixed farming was practised, with wheat, rye and oats as the principal grain crops. Animal husbandry, comprising poultry, pigs and sheep, was important. Poultry were kept largely for use by the abbey. The pigs would have been fattened in the forest in the north of the parish. Sheep were fattened on the marshes for their milk, which was made into cheese, and their wool, which was frequently taxed during the early years of the war. In 1347, for instance, the abbess, like other heads of religious houses, was asked to lend 20 sacks of wool to the king, presumably to raise money for the war.[70] As in St Osyth, few manorial documents survive for Barking for the fourteenth century, but it is likely that farming, trading and religious life continued normally during the Hundred Years War. Whether there were tensions between the abbey and its peasants is unknown. In 1381 rebels, possibly including abbey tenants, entered the abbey on 15 June and destroyed its records.[71]

A small fishing and trading town had grown up around the abbey that dominated the town. The abbey owned the market, which had been in existence since the twelfth century. Some of the town's inhabitants were probably employed as servants at the abbey; Henry atte Coventekechene was mentioned in 1327. Trades in the town are indicated by the names of 1327 taxpayers, such as Vincent le Glovere, Walter le Coupere and William le Pottere. The name John le Wolmongere – a man who paid six shillings in tax – suggests that some wool was shipped out of the port of Barking.[72] The leather trades were probably important; the import of hides was referred to in 1367 and Henry Noble was a tanner there in 1371.[73] In 1327 119 taxpayers were listed for Barking, assessed to pay £17 17s 6½d. Few taxpayers were assessed at the lowest rate of 6d, and most paid between 1s and 4s. From 1334 Barking was assessed at £22 15s 0¾d.[74] No poll tax returns survive for Barking. The abbey paid separately, as ecclesiastical taxes were granted in convocation (the assembly of the clergy for the Canterbury province) and not in parliament.

Both river and sea fishing were important to the town in the fourteenth century. On occasion this brought them into conflict with London over the illegal use of nets with too small a mesh.[75] Many fishermen were called on during the Hundred Years War to serve as mariners on ships impressed for service as troop transports or for battle, and the shipping survey of 1372 listed nine mariners at Barking.[76] In 1355 two royal commissions were issued to raise 120 mariners from places along the Thames between London and the sea, and to take them to Flanders.[77]

From the abbey's point of view, its greatest problem in the later fourteenth century had nothing to do with the Hundred Years War but was rather the loss of land as a result of flooding; this led, inevitably, to a diminution of income. After the bad floods of 1377 Edward III allowed the abbey to be exempt from the array of men-at-arms for the defence of the realm on their Essex estates. The king had been informed in the abbey's petition that because of the Thames flooding the abbey had lost much of its profits and was spending heavily on the repair of dykes.[78]

Three years later, in 1380, the abbey's seawall along the Thames was seriously breached, resulting in a great lake forming. The king ordered the repair of the seawall 'with all speed'. A further problem aroused the anger of the mayor of London, as the abbey's tenants set fish traps and used small-mesh nets to catch fish in the lake. As a result of the mayor's protest, a royal order was sent to the abbey to remove them. According to the mayor, fish spawning in the lake were being caught before they were big enough to eat and being used by the tenants to feed their pigs. The breach was also causing difficulties for navigation to the port of London.[79] Flooding continued to be a problem well into the fifteenth century.[80]

Great Bardfield

Great Bardfield, in the north of Essex, comprised a manor that was exploited directly by its lords and also a small borough with a market established in the thirteenth century. It was held by the Clare family from the Norman Conquest to 1314, when the last Gilbert de Clare, earl of Gloucester and Hertford, was killed at Bannockburn. Bardfield then passed to his youngest sister, Elizabeth de Burgh, and on her death in 1360 it was held by her granddaughter Elizabeth, countess of Ulster, and her husband Lionel, duke of Clarence, second son of Edward III. It then passed by marriage to the Mortimer family.[81] Elizabeth de Burgh in particular used Bardfield Hall as a favourite residence and extended the house in the 1340s, making it a suitable residence for a member of the higher nobility. Its great gate led into an outer courtyard where, presumably, the offices of the household were to be found. The inner court would have contained the hall, the chapel and Elizabeth's own chamber. References are also made in the accounts to the king's chamber and the Ferrers and Marshal chambers: the former for Elizabeth's daughter, Isabella de Ferrers, and her husband and the latter for Robert Marshal, Elizabeth's chief councillor, and his wife, one of her ladies-in-waiting.[82]

The size of Bardfield's population is uncertain but was probably sizable before the Black Death. Twenty-four taxpayers were listed in 1327, assessed to pay £3 9s 10½d. It is likely that these mostly represented the better-off inhabitants, as only three people paid the lowest amount of 6d. In view of the fact that Earl Gilbert's inquisition post mortem referred to 40 unfree tenants in 1314, it is likely that most of the poorer tenants were omitted from the tax return. The vill was assessed in 1334 for £4 14s 3d. The poll tax of 1377, levied on men and women over the age of 14, was more realistic; 291 people were taxed, suggesting a population of 400 or more. It was probably considerably higher before the Black Death.[83] Most people lived and worked on the manor. The borough, valued at £9 10s 10d in 1329–30, was small. There was a little industry: a court case in 1350 referred to 15 ells of cloth handed over for fulling and not returned.

In contrast to St Osyth and Barking, there is little sign of the impact of war on the normal routine of manor and borough; there is no sign of major problems, such as the flooding the other two places experienced. Surveys of the manor in the late 1320s and 1330s show that mixed faming was practised on the Lady's demesne. Thus, in 1336, 253 acres of the demesne were sown with wheat and 214½ acres with oats, with small acreages of maslin (a mixture of wheat and rye), peas and barley. It was estimated that 41 acres of meadow would be mown as hay. Livestock included the animals needed to work on the estate: five carthorses, 24 draught animals and 15 oxen. There were herds of 36 cows and 45 pigs. There were also 282 hoggets – two-year-old sheep – and this reflects Elizabeth de Burgh's policy of developing sheep farming on her demesne manors at a time when wool commanded high prices.[84] Diversification and close attention to farming by the officials were essential at a time when agricultural profits were falling.

Much of the agricultural labour on the lord's lands was supplied by the services of unfree tenants, and the court roll of 1350–51, soon after the Black Death, shows that strong lordship was maintained. The court, held every three weeks, was used, in addition to the cases between the tenants themselves, by the Lady to enforce her rights. For instance, in April 1351, the whole body of suitors was ordered to certify at the next court the number of labour services due from one unfree virgate and from half a virgate of land. Suitors were fined for non-attendance at the court and brewers for breaking the assize of bread and ale. Heriots were collected (the best beast due on the death of a villein), such as the foal handed over for Alice Crowe, who had held one messuage and 30 acres of land, which were taken into the hands of the Lady. Reliefs and entry fines were levied; John le Roo junior fined for entry on three acres of land and meadow acquired from Richard Thurston, and four tenants paid 6s 9d relief for the tenement once held by John Hook. Trespasses by animals on the Lady's crops were punished. There are possible signs of grievance over services; in a few cases tenants refused to perform the works they owed.[85] It is also possible that there had been disruption during the Black Death; a petition of 1351–2 was sent to the Lady by members of the peasantry who had not been paid for work they had done for wages.[86] There is no record that Great Bardfield took part in the 1381 revolt, and the court roll of 1384–5 makes no reference to rebels.[87]

There is only one incident related to the war which interrupted normal routine. A French invasion was threatened in the spring of 1360, and Elizabeth de Burgh sent a strong protest to Edward III over the activities of commissioners of array on her manors, namely Great Bardfield and Claret in Ashen in Essex, and Clare, Hundon, Stradishall, Denston and Sudbury in Suffolk. She asserted that Clare Castle was near the sea and that her large force of men-at-arms and archers in the castle would defend the coastal area if the French dared to attack. As she was ready to do this at her own expense, the king ordered the commissioners not to interfere further on her manors.[88]

For many people at St Osyth, Barking and Great Bardfield life continued much as usual despite the French war; at St Osyth and Barking the problem of flooding in the late fourteenth century must have seemed as serious as the war, if not more so. Normal routine was probably the usual state of affairs for the civilian population away from the coast in wartime down to the twentieth century. How well informed were the people in these places as to what was going on? Much must have depended on oral reports passed from one group of people to the next. All three places were well served in this respect. Elizabeth de Burgh frequently entertained visitors at Bardfield Hall, including her cousin, William de Bohun, earl of Northampton, who was a prominent leader in the Hundred Years War, and Ralph, earl of Stafford, who married her niece, Margaret Audley. The Black Prince was also a frequent visitor.[89] One can imagine the conversations between the visitors' servants and Elizabeth's, the tales that were told of the battles of Crécy and Poitiers and life in France, and the way the stories were passed around the village.

The communities of St Osyth and Barking would also learn much from the oral reports of merchants, sailors and fishermen. The close proximity of London meant that Barking men were well informed and news of the war probably circulated widely. Barking and London men did business with each other, Londoners held property in Barking and the abbey held property in London. St Osyth men would get reports when they traded in the Colchester markets and fairs. Reports would spread from what the abbot and canons learned from visitors and letters.

Prayers were considered an integral part of the war effort and were highly valued. At Barking the nuns were drawn from the nobility and gentry and would learn of what was happening in the war from letters and visits. The fourteenth-century abbesses were elected from leading families. For instance, two members of the Sutton family, prominent members of the Essex gentry, served as abbess: Yolande between 1329 and 1341, and Katherine between 1358 and 1377. Three abbesses belonged to the Montagu family: Matilda and Isabella, who headed the abbey in the 1340s and 1350s, were sisters of William de Montagu, earl of Salisbury, who served Edward III until his death in the early 1340s; and Matilda, who was abbess between 1377 and 1393, was their niece. At the end of the fourteenth century Sibyl de Felton was the daughter of Sir Thomas de Felton and widow of Sir Thomas Morley. Sir Thomas de Felton served the Black Prince; he was prominent in the government of Aquitaine between 1369 and 1377. Sibyl established a chantry for her parents in 1397 at St Æthelburga's shrine in the abbey church.[90] Although there were strict rules of enclosure for nuns, they remained in close touch with their families. In one way or another, news of the war would spread.

Life apparently continued normally, but there are signs of the pressure placed on Essex people by taxation and the royal demands for soldiers and mariners. In addition, the Black Death and subsequent plagues opened up new opportunities for the surviving population in town and country to gain land, engage in industry and move to the towns in order to shake off servile obligations, which were an undoubted cause of grievance; serfdom gradually disappeared during the fifteenth century. The impact of the Hundred Years War on three places has been considered here, but more research is needed by local historians to assess the impact across Essex.

Notes

1 J.C. Holt, *Magna Carta*, 2nd edn (Cambridge, 1992), p. 221; D. Carpenter, *The Struggle for Mastery. Britain 1066–1284* (London, 2003), p. 286.

2 Holt, *Magna Carta*, pp. 454–5; H. Rothwell (ed.), *English Historical Documents: Vol. III 1189–1327* (London, 1975), p. 318. These provisions were omitted from all reissues of Magna Carta, but the principle of consent for taxation was established.

3 Rothwell, *English Historical Documents*, pp. 355–7.

4 *Ibid.*, pp. 310–11, 319.

5 *Ibid.*, pp. 469–72.

6 Carpenter, *Struggle for Mastery*, pp. 395–410.

7 W. Page and J.H. Round (eds), *VCH Essex*, Vol. 2 (London, 1907), pp. 210–12; M. Osborne, *Defending Essex. The Military Landscape from Prehistory to the Present* (Stroud, 2013), pp. 21–31.

8 For the general context: J.R. Alban, 'English Coastal Defence: Some Fourteenth-Century Modifications within the System', in R.A. Griffths (ed.), *Patronage, the Crown and the Provinces in Later Medieval England* (Gloucester, 1981), pp. 57–9, 71–2.

9 J.C. Cooper, 'Medieval Colchester', in J.C. Cooper (ed.), *VCH Essex*, Vol. 9 (London, 1994), pp. 21–2; J.C. Cooper, 'Castle', in *ibid.*, pp. 241–8.

10 J.C. Cooper, 'Walls, Gates and Posterns', in J.C. Cooper (ed.), *VCH Essex*, Vol. 9 (London, 1994), pp. 248–50 (see also map, p. 43); H.L. Turner, *Town Defences in England and Wales* (London, 1971), p. 125.

11   Cooper, 'Walls, Gates and Posterns', pp. 248–9; Turner, *Town Defences*, p. 125.

12   Cooper, 'Medieval Colchester', p. 25.

13   H.M. Colvin (ed.), *The History of the King's Works. The Middle Ages* (London, 1963), vol. 1, pp. 161, 236–7, and vol. 2, pp. 659–6; P.L. Drewett, 'Excavations at Hadleigh Castle, Essex, 1971–2', *Journal of the British Archaeological Association*, 38 (1975), pp. 90–154; J. Bettley and N. Pevsner, *The Buildings of England. Essex* (New Haven, CT and London, 2007), p. 438; I. Yearsley, *Hadleigh Past* (Chichester, 1998), pp. 8–17.

14   J. Sumption, *Divided Houses. The Hundred Years War, vol. III* (London, 2009), p. 386.

15   L.T. Weaver, *The Harwich Story* (Harwich, 1975), pp. 7–9; M. Oppenheim, 'Maritime History', in W. Page and J.H. Round (eds), *VCH Essex*, Vol. 2 (London, 1907), pp. 262–5.

16   J. Sumption, *Trial by Battle. The Hundred Years War, vol. I* (London, 1990), p. 324; Weaver, *The Harwich Story*, p. 9.

17   M. Hughes, 'The Fourteenth-Century French Raids on Hampshire and the Isle of Wight', in A. Curry and M. Hughes (eds), *Arms, Armies and Fortifications in the Hundred Years War* (Woodbridge, 1994), pp. 121–32; Sumption, *Trial by Battle*, pp. 226–8, 246–51, 261, 263; Weaver, *The Harwich Story*, pp. 8–9; Oppenheim, 'Maritime History', p. 263.

18   *CPR*, 1338–40, p. 88, 109, 556; *ibid.*, 1350–54, p. 316; Turner, *Town Defences*, pp. 14, 24–5, 126; P. Davis, 'English Licences to Crenellate 1199–1567', *Castle Studies Group Journal*, 20 (2006–7), pp. 241 (226–45); Oppenheim, 'Maritime History', p. 263.

19   Sumption, *Divided Houses*, pp. 281–3, 286.

20   *CPR*, 1377–81, p. 162; *ibid.*, 1405–08, 3–4; Weaver, *Harwich Story*, p. 9; Davis, 'English Licences to Crenellate', pp. 230, 243. We are grateful to Neil Wiffen for his advice and contribution of material to this paragraph.

21   BL, Cotton Augustus I.i, ff.58 (1539), 56 (1543); TNA, MPF/1/25, 'A trick of Harwich', [?Eliz I]; B. Ayers, R. Smith and M. Tillyard, 'The Cow Tower, Norwich: A detailed survey and partial reinterpretation', *Medieval Archaeology*, 32 (1988), pp. 184–207; O. Creighton and R. Higham, *Medieval Town Walls. An Archaeology and Social History of Urban Defence* (Stroud, 2005), pp. 222, 224, 264; J.R. Kenyon, *Medieval Fortifications* (Leicester, 1990), p. 195.

22   Alban, 'English Coastal Defence', pp. 59–71. See also below, Chapter 2, p. 34.

23   *CPR*, 1377–81, pp. 2, 6.

24   *CCR*, 1377–81, p. 77; Sumption, *Trial by Battle*, pp. 226–7; Froissart, *Chronicles*, ed. G. Brereton (London, 1968), p. 307. See also: F. Kitchen, '"The Ghastly War Flame": The Beacon System in Essex', *Essex Journal*, 23 (2) (Summer 1998), pp. 41–4; J. Kemble, 'Essex Beacons and Look-Outs: A Multi-period Place-Names Study', *Essex Journal*, 42 (1) (Spring 2007), pp. 11–15.

25   Brooks, N., 'The Organisation and Achievements of the Peasants of Kent and Essex in 1381', in H. Mayr-Harting and R.I. Moore (eds), *Studies in Medieval History presented to R.H.C. Davis* (London and Ronceverte, 1985), pp. 251, 253, 255. For further discussion of Fobbing, below, Chapter 6, pp. 127, 129–30, 133–4.

26   Between 1352 and 1359 the labour legislation was enforced by separate commissions of justices of labourers, chosen by the crown from the county gentry; E.C. Furber (ed.), *Essex Sessions of the Peace, 1351, 1377–9*, Essex Archaeological Society, Occasional Publication no. 3 (Colchester, 1953).

27   The amount of land which men were expected to have varied.

28   www.medievalsoldier.org.

29   There are no returns for the 1379 poll tax for Essex.

30   Gibbs supplies a detailed account of his methodology.

31   TNA, C47/2/46.

32   G.L. Harriss, *Shaping the Nation. England 1360–1461* (Oxford, 2005), p. 414.

33   Ipswich was one of the places listed which lies outside the county.

34 The last Earl Humphrey de Bohun died in 1373, and his place in Essex was taken by Thomas of Woodstock, youngest son of Edward III, who married Earl Humphrey's elder daughter, Eleanor.

35 *CPR*, 1272–1399, 31 vols (London, 1891–1916); *CCR*, 1272–1399, 29 vols (London, 1892–1927).

36 Page and Round, *VCH Essex, vol. 2*, pp. 157–62.

37 J. Ward (ed.), *The Medieval Essex Community. The Lay Subsidy of 1327*, Essex Historical Documents 1, Essex Record Office Publication 88 (Chelmsford, 1983), pp. 7–16.

38 C. Fenwick (ed.), *The Poll Taxes of 1377, 1379 and 1381*, British Academy Records of Social and Economic History, new series, vol. xxvii (Oxford, 1998), part i, pp. 178–9. Assuming a total population multiplier of somewhere between 1.5 and 2.0.

39 Anon., 'St Osyth Priory', *Essex Review*, 30 (1921), pp. 1–13, 121–7, 205–21; C.C. Thornton, 'St Osyth', in C.C. Thornton (ed.) *VCH Essex*, Vol. 12 (forthcoming 2017/18).

40 S. Letters (ed.), *Gazetteer of Markets and Fairs in England and Wales to 1516*, 2 vols, List and Index Society, Special Series 32–3 (London, 2003), Part 1, p. 135; L. Landon (ed.), *The Cartae Antiquae Rolls 1–10*, Pipe Roll Society, 17 (London, 1939), pp. 85–6 (nos 171–2).

41 R.H. Britnell, *Growth and Decline in Colchester, 1300–1525* (Cambridge, 1986), p. 45; A. Bell, C. Brooks and P. Dryburgh (eds), *Advance Contracts for the Sale of Wool c. 1200–c. 1327*, List and Index Society 315 (2006), pp. 198–9.

42 Britnell, *Growth and Decline*, p. 13.

43 TNA, E122/159/2 (account of Tunnage and Poundage for the port of St Osyth, 11 Richard II).

44 *Calendar of Inquisitions Miscellaneous*, 1348–77, pp. 406–7; *CPR*, 1374–7, p. 489.

45 TNA, SC8/194/9654; M. McKisack, *The Fourteenth Century, 1307–99* (Oxford, 1959), p. 11.

46 *CPR*, 1324–7, p. 311. The other places were Harwich, Colchester, Manningtree, Maldon, Salcott, Tollesbury, Mersea, Fingringhoe and Foulness.

47 *CCR*, 1323–7, pp. 643–4.

48 McKisack, *The Fourteenth Century*, p. 83; Oppenheim, 'Maritime History', p. 262 and footnote 12 citing J.H. Round, 'The Landing of Queen Isabella in 1326', *English Historical Review*, 14 (1899), p. 104.

49 *CPR*, 1338–40, p. 223.

50 Sumption, *Trial by Battle*, pp. 178–9.

51 *CPR*, 1345–8, p. 492. For the Normandy landings, see Sumption, *Trial by Battle*, pp. 497–502.

52 TNA, C47/2/46/6. For the 1372 returns, see below, Chapter 6, pp. 100–05, 125–9.

53 *Calendar of Inquisitions Miscellaneous*, 1348–77, pp. 406–7.

54 Sumption, *Trial by Battle*, pp. 174–8.

55 TNA, E122/159/2.

56 *CPR*, 1391–6, p. 344. For Thomas Swynborne's memorial brass, see below, p. 30, Fig. 2.1.

57 *CCR*, 1389–92, p. 275; *ibid*, 1392–6, p. 140.

58 *Ibid.*, 1392–6, p. 260; Thornton, 'St Osyth' (forthcoming, 2017/18).

59 G.O. Sayles (ed.), *Select Cases in the Court of King's Bench, Richard II, Henry IV and Henry V*, vol. vii, (Selden Society 88, 1971), pp. 151–5; *CPR*, 1401–5, pp. 432, 468, 487; J. Ross, 'Seditious Activities? The Conspiracy of Maud de Vere, Countess of Oxford, 1403–4', in L. Clark (ed.), *The Fifteenth Century, 3: Authority and Subversion* (Woodbridge, 2003), pp. 25–41.

60 *CPR*, 1345–8, p. 492.

61 *CPR*, 1377–81, p. 637; *CPR*, 1396–7, p. 178.

62 *CCR*, 1307–13, pp. 260, 265.

63 *CCR*, 1346–9, p. 467.

64 *CPR*, 1374–7, p. 101.

65 *CPR*, 1361–4, p. 283. The other ports were Colchester, Alresford, Brightlingsea, East Mersea, West Mersea, Fingringhoe, Peldon, Pete (Pete Hall, Peldon), Wignorough, Salcott, Tollesbury and Goldhanger.

66 W.R. Powell, 'Lionel de Bradenham and his Siege of Colchester in 1350', *Essex Archaeology and History*, 3rd series, 22 (1991), pp. 67–70.

67 TNA, KB145/3/5/1; KB145/3/6/1; King's Bench Recorda Files, unnumbered.

68 TNA, KB/145/3/6/1/; E136/77/1; A. Prescott, 'Essex Rebel Bands in London', in W.H. Liddell and R.G. Wood (eds), *Essex and the Great Revolt of 1381* (Chelmsford, 1982), pp. 60, 95.

69 W. Dugdale, *The History of Imbanking and Draining of Divers Fens and Marshes*, 2nd edn (London, 1722), pp. 80–81; P.H. Reaney, 'Earthquake and Inundations at St Osyth', *Transactions of the Essex Archaeological Society*, new series, 21 (1937), pp. 136–7; *CPR*, 1381–5, p. 269.

70 *CCR*, 1346–9, pp. 265, 383; TNA, SC6/849/11; ERO, T/A 233/1; R.B. Pugh (ed.), *VCH Essex*, Vol. 5 (London and Oxford, 1966), pp. 184, 235.

71 W.H. Liddell and R.G. Wood (eds), *Essex and the Great Revolt of 1381*, Essex Record Office Publication 84 (Chelmsford, 1982), p. 86.

72 Ward, *The Medieval Essex Community*, pp. 105–6.

73 *CCR*, 1364–8, p. 328; *CCR*, 1369–74, p. 291.

74 R.E. Glasscock (ed.), *The Lay Subsidy of 1334*, British Academy Records of Social and Economic History, new series 2 (Oxford, 1975), p. 81.

75 H.T. Riley (ed.), *Memorials of London and London Life, 1276–1419* (London, 1868), pp. 135, 244–5; H.T. Riley (ed.), *Munimenta Gildhallae Londoniensis* (3 vols, Rolls Series, London, 1860–62), vol. iii, pp. 207–11; CPR, 1405–8, pp. 232, 309.

76 See below, pp. 100–01.

77 *CPR*, 1354–8, p. 155.

78 ERO, D/DHf T90; *CCR*, 1377–81, p. 16.

79 *CCR*, 1377–81, pp. 402–3.

80 Pugh, *VCH Essex*, Vol. 5 p. 238.

81 J. Ward, 'Elizabeth de Burgh and Great Bardfield in the Fourteenth Century', in K. Neale (ed.), *Essex Heritage* (Oxford, 1992), pp. 47–60.

82 TNA, E101/459/24, m. 3; SC6/1110/10, m. 5; SC6/1110/12, m. 2.

83 Ward, *Medieval Essex Community*, p. 54; TNA, C134/42, m. 3; Glasscock, *The Lay Subsidy of 1334*, p. 87; Fenwick, *The Poll Taxes of 1377, 1379 and 1381*, part i, p. 177. There is no poll tax return for 1381.

84 TNA, SC6/1110/3, m. 3d; SC11/799; SC2/171/16, m. 3.

85 TNA, SC2/171/16, m. 2–7.

86 TNA, SC6/1110/25, m. 1.

87 ERO, D/DHf M58.

88 J. Ward (ed.), *Elizabeth de Burgh, Lady of Clare (1295–1360). Household and Other Records*, Suffolk Records Society lvii (Woodbridge, 2014), pp. 139–40.

89 TNA, E101/92/12, m. 5; 92/24, m. 2–10; 93/20, mm. 8–26, 23d–25d.

90 E.A. Loftus and H.F. Chettle, *A History of Barking Abbey* (Barking, 1954), pp. 34–48.

Chapter 2

Essex and the Hundred Years War:
taxation, justice and county families
Jennifer Ward

The late thirteenth and the fourteenth centuries, covering the reigns of the three Edwards and Richard II, can justifiably be described as an age of warfare: it was the time of the Welsh and Scottish wars of Edward I, the latter continuing through Edward II's reign and well into Edward III's. There were periodic crises over the king's French lordship of Gascony in 1294–8 and 1323–5, and it was the confiscation of Gascony by the French king, Philip VI, that sparked off the Hundred Years War in 1337, a war which was to last on and off until 1453. Most of the fighting in the fourteenth century took place between 1337 and 1360, and then between 1369 and 1389. Whereas the 1340s and 1350s were a time of good fortune for the English, with victories at Crécy in 1346 and Poitiers in 1356, the period after 1369 was a time of defeats and losses for the English crown, and of mounting criticism of royal government. The fourteenth-century wars have to be set against the background of the famine years of 1315–16, and, with more long-lasting effect, the Black Death of 1348–9 and the subsequent outbreaks of bubonic plague which affected England, France and Scotland and most of Europe. In England, before the Black Death, it is likely that the population had reached about five million, but it had probably halved by 1377. War and plague ushered in a time of revolt in fourteenth-century Europe, as in England in 1381, and the fall of population brought about an era of better fortune for the English peasantry and increasing economic problems for the lords.

County administration and local office
In order to fight the wars the role of the 'home front' was vital, and the people of Essex felt the full burden of taxation, purveyance and array, as money, supplies and men were needed. No king could fight a war in the fourteenth century without levying taxes, and this was done using the county as the administrative

unit. He also needed to raise an army and ensure transport, whether across the Channel or the North Sea. No king wanted to get news of outbreaks of disorder when he was fighting abroad, and he therefore needed a system of justice that would ensure that the peace was kept during his absences. Again, the county was the obvious unit for this. The king had his officials in the chancery, exchequer and other departments of government, and professional justices in his central courts of King's Bench and Common Pleas, while the sheriff remained the principal royal appointment in the counties, although by 1300 gentry were coming to be used increasingly on commissions. This practice was to grow substantially in the fourteenth century, as county gentry were used in the fields of taxation and justice as well as to raise military forces and to perform military service themselves.

The king was always expected to be an effective ruler – to protect his subjects, lead his army into battle, formulate policy, issue and enforce laws and maintain order. He received his authority from God at his coronation when he was anointed and swore the coronation oath.[1] Edward II promised to enforce the laws and customs granted by his predecessors; to keep the peace for the benefit of the Church, clergy and people of the realm; to exercise justice impartially; and to preserve 'the laws and rightful customs which the community of the realm shall have chosen'. This last promise was new at the coronation in 1308 and has led to much debate among historians. It has recently been suggested that it was aimed at ensuring that Edward II would not break his promises as his father Edward I had done, a practice which had caused considerable disquiet among the nobility.[2]

The oath shows conclusively that no king could do as he liked. He was subject to the law of the land and, as Archbishop Thomas Arundel put it in 1399, he was expected to govern with the counsel of 'the honourable, wise and discreet persons of his realm'.[3] He had to have at least the tacit consent of the powerful men of England, clerical and lay. Otherwise, as Edward II and Richard II found to their cost, there would be a major opposition crisis. For much of his reign Edward III was able to take his realm along with him, his qualities of leadership, courage and chivalry and his execution of justice enabling him to do this. King, nobles and knights all subscribed to the code and virtues of chivalry in war and peacetime; the chivalrous king was expected to show leadership in war and peace, while the noble and knight were expected to be valiant fighters and just administrators.[4]

Although the king had his own revenues, including the royal lands and customs duties, especially on the export of wool, his resources were inadequate for waging war. Taxation required consent,[5] and under Henry III (1216–72) this was granted or refused by the great council of leading churchmen and barons, who made the decision on behalf of the community of the realm.

Consultation broadened during the thirteenth century, as parliament evolved out of the great council and counties became increasingly involved in the affairs of the realm. Assemblies of knights met occasionally before 1250, but Simon de Montfort initiated the systematic representation of counties and boroughs by summoning knights and burgesses to his councils of 1264–5. Under Edward I it was usual to summon two knights from each county and two burgesses from each borough, and this was accepted practice by 1327, the year of Edward III's accession.[6] From 1295 these men were instructed to come 'with full power' to bind their counties and boroughs to abide by the decisions reached in parliament. By the time of the outbreak of the Hundred Years War in 1337, parliament comprised the king, lords and commons.[7] The assent of the commons, composed of the knights and burgesses, was essential for taxation and normal for legislation. By 1340, when Edward III had achieved nothing in the war and was bankrupt, the commons were linking consent to taxation with redress of grievances, a procedure which was to be taken much further in the future. Parliament was both a forum for the king to publicise his policies, grant laws and get consent to taxes, arguing that they were necessary for the preservation of the realm, and also the place for his subjects to put forward their own views and to find out what the king had in mind.

Essex was represented in the commons by two knights of the shire and two burgesses each from Colchester and Maldon. During the fourteenth century burgesses usually represented the town where they lived. The knights of the shire were either knights or esquires, who were regarded as having a lower standing than the knights and were usually less wealthy. Both groups, however, enjoyed status in the county and had experience in both war and local affairs.[8] Many served as knights of the shire several times, as well as in county offices. Thomas Gobion, summoned as a knight to the great council of 1324, was a knight of the shire for Essex in 1328, 1336, 1337 and 1340, and served as sheriff, commissioner of array and for taxation, and as keeper of the peace.[9] John de Coggeshale of Great Codham Hall in Wethersfield and Robert de Swynborne of Little Horkesley (whose memorial brass is illustrated in Figure 2.1) served six and five times respectively;[10] John de Coggeshale dominated Essex affairs during the 1330s and 1340s. Knights of the shire elected later in the fourteenth century included Robert Marny of Layer Marney, who served 12 times between 1369 and 1390. Such men built up considerable parliamentary and county experience and had ample opportunity to present petitions on behalf of the Essex community, as well as to pursue their own business and improve their social contacts.

It is rare to have details of the debates of the commons. The office of Speaker dates from the Good Parliament of 1376, and John de Gildesburgh of Wennington in south Essex acted in this capacity in 1380. Discussions between lords and commons frequently took place, and John was a member of

Figure 2.1. Double brass of Robert and his son Thomas Swynborne, who both served in the Hundred Years War and were buried at Little Horkesley in 1391 and 1412 respectively. The brass was badly damaged by a bomb in 1940 but has been extensively repaired. Robert came from a Northumbrian family and acquired lands in Essex through inheritance, purchase and marriage. He served the Black Prince in the Poitiers campaign and in Spain, and later in life became involved in Essex affairs. His son Thomas pursued a military career, serving in northern France and in Aquitaine.

the commission chosen from both houses to investigate the state of the realm, the royal revenues and Richard II's ministers.[11] The Speaker in the autumn of 1381 after the Great Revolt was Richard Waldegrave, a knight with land in Essex and Suffolk who carried out some work in Essex. His views on the causes of the Revolt were recorded: he blamed excessive taxation, the royal court's extravagance, the failure to defend the coast against French and Castilian ships and the illegal maintenance of retainers by the nobility.[12]

Representation in parliament constituted only a small part of the gentry's work for the crown, and knights and esquires in particular found themselves increasingly involved in local office and on county commissions, both of which underwent considerable evolution during the late thirteenth and fourteenth centuries. Much of their work related directly or indirectly to the Scottish and French wars. The office-holders comprised the sheriff, escheator and coroner. The sheriff's office dated back to Anglo-Saxon times, and his power had declined somewhat by the fourteenth century. However, he remained the most important county official, responsible for the two counties of Essex and Hertfordshire. He was appointed by the crown, except in 1339–40,[13] received and carried out royal orders and writs, and was responsible for the farm of the county, the fixed sum due each year from the county which was paid to the exchequer. He held the county court, where elections of knight of the shire to parliament took place. The sheriff was often a knight; according to the statute of 1371 he was expected to hold land worth £20 a year. Many sheriffs held office once for about one year, but John de Coggeshale held the office frequently over a period of 20 years between 1334 and 1354.[14]

Possibly the most unpopular royal order the sheriff had to carry out concerned the purveyance of food, armaments and fodder for the king's household and armies when purveyors, appointed by the king and helped by the sheriffs, bought up goods compulsorily for the army's use. The sheriffs also usually arranged for the transport of goods. The crown worked out what was needed, but did not necessarily get as much as it wanted. Purveyance was unpopular, especially when it coincided with taxation,[15] and the government increasingly turned to the purchase of food supplies. In 1355 John de Coggeshale was buying up beef, bacon, wheat and peas and having the goods transported to Maldon, where they were loaded onto two ships and taken to Calais.[16]

The sheriff was also responsible for securing war supplies. In the spring of 1340, when the king was preparing to ship an army to Flanders, William de Wauton, sheriff of Essex, was ordered to secure what was needed for the transport of the horses. Four gangways, 30 feet long and five feet wide, were made, timber was purchased to make hurdles and racks, canvas and rope for making mangers, and two barrels to hold staples, rings and nails. Everything was taken to the port of Manningtree, where it was stored. Two large boats were hired at Ipswich for six journeys to Orwell, where the fleet was being assembled, and the goods were stored at Harwich until the fleet set sail.[17]

The escheator was responsible for taking inquisitions post mortem, compiling descriptions of the lands held by deceased tenants-in-chief of the crown and taking proofs of age as to whether male heirs had reached the age of 21; the crown had the right of wardship over heirs who were minors. In the case of co-heiresses, the inheritance was divided into equal shares and the escheator was responsible for making the partition. Any revenue from lands received by the escheator was accounted for at the exchequer.[18] Like the sheriff, the escheator was expected to have £20 worth of land, according to the statute of 1371. The area that the escheator was responsible for changed several times over the fourteenth century. Before 1340, except for the years 1323–7, 1332–5 and 1340–41, Essex was handled by the escheator appointed for the whole of England south of the river Trent; during the exceptions Essex was part of a group of six eastern counties. The office was combined with that of sheriff between 1341 and 1356, then between 1357 and 1369 Essex and Hertfordshire were joined with Norfolk and Suffolk under one escheator. After 1369 Essex and Hertfordshire had their own escheator, although each county had its own escheator for about three months after the Great Revolt, with supervisors also being appointed.

The coroner was expected to be a landholder and was elected in the county court; he served in a single county and several coroners were usually appointed. Normally, the coroner held office for life. His most notable duties were the holding of inquiries in the event of sudden death, whether by accident or violence, and the keeping of the record of the pleas of the crown until the arrival of royal justices in the county, when the pleas were heard and determined.[19]

Taxation and array

Members of parliament, sheriffs, escheators and coroners dealt with much of the county business, but when there was a need to carry out a particular task ordered by the king a commission of local nobles, gentry and sometimes churchmen would be appointed by the crown. These commissions covered a wide variety of matters, from the maintenance of sea-walls to the investigation of smuggling, but two stand out as important for the king's wars, namely commissions for taxation and for array, which were designed to meet the king's needs for money and men. Taxes were granted in parliament on the plea of the king's necessity, usually war. They became increasingly frequent after 1290, when Edward I was faced with Welsh rebellion, war in Gascony and especially the Scottish wars, which continued under Edward II and beyond. Further crises erupted in Gascony in 1324–5 as well as in 1337, which marks the beginning of the Hundred Years War.

Down to 1334, the tax consented to by parliament comprised a tax on a proportion of a man's personal property, described as his movable goods. The proportion varied from one levy to the next and each tax was separately assessed. In 1332 the one-fifteenth of men's movables in rural areas and the one-tenth of movables in the boroughs brought in about £38,000; fifteenths and tenths, as the tax was called, continued to be levied until the early seventeenth century. Certain goods were exempt: armour, horses and treasure in rural areas and, in the towns, one outfit of clothes each for a man and his wife, a bed, a drinking cup and a few ornaments. In practice, household goods, food and tools were not taxed and grain and livestock were taxed at less than the market valuation. The poorest people in the community did not pay tax.[20] For Essex in 1327 the local assessment for Waltham Holy Cross survives,[21] and shows that people were taxed on wheat, barley and oats, hay and beans, livestock, brass vessels, salted meat and a cart.

In order to assess and collect the tax, a commission was appointed of two or three local men of standing. For the tax of one-twentieth of 1327 the commissioners were Thomas Gobion, Ralph Giffard and Nicholas de Storteforde. All three were prominent in county affairs. Ralph Giffard was sheriff of Essex and Hertfordshire in 1319. Nicholas de Storteforde served in the 1320s on commissions of oyer and terminer (commissions to hear and determine pleas of the crown and complaints from individuals). Thomas Gobion ranked as a knight and had been appointed steward to Humphrey de Bohun, earl of Hereford and Essex, in 1314. He was on the commission to collect the tax of one-tenth and one-sixth in 1322 and served as sheriff the following year and as a member of the commission of the peace six years later. He was often appointed to commissions of array and commissions of oyer and terminer in the 1320s.[22]

The procedure for raising the tax was laid down by the exchequer in 1297. The commissioners appointed four or six men of each village or borough to assess the tax and to return their list to the commissioners as soon as possible. These local rolls were scrutinised by the commissioners; it is not known how accurate they were, but in at least some cases under-assessment is likely, and assessments are suspiciously low for many knights and gentry. The yields of taxation declined when taxes were frequent and economic conditions bad, indicating concealment in the localities. The local assessments were copied onto two county rolls, one kept locally and the other passed on to the exchequer. The first half of the 1327 tax, for instance, was due to be delivered in February 1328 and was in fact handed over in November 1330.[23]

What was the impact of these taxes on Essex people? In 1327 Boxted, for example, had 33 taxpayers and was assessed to pay £2 16s ¼d in tax.[24] Those who owned goods worth less than 10s were exempt; for the tax of one-twentieth of 1327 the lowest tax paid was 6d. The lords of the manor of Boxted Hall and Rivers Hall, which headed the list, were assessed at between 5s 6d and 7s 8d. At the bottom of the list three people were assessed at 6½d, five at 7d, and six at sums between 8d and 9½d. All the others were assessed at between one and three shillings. It is likely that a large number of people were excluded from the tax because of poverty. A comparison of the 1327 roll with others near to it in date shows that names and the amounts of assessment varied, in some cases markedly, pointing to the possibility of corruption at local level.

It was because of suspected corruption in 1332 that the system of assessing and collecting the fifteenth and tenth was changed in 1334. Separate assessments for each tax were abandoned and quotas based on the fifteenth and tenth of 1332 were imposed on villages and boroughs.[25] Although the figures for the quotas are known, there is little information surviving to indicate how it was divided up among the inhabitants. However, one fourteenth-century assessment survives for Boxted.[26] This shows that the tax was assessed on landholding, not on movable goods. A total of 112 holdings were listed for the two manors: the name of the holder was given, followed by the assessment; some men held more than one holding and consequently paid more tax. The quota for Boxted amounted to £3 12s 11½d. A much higher proportion of the population contributed to the tax compared with 1327, and those who had only a single holding and paid 1d or 2d were probably poor. It is likely that the very poor were still exempt, and this is supported by the poll tax figures for 1377, levied on men and women over the age of 14. By 1377 the Black Death and subsequent plagues had wiped out up to half of the Essex population, but Boxted still had 115 taxpayers.[27]

County gentry were not only appointed to the taxation commissions but were also commissioners of array, responsible for raising foot soldiers in the county as required by the king. In both cases appointments were made by the crown and the commissions were enrolled on the Patent Rolls. The commissioners surveyed the able-bodied men between 16 and 60 years old, and picked the best to serve at the king's wages. These men fought alongside the retinues of knights and men-at-arms, particularly in the late thirteenth and first half of the fourteenth centuries, including the battle of Crécy, but played little part in the war in France by the 1370s.[28] By then mounted archers as well as men-at-arms were recruited by leaders of retinues, which had become larger.[29] Most of the later fourteenth-century commissions of array recruited men to defend the coast against French raids, and in 1381 a commission was appointed to array men to fight against the rebels.[30] The commissions grew in size by the late fourteenth century, but were still served by men engaged in other county work. Thomas Gobion, William Marny, John de Coggeshale and William FitzRalph (for whose memorial brass see Figure 2.2) all served as commissioners.[31]

Figure 2.2. Engraving of a brass of William FitzRalph, dating from *c.*1331–8. This is a reconstruction of a partially damaged brass with missing elements accurately restored. The date of Fitzralph's death is uncertain, but he was taking part in county affairs in the early fourteenth century. His family had been established at Pebmarsh and at Little Waldingfield in Suffolk since the early twelfth century, holding their lands of the lords of Clare. They also had close ties with the de Veres and were patrons of Colne Priory.

Taking taxation, purveyance and array together, a considerable burden was placed on Essex people, especially the poor. In 1337 the fifteenth and tenth was granted for three years. In addition, men were arrayed for the royal army, the royal right of purveyance meant that foodstuffs were being seized for the army, and there were also seizures of wool as Edward III tried to maximise his revenue from wool exports. All this was happening when England was in a poor economic state. Coinage was in short supply. The year 1338–9 saw a wet autumn and a cold winter, followed by a bad harvest in 1339. Taxpayers still had to pay their rents and tithes, and needed cash for their families. Edward III, who had hoped for a quick war, had no success and was bankrupt in 1340. No wonder he faced opposition in parliament in 1340–41.[32]

The situation improved during the 1340s and 1350s, and the war grew in popularity, partly as a result of the successful campaigns leading to victories at Crécy and Poitiers. Yet the mass of population remained heavily burdened, with taxes being levied almost every year.[33] The Black Death and the consequent fall in population apparently did not affect recruitment for the war.[34] The treaty of Brétigny was concluded in 1360, but war broke out again in 1369. The fighting was intensive, with frequent, unsuccessful campaigns and greater naval activity than earlier. Military defeat and increasing demands for money contributed, as in the late 1330s, to growing discontent. In addition, there was increasing restiveness among the peasantry, wheat prices were exceptionally high in 1370 after the harvest failure of 1369, and trade was in recession. In addition, by the 1370s Edward III was showing signs of senility, and the Black Prince was suffering from terminal illness. Rumours of corruption were to reach a crescendo in the Good Parliament of 1376.

The fifteenth and tenth continued to be raised as in 1334, with no allowance for the drop in population; it was remarked in the parliament of 1380 that it was 'in many ways oppressive to the poor commons'.[35] Parliament tried out new taxes, notably the poll taxes of 1377, 1379 and 1380–81. At that time, many should have been better able to pay them than in the 1330s. Harvests were good from 1375 and, with the fall in population, wages and diet for the majority of the population were improving and there were better opportunities to acquire land. On the other hand there was military defeat and the threat of invasion, a lack of political leadership and grievances over servile tenure. The poll tax represented a new and considerable burden. In 1377 men and women aged 14 and over had to contribute 4d each; the tax in 1379 was graduated, and levied on men and women aged 16 and over;[36] the tax of 1s on men and women aged 15 and over in 1380–81 was widely ignored; and the investigation of non-payment by John Bampton at Brentwood on 30 May 1381 sparked off the Great Revolt. The degree of tax evasion should have warned the government of serious discontent.[37] In Essex, for example, in 1377 Boxted paid £1 18s 4d from 115 taxpayers; for 1381, there is no information from this parish. A comparison, however, can be made in two places: Castle Hedingham paid £4 2s 4d in 1377 from 247 people taxed and £5 in 1381 from 100 taxed; at Bocking, 318 taxpayers in 1377 paid £5 6s; in 1381, 216 were taxed, paying £10 16s.[38] There is little doubt that the poll tax contributed to the outbreak of the Great Revolt.

Justice

In addition to relying on county gentry for the raising of taxes and soldiers, it was also essential for the king to ensure that England would be governed effectively and law and order maintained while he was campaigning overseas. Moreover, there was a strong demand for justice from the localities, and the fourteenth century saw a marked increase in legal business and the forms of actions that could be brought. Lawyers and the common law courts of King's Bench and Common Pleas were becoming more professional.[39] A workable judicial system evolved after considerable experiment, combining demand from the localities for effective justice in the counties with central control by the king and his courts in London, which the government regarded as essential.

Law enforcement in the Middle Ages was the responsibility of numerous local courts among which the county court had a key role, meeting every four weeks under the presidency of the sheriff, usually at Chelmsford.[40] During the twelfth and thirteenth centuries the king had sent royal justices out to the counties at intervals; this general eyre dealt with royal rights, crime and other pleas. The eyre was a victim of its own success; the whole system clogged up, became unpopular and virtually ceased after 1294.[41] Once it was clear that the eyre could not be revived the Crown experimented with various commissions, such as the commission of oyer and terminer and commissions of trailbaston, which dealt with cases of trespass, disturbers of the peace and those who maintained criminals and interfered with juries. Trailbaston commissions proved unpopular, except in the aftermath of the Peasants' Revolt, partly because they were seen as condoning violence by powerful men in the locality.[42]

The permanent solution, however, lay in the development of the keepers of the peace, who were appointed from the county gentry. Such men had been appointed at times of crisis in the thirteenth and early fourteenth centuries to help the sheriff to maintain order; in 1316, for instance, they were appointed to arrest suspects and inquire into felonies and trespasses.[43] During the early years of Edward III's reign various methods were tried to keep the peace, one method succeeding another in quick succession. Experiment continued in the 1330s and 1340s, although the gentry were increasingly used as keepers and occasionally as justices of the peace, as in 1332 and 1338–44.[44] Major changes came in the aftermath of the Black Death, the labour shortage and the issue of the Ordinance and Statute of Labourers in 1349 and 1351, freezing wages at pre-Black Death levels. The peace commissions of 1350 gave justices of the peace the right to hear and determine felonies and trespasses with a quorum of professional, experienced lawyers. They were also responsible for enforcing the labour legislation, although this was hived off to commissions of labourers between 1352 and 1359.[45] The two commissions were combined in 1359, although at the same time the justices lost their responsibility for array. The statute of 1361 confirmed the determining power of the justices of the peace, who retained this until 1400 and beyond, although special commissions were appointed after the Great Revolt.[46] Some changes continued to be made but essentially the commission continued in a similar form to the end of the sixteenth century. Central control was supplied not only by the quorum but by regular visitations of the counties by royal justices of assize, a practice established by the 1360s.

County gentry were therefore involved in local commissions of justice throughout the fourteenth century, although it is only in the second half of the century that their powers of determining cases were assured. In addition to their responsibility for enforcing the labour legislation, they became increasingly responsible for enforcing statute law. Local justice was administered at quarter sessions by men who knew their county, lived locally and were used to working together.[47] At the same time supervision by the crown was provided, justices of the peace were appointed by the royal chancery and the personnel changed from one commission to the next.

Essex sessions of the peace survive for 1351 and 1377–9 and have been published;[48] the originals are housed in the National Archives. The commission of the peace for 1351 listed the justices who were responsible for keeping the peace, determining felonies, trespasses and array, and enforcing the Ordinance and Statute of Labourers; fines for breaking the labour laws were to be used as a contribution towards payment of the fifteenth and tenth. The roll for 1351 contains indictments for felonies and trespasses. There is hardly any reference to the labour legislation, but an estreat roll survives which lists the labour fines levied by the justices. The justices of 1377–9 exercised similar powers to those of 1351. The surviving roll again contains indictments, including labour cases, and more ancillary information is given, including the action taken by the justices of the peace.[49]

Although the majority of offenders were peasants or artisans, the 1351 indictments make it clear that the worst offender was John Lord Fitzwalter, noted for his fighting with the Black Prince at the battle of Crécy and in the siege of Calais in 1346–7. According to the 1351 roll, he rampaged through the county from 1342, besieging Colchester the following year and harassing and threatening Dunmow priory; even more crimes emerged when he was tried in 1351 in King's Bench. He was imprisoned and his estates confiscated, but he was pardoned by the king the following year and heavily fined.[50] He spent the rest of his life paying the fine. He was not the only member of the Essex nobility and gentry to indulge in crime. Lionel de Bradenham of Langenhoe and Robert Marny were with Fitzwalter at the siege of Colchester in 1343, while Lionel lord of Langenhoe besieged Colchester for nearly three months in 1350, probably in a dispute over fishing rights in the River Colne.[51] There was a real need for the crown to supervise noble and gentry activity.

Most of the indictments of 1351 concerned men of lower social status, such as John Henham of Thaxted, who feloniously broke into the house of John Cartere of Asheldham and robbed him of woollen and linen cloths and other goods worth 5s.[52] Thomas le Walshe and others assaulted John de Leghes at Shelley, and beat, wounded and maltreated him contrary to the peace. The indictment commented that Thomas was a common malefactor and disturber of the peace.[53] At Manningtree the sub-constables arrested John son of John Alote Gernon for an assault on Thomas Sandre, chaplain; Robert de Mistelegh prevented them from doing their office and rescued John.[54] Although the justices had no jurisdiction over forestalling, John Arwesmyth of Great Leighs was accused of being a common forestaller of victuals and paid his employees excessive wages contrary to the king's Ordinance of Labourers.[55]

When the 1351 estreat roll listing fines for labour offences is examined it is easy to understand the depth of grievance among the working population. At a time of labour shortage and given the willingness of lords, bailiffs and others to pay higher wages in order to secure workers it must have been galling when men receiving or offering 'excessive' wages were indicted and fined. The estreat roll lists 7,576 people who paid fines totalling £719 10s. In all probability this was not the total for the whole county, as Furber has shown that the estreat roll did not cover the hundreds of Dunmow, Becontree, Chafford, Harlow, Ongar, Clavering and Waltham. According to the estreat roll the total number of people fined in each hundred varied widely, from 160 for Barstable to 1,167 for Dengie and 1,408 for Rochford.[56]

Examples of wages offences entered on the roll for 1377–9 include Peter Colman, labourer, accused of taking 2d a day in winter and 3d and food in summer, when his pay should have been limited to 1½d or 2d respectively. John Pete of Finchingfield, a feeble carpenter, was taking 1s 6d a week in winter, although he should not have received more than 1s, while Alice Gylot of Ashen took excessive wages of 4d a day at harvest time and also moved from place to place; according to the statute, she should not have received more than 2d or 3d[57] and should have worked on the manor where she lived instead of going elsewhere to gain a higher wage. Those who paid excessive wages, as well as those receiving them, were fined. Richard Boyn of Finchingfield, mower, hired two men for excessive wages for haymaking. John, the bailiff of Wendens

Ambo (or Wendon Lofts), and his ploughman, John Sweyn, were both fined for giving and receiving excessive wages.[58]

The justices of the peace were chosen by the crown from the elite of the county gentry and usually ranked as knights and esquires; they also often served as knights of the shire in parliament, as sheriffs and escheators and on commissions. The number of men on the commission of the peace grew during the fourteenth century. The Essex sessions of the peace indicate that the commission of 1351 numbered 10 justices.[59] Four royal justices constituted the quorum, namely Richard de Wylughby, Henry de Grene, William de Notton and John de Cavendish. The rest were county gentry: Sir John de Sutton of Wivenhoe, Sir John de Coggeshale of Great Codham Hall in Wethersfield, John de Goldyngham of Chigwell, who also served in the Commons in February 1351, Robert de Teye of Marks Tey and John de la Grove of Great Oakley. William de Lavenham was added to the commission two months later.[60] The commission of 1376 was headed by Thomas of Woodstock, youngest son of Edward III and earl of Buckingham, who had married Eleanor de Bohun and served as constable of England. Two professional lawyers were appointed: Robert Bealknap, chief justice of the court of Common Pleas, and Henry de Asty, chief baron of the Exchequer. The gentry comprised Thomas de Mandeville of Black Notley, William de Wauton of Willingale Doe, Richard de Sutton, John de Mounteney of Mountnessing, Geoffrey de Dersham and Robert Rikedon of Witham; John de Bampton was added in July 1377 on Richard II's accession.[61] The structure of these two commissions was typical of the period after 1361, and continuity of service became more marked, as in the case of John de Gildesburgh, who served on six successive commissions from May 1380 to July 1387. Altogether 35 men served as justices of peace in Essex under Richard II, sometimes only once, as in the case of Richard de Waldegrave, but in other cases as many as nine times, as with Clement Spice.[62]

The variety of the gentry's administrative and judicial duties can best be summed up by looking at the career of John de Coggeshale (c.1301–1361), one of the most active Essex knights of the fourteenth century.[63] John succeeded his father as a minor in 1319 and came of age three years later. He was first appointed sheriff of Essex and Hertfordshire in 1334 and held the office until 1339; he was again sheriff between 1340 and 1341, 1343 and 1348 and 1352 and 1354. These long periods ran contrary to the statute of 1340, which stated that the sheriff was to serve for only one year. He was appointed escheator of Essex, Hertfordshire and Middlesex in 1343, holding the office for five years, and of Essex and Hertfordshire between 1351 and 1354; in both these periods it was usual for the office of escheator to be combined with that of sheriff. His work on commissions overlapped with that as sheriff, and was closely linked to the Scottish and French wars. He was engaged in levying hobelars (lightly armed horsemen) and archers in 1335 for the Scottish war, and with the array of soldiers and the defence of the coast in 1346–7. In 1349 he was inquiring into money which had been raised to pay archers but had never been sent to Calais, in 1353, 1354 and 1357 he was investigating cases of non-payment of customs duties on wool, and in 1358 he was examining a case of fraud over the cloth subsidy. He was also involved with purveyance and in 1355 was responsible for sending purveyed food supplies to Calais. As sheriff he had responsibilities for keeping the peace, a task which must have been difficult during the years of John Fitzwalter's gang warfare in the 1340s. He was appointed to commissions of the peace in 1351 and 1356. He acted as a commissioner of sewers (channels of water) for the hundred of Rochford in 1338 and for Dengie in 1355; these commissions, appointed by the crown, were responsible for sea and river defences. He served in parliament as one of the two knights of the shire for Essex in February 1334, May 1335, September 1336, February 1339, April 1343 and February 1358. Men such as John de Coggeshale can be said to have merited the title of 'maid of all work' long before it was coined to describe the work of the Tudor justices of the peace.

The Essex gentry

The term 'gentleman' first came into use in official documents as a result of the statute of 1413, which required men involved in litigation to describe their status, but historians use it at a much earlier date to describe landowners below the rank of nobility who were lords of manors and involved in local affairs. As far as landholding and wealth were concerned, there were great differences among the landowning class and, although the terms 'gentlemen' and 'gentry' are used to denote the whole group, it can be divided by legal and social status into knights, esquires and gentlemen. The gentry as a whole are also subdivided by historians into the 'county' and the 'parish gentry', depending on whether they were wealthy and influential enough to have a say in county affairs or whether they limited their interests to the one or two parishes where they held land; the 'county gentry' was largely made up of knights and esquires. Needless to say, there was much overlap between these groups and considerable upward and downward mobility. H.L. Gray, in his article on incomes from land in 1436, distinguished between knights, esquires and gentlemen. He reckoned that greater knights enjoyed an average income of £208 a year, lesser knights £60 and esquires £24.[64] Gentlemen had lower incomes than the esquires, many of them receiving between about £7 and £15 a year; most men in this income bracket would be considered by historians as 'parish gentry'. The wealthier groups often held land in more than one county, but to have a role in county affairs it was important that they should be resident mainly in Essex, that their interests should be focused on the county and that they were well known inside and outside the county.

These men would not always be law-abiding. Society was violent in the fourteenth century, both in warfare and on the 'home front'. Gentry were above all concerned for the well-being, wealth and status of their own nuclear families; they were ambitious to increase the family lands and ensure that they enjoyed as prominent a position as possible. Lands could be increased by marriage, by inheritance and by purchase, grant or exchange. All these were perfectly legal means, but if legal means failed shady practices or violence were an acceptable alternative. Robert Marny had a turbulent career in warfare and land acquisitions from the 1340s into the 1360s. In 1360 he began to get a foothold in the Bruyn lands when he secured a £40 rent in South Ockendon; the Bruyn family had estates in Hampshire and single manors in Dorset, Kent and Essex. William Bruyn died in 1362, leaving an eight-year-old son and heir, Ingram; at least some of the land had been held jointly by William and his wife Alice. In the next year Robert and Alice purchased Ingram's wardship from the crown and married. When Ingram came of age, he granted his lands to Robert and Alice for life. Alice was coheiress to her father's inheritance in London and Kent; Robert negotiated the partition between her and her sister in his favour. These acquisitions did not involve violence, but there was a certain amount of sharp practice.[65] In an ambitious and competitive society where force was seen as part of life many men, such as Lionel de Bradenham, would resort to violence when they felt that their rights were under attack and no legal means were open to them.[66]

The fourteenth-century Essex gentry were a fluid group, frequently reinforced by newcomers. Some twelfth- and thirteenth-century families, such as the Coggeshales and the Marnys, continued in the male line throughout the fourteenth century and beyond. The foundations of the success of the Coggeshale family were laid by John de Coggeshale's grandfather, Ralph (d. 1305), who acquired major landholdings including Great Codham Hall in Wethersfield, which became the main family residence. He was probably responsible for arranging the marriage of his son John (d. 1319) to Sarah, daughter of Laurence de Plumbergh, who was heiress to North Benfleet and Paglesham in south Essex. In the next two generations further good marriages were made by John (d. 1361) and his sons Henry, who married Joan, daughter of William de Welle, and Thomas, whose wife was the widow of Hugh de Badewe; widows who held land in dower and possibly some land of their own inheritance were in demand as marriage partners. Both Henry and Thomas were involved in county affairs. Family fortunes suffered a temporary reverse in 1375 when Henry died deeply in debt. His son and heir, William, went out to Italy to fight in the company of Sir John Hawkwood and married his daughter, Antiocha. On his return he became immersed in county affairs and was elected to parliament in 1397.[67]

Other families died out, usually because of failure in the male line, as when William de Horkesleigh died in 1332.[68] This meant that the family name and lineage would disappear and, if there were daughters, the estates would be divided and the lands taken on marriage into other families, as was the case after the death of William de Coggeshale in 1426. Even if a son was living at the time of his father's death, he might die during his minority or before children were born to a marriage, as happened with the Filliol family of Kelvedon, where the heiress Cecily married John de Bohun.[69] Ambitious husbands on the lookout for marriage to an heiress or wealthy widow were an important factor in social change. This was a way in which younger sons became established in county society, as when William son of Robert Bourchier married Eleanor, heiress to the Loveyn family of Little Easton, in the mid-fourteenth century.[70]

It has often been pointed out that newcomers became gentry after a career in trade or the law. This is occasionally found in the fourteenth century, often coupled with an advantageous marriage. In the early fourteenth century John Bousser (d. 1329), a judge in the court of Common Pleas, secured the manor of Stanstead Hall in Halstead as a result of his marriage to Helen, daughter and heiress of Walter of Colchester, and founded the Bourchier family, as his descendants came to be called. His son Robert served as knight of the shire for Essex in four parliaments between 1329 and 1339, fought in the Hundred Years War, including the battle of Crécy, and was Edward III's chancellor in 1340–41. Robert married Margaret, daughter and heiress of Thomas Praers of Sible Hedingham, and rose into the nobility. His son John married Matilda de Coggeshale, and his younger son William, Eleanor Loveyn.[71]

John Hende, draper and citizen of London, built up an estate of eight Essex manors by the time of his death in 1418 in addition to his property in London and Kent. His second marriage to Katherine, widow of Thomas Baynard of Messing, gave him an interest in the Baynard lands during Katherine's lifetime; Katherine's and Thomas's son, Richard, was orphaned at an early age and trained as a lawyer before securing the bulk of his inheritance at the age of 21; his lands were concentrated in the area round Messing.[72]

Sir Robert Swynborne (c.1327–91) was an incomer from Northumberland who obtained lands in Essex as a result of inheritance, purchase and marriage. His grandfather bought the reversion of Wiston manor in Suffolk and Little Horkesley in Essex, and both manors were inherited by Robert. He gained further land in Essex as a result of his second marriage to Joan Botetourt, who inherited some of the Botetourt lands, including Gosfield, Belchamp Walter and Gestingthorpe in Essex. She was also co-heiress to her grandfather, Sir John Gernon, who held lands in the Midlands as well as Essex. Joan received Bakewell in Derbyshire and estates in Lincolnshire and Cambridgeshire as well as in Essex.[73] Robert added other Essex manors by purchase, such as East

Figure 2.3. Brass of John de Wauton and his wife Ellen (Elizabeth). John fought in Edward III's campaigns in Scotland and during the early stages of the Hundred Years War; he was present at the battle of Crécy and died in 1347 during the siege of Calais. He was probably a younger son who established himself in county affairs through his service to the Fitzwalter family and to Elizabeth de Burgh, representing Essex in parliament and serving as sheriff and on royal commissions. He lived at Tiptofts in Wimbish where the surviving hall and cross-wing date from the late thirteenth century, and was buried in Wimbish church. The figures are placed in the head of a cross; much of the cross and the marginal inscription are missing.

Mersea. He served the Black Prince in the Poitiers campaign and also in Spain. He became active in Essex affairs in the 1370s and 1380s and represented the county in parliament.[74] Here was a newcomer who became fully involved in the county where he had gained estates.

Any ambitious member of the gentry who wished to further his career in war or at home needed to build up his contacts with the royal court and the nobility. Retainer relationships were to be found throughout noble and gentry society, in military retinues, the management of noble households and estates and in the king's service, where, particularly under Richard II and later, members of the gentry were recruited as king's knights. Information is plentiful for the de Bohuns, who were the leading noble family in Essex, and men were attracted to the followings of Humphrey, earl of Hereford and Essex (d. 1322), his younger son William, earl of Northampton (d. 1360), and William's son Humphrey, earl of Hereford, Essex and Northampton (d. 1373).[75] Some families, such as the Engaines, served the Bohuns over more than one generation.[76]

Earl William played an important part in the Scottish wars of the 1330s, the war in Brittany in the 1340s and the Crécy campaign of 1346–7.[77] Many of the Essex gentry in his retinue served with him on several campaigns: John de Wauton, for example, had been in the retinue of Robert Fitzwalter in 1322, served in William's retinue early in the Hundred Years War, fought with him at Crécy and died at the siege of Calais. His memorial brass is shown in Figure 2.3.[78] John Fitzwalter and Robert Marny served with him as esquires between 1337 and 1339.[79] Families long connected with the Bohuns are found in the retinue of Earl Humphrey in 1371–2, notably Sir Thomas Mandeville, father and son;[80] the Mandeville family were long-standing retainers of the Bohuns.

Through these ties the gentry were bound into networks with the king, the nobility and each other. Most were involved in military campaigning, some for a short time, possibly in early adulthood, such as John de Coggeshale in the 1320s, while others interspersed military service with county duties. Some were seasoned soldiers, such as Robert Marny, John Fitzwalter and John Bourchier. There is little sign of reluctance to serve. Membership of networks facilitated social as well as political contacts. John de Coggeshale came into royal custody on the death of his father in March 1319 and in May his marriage was granted to Bartholomew de Badelesmere, at that time a powerful man at court. By the time that Bartholomew was executed as a traitor in 1322 it is likely that John had forged close ties at court, with the Burghersh family and possibly with the future Edward III. When John, as sheriff of Essex, was accused of extortion in the inquiry into local government in 1340–41 the king intervened, John was ordered to appear before the chancellor and the keeper of the privy seal – the chancellor being Robert Bourchier, whom he knew in Essex – and the king stipulated that any fine was to be very reasonable.[81]

Gentry also forged ties among themselves, often through marriage alliances. Once children were born the ties could be strengthened, with gentry or their wives being invited to act as godparents; William de Wauton was godfather to William de Coggeshale, the baptism taking place at Great Codham.[82] Gentry also helped their friends and neighbours by acting as witnesses to deeds or as feoffees (trustees); when Henry de Coggeshale was dying it was his feoffees who were urged to do their best to provide for his family.[83] Retainers might be rewarded by their lords. Robert Fitzwalter granted Wimbish to John de Wauton five years after John had served with him on the Scottish campaign. John also served Elizabeth de Burgh, Lady of Clare, in the running of her estates and held land of hers in Steeple Bumpstead and Birdbrook.[84] As a younger son he built up his career by serving several lords, fighting throughout his life, and also by serving as sheriff of Essex and as a knight of the shire. His funeral, in 1347, took place at Wimbish, where his memorial brass survives in the church and much of his house, Tiptofts, still stands.

Both kindred relationships created by the intermarriage of families and the tie of retaining helped to bond the county gentry in both war and peacetime activities. Unfortunately, relatively little is known about the social occasions where these ties could be fostered because few records of these survive. The fourteenth-century nobility and gentry lived very much under the public gaze, and in their houses the great hall was the centre of hospitality. These halls survive at Tiptofts, Southchurch Hall and Great Codham Hall, among other places, and would have witnessed meetings and feasting by the gentry.

Details of feasts are sometimes included in household accounts, such as those of Elizabeth de Burgh, which give an account of the funeral of Sir Edward de Monthermer, who was mortally wounded at Vironfosse in October 1339. He died at Clare castle, the home of his half-sister, Elizabeth de Burgh, probably on 11 December, when loaves and herring were distributed to the poor to pray for his soul. In the days that followed invitations to the funeral were sent out, including to the dowager Queen Isabella, Lord Morley, Lord Fitzwalter and other knights of Essex and Suffolk. Edward's brother, Sir Thomas, was notified, but, as he lived in south Devon, would not have received the news before the funeral on 16 December. Edward was buried in Clare Priory church, with the funeral probably conducted by the abbot of Bury St Edmunds. A great feast followed the funeral. There is no information about the number of people who attended, but 192 horses and 15 hackneys were fed in the stables, three carpenters spent six days making boards and trestles, 300 wooden dishes were made and 500 bought, and 200 wooden goblets were made and 194 bought. The meat and fish served included boar, venison, sturgeon, salmon and 2,000 oysters. Several types of bird were served, including 80 hens, 63 partridges and plovers and 32 geese. In addition, 1,600 eggs, 18 cheeses and eight gallons of milk were purchased.[85] Did the guests talk about the early failures of the Hundred Years War? We shall never know.

The 'home front' in Essex was vital for the prosecution of the Scottish and French wars of the late thirteenth and fourteenth centuries. The county provided money, men and supplies for the wars, despite the occasional upheaval that took place as a result of plague and rebellion. The nobility and gentry raised or served in war retinues that were essential to winning victories such as Crécy. Their administrative and judicial work underwent considerable development over the period, as they strove to meet the king's demands and to keep order. The pattern of county government that was set by 1400 was to last into the 1800s. Throughout the fourteenth century, nobles and gentry supported royal ambitions in France and were loyal to the royal cause.

Notes

1 H. Rothwell (ed.), *English Historical Documents: Vol. III, 1189–1327* (London, 1975), p. 525; A.R. Myers (ed.), *English Historical Documents: Vol. IV, 1327–1485* (London, 1969), pp. 403–5.

2 S. Phillips, *Edward II* (New Haven, CT and London, 2010), pp. 140–44.

3 A.P. d'Entrèves (ed.) and J.G. Dawson (trans.), *Aquinas. Selected Political Writings* (Oxford, 1965), pp. 139–40; Myers (ed.), *English Historical Documents*, p. 415.

4 M. Keen, 'Chivalry and English Kingship in the Later Middle Ages', in C. Given-Wilson, A. Kettle and L. Scales (eds), *War, Government and Aristocracy in the British Isles, c. 1150–1500* (Woodbridge, 2008), pp. 252–5. Edward III's personality is discussed in W.M. Ormrod, *Edward III* (New Haven, CT and London, 2011), pp. 92, 104–6.

5 See Magna Carta, 1215, c. 12, 14, in J.C. Holt, *Magna Carta*, 2nd edn (Cambridge, 1992), p. 455; Rothwell (ed.) *English Historical Documents*, p. 318.

6 There was a certain amount of variation in the choice of boroughs under Edward I, but the list had been stabilised by 1327.

7 The Lords comprised bishops, mitred abbots and barons. During the fourteenth century the practice of sending individual summons to particular lords led to the evolution of the parliamentary peerage. Within the Commons the burgesses were regarded inferior to the knights. The development of parliament is discussed in depth by R.G. Davies and J.H. Denton (eds), *The English Parliament in the Middle Ages* (Manchester, 1981), pp. 29–60, and G.L. Harriss, *King, Parliament and Public Finance in Medieval England to 1369* (Oxford, 1975), pp. 231–312.

8 The term gentry is used by historians to include knights, esquires and gentlemen; as far as office-holding was concerned, the knights, esquires and wealthiest gentlemen held office and constituted the county elite, and this group was by no means static during the late thirteenth and fourteenth century. A. Musson, *Public Order and Law Enforcement. The Local Administration of Criminal Justice, 1294–1350* (Woodbridge, 1996), pp. 125–46.

9 F. Palgrave (ed.), *Parliamentary Writs and Writs of Military Summons*, Record Commission (London, 1827–34), vol. iii, part ii, pp. 637, 651–2; *Return. Members of Parliament, part i, Parliaments of England, 1213–1702* (London, 1878), pp. 81, 111, 116, 128; *List of Sheriffs of England and Wales from the Earliest Times to 1831*, Public Record Office, Lists and Indexes, ix (London, 1898), p. 44; *CPR, 1321–4*, pp. 124, 130, 213, 225, 424; *CPR, 1327–30*, pp. 172, 431; *CPR, 1330–4*, pp. 57, 286; *CPR, 1334–8*, pp. 132, 139, 208, 298, 370–71, 504; *CPR, 1338–40*, pp. 76, 139.

10 J. Ward, *The Essex Gentry and the County Community in the Fourteenth Century*, Studies in Essex History 2 (Chelmsford and Wivenhoe, 1991), p. 6; *Return. Members of Parliament*, pp. 102, 106, 111, 124, 136, 161, 182, 184, 186, 193, 195, 197, 202, 206, 212, 217, 223, 228, 237.

11 Ward, *Essex Gentry*, p. 6; *CPR, 1377–81*, p. 459; A.I. Dasent, *The Speakers of the House of Commons* (London, 1911), p. 54; J.S. Roskell, L. Clark and C. Rawcliffe (eds), *The History of Parliament: The House of Commons 1386–1421* (Stroud, 1992), vol. iii, pp. 185–7.

12 W.H. Liddell and R.G. Wood (eds), *Essex and the Great Revolt of 1381*, Essex Record Office Publication 84 (Chelmsford, 1982), pp. 7–8; Roskell *et al.*, *The House of Commons 1386–1421*, vol. iv, pp. 735–9.

13 The Walton Ordinances of 1338 provided for sheriffs to be elected in the counties. William de Wauton was elected in the county court and served in 1339–40.

14 H.M. Jewell, *English Local Administration in the Middle Ages* (Newton Abbot and New York, 1972), pp. 121–2, 186–90; Ward, *Essex Gentry*, pp. 4–6; J. Ward, 'Sir John de Coggeshale: An Essex Knight of the Fourteenth Century', *Essex Archaeology and History*, 3rd series, 22 (1991), pp. 62–3.

15 M. Prestwich, *Plantagenet England 1225–1360* (Oxford, 2005), p. 77; TNA, E101/621/3.

16 TNA, E101/619/15.

17 H.J. Hewitt, *The Organisation of War under Edward III* (Manchester, 1966), pp. 180–81.

18 Jewell, *English Local Administration*, pp. 95–6, 99–102; Ward, *Essex Gentry*, pp. 4–5; Ward, 'John de Coggeshale', p. 63.

19 Jewell, *English Local Administration*, pp. 153–7; Ward, *Essex Gentry*, p. 5.

20 J. Ward (ed.), *The Medieval Essex Community. The Lay Subsidy of 1327*, Essex Historical Documents 1, Essex Record Office Publication 88 (Chelmsford, 1983), p. iii; M. Jurkowski, C.L. Smith and D. Crook, *Lay Taxes in England and Wales, 1188–1688*, Public Record Office Handbook 31 (London, 1998), pp. xxvi–xxxi.

21 Ward (ed.), *The Medieval Essex Community*, pp. 108–10; TNA, E179/107/14.

22 Ward (ed.), *Medieval Essex Community*, p. i. 'Oyer et terminer' means 'to hear and determine' a case. Jewell, *English Local Administration*, p. 142; R.W. Kaeuper, 'Law and Order in Fourteenth-Century England – Special Commissions of Oyer and Terminer', *Speculum*, 54 (1979), pp. 734–84.

23 Ward (ed.), *Medieval Essex Community*, pp. i–ii, 34–6, 108–10; TNA, E179/107/12, 13.

24 Ward (ed.), *Medieval Essex Community*, pp. 17–18.

25 R.E. Glasscock (ed.), *The Lay Subsidy of 1334*, British Academy Records of Social and Economic History, new series, 2 (Oxford, 1975), pp. xv–xxxii, 79–89; Jurkowski *et al.*, *Lay Taxes in England and Wales*, pp. xxxi–iv.

26 ERO, D/DRg 1/35; the document is undated but belongs to the fourteenth century.

27 C. Fenwick (ed.), *The Poll Taxes of 1377, 1379 and 1381*, British Academy Records of Social and Economic History, new series, vol. xxvii (Oxford, 1998), part i, p. 177.

28 A. Ayton and P. Preston, *The Battle of Crécy, 1346* (Woodbridge, 2005), pp. 176–88.

29 A. Ayton, 'Armies and Military Communities in Fourteenth-Century England', in P. Coss and C. Tyerman (eds), *Soldiers, Nobles and Gentlemen. Essays in Honour of Maurice Keen* (Woodbridge, 2009), pp. 217–19; A. Ayton, 'Military Service and the Dynamics of Recruitment in Fourteenth-Century England', in A.R. Bell and A. Curry (eds), *The Soldier Experience in the Fourteenth Century* (Woodbridge, 2011), pp. 30–33. Commissions of array were occasionally used to recruit mounted archers.

30 Ward, *Essex Gentry*, pp. 7–9. Array was added to the commission of the peace in 1338 and between 1346 and 1359.

31 Ward, *Essex Gentry*, p. 8.

32 J.R. Maddicott, *The English Peasantry and the Demands of the Crown 1294–1341*, Past and Present, Supplement 1 (1975), pp. 45–67.

33 Prestwich, *Plantagenet England 1225–1360*, p. 279.

34   Ayton, 'Military Service and the Dynamics of Recruitment', p. 38.

35   *Rotuli Parliamentorum* (London, 1783), vol. iii, p. 90; G.L. Harriss, *Shaping the Nation. England 1360–1461* (Oxford, 2005), p. 60n.

36   No Essex returns have survived for the poll tax of 1379.

37   Harriss, *Shaping the Nation*, p. 229, points out that in London and south-east England 102,500 of the 1377 taxpayers had disappeared.

38   Fenwick (ed.), *The Poll Taxes of 1377, 1379 and 1381*, pp. 176, 177, 180, 181. The £5 from 100 taxpayers at Castle Hedingham looks suspiciously like a fabricated number.

39   C. Carpenter, 'War, Government and Governance in the Later Middle Ages', in L. Clark (ed.), *The Fifteenth Century VII* (Woodbridge, 2007), p. 316; A. Musson and W.M. Ormrod, *The Evolution of English Justice. Law, Politics and Society in the Fourteenth Century* (Basingstoke, 1999), pp. 115–54.

40   J.R. Maddicott, 'The County Community and the Making of Public Opinion in Fourteenth-Century England', *Transactions of the Royal Historical Society*, 5th series, 28 (1978), pp. 27–43.

41   Musson and Ormrod, *The Evolution of English Justice*, pp. 43–5.

42   Jewell, *English Local Administration*, p. 142; Ormrod, *Edward III*, p. 73.

43   Jewell, *English Local Administration*, p. 145.

44   Prestwich, *Plantagenet England 1225–1360*, pp. 520–21; Musson, *Public Order and Law Enforcement*, pp. 11–82, 169–86; E. Powell, 'The Administration of Criminal Justice in Late Medieval England: Peace Sessions and Assizes', in R. Eales and D. Sullivan (eds), *The Political Context of Law* (London, 1987), pp. 50–51. Keepers of the peace were empowered to hear and inquire into cases; justices of the peace had the additional power to determine them.

45   Powell, 'The Administration of Criminal Justice', pp. 51–3; Musson, *Public Order and Law Enforcement*, pp. 49–82.

46   Musson and Ormrod, *The Evolution of English Justice*, p. 155; Powell, 'The Administration of Criminal Justice', pp. 53–6.

47   Quarter sessions were held from 1362. The county town was the normal meeting place, but the court did meet at other places as well; E.C. Furber (ed.), *Essex Sessions of the Peace, 1351, 1377–9*, Essex Archaeological Society, Occasional Publication no. 3 (Colchester, 1953), pp. 28–9, 71–3.

48   The rolls have been edited by Furber, *Essex Sessions of the Peace*.

49   *Ibid.*, pp. 10–14.

50   *Ibid.*, pp. 61–5, 81–90; *Oxford Dictionary of National Biography* (Oxford, 2004), vol. 19, p. 948.

51   W.R. Powell, 'Lionel de Bradenham and his Siege of Colchester in 1350', *Essex Archaeology and History*, 3rd series, 22 (1991), pp. 68–72. A further troublemaker was Hugh de Badewe: see below, pp. 65–77.

52   Furber, *Essex Sessions of the Peace*, pp. 99–100.

53   *Ibid.*, p. 107.

54   *Ibid.*, p. 109.

55   *Ibid.*, pp. 111–12.

56   The estreat roll was an extract from the court record which was sent to the exchequer for prosecution; the fines would then be levied by the exchequer. Furber, *Essex Sessions of the Peace*, pp. 13, 47–55, 74–5, 79. About £675 was allocated to communities as a contribution towards the fifteenth and tenth of 1352–3.

57   *Ibid.*, pp. 158–9. The bailiff's surname is not recorded.

58   *Ibid.*, pp. 157–8, 164.

59   *Ibid.*, pp. 14–21.

60   *CPR*, 1350–4, p. 86. William's identity is uncertain.

61   Furber, *Essex Sessions of the Peace*, pp. 21–5. From 1361 it was usual for an Essex noble to head the commission of the peace.

62 Ward, *Essex Gentry*, p. 12, gives a table of the Essex gentry who served as justices of the peace between 1377 and 1397, and the number of commissions of which they were members. See also C. Starr, *Medieval Lawyer. Clement Spice of Essex*, Essex Society for Archaeology and History, Occasional Papers, new series, no. 2 (Colchester, 2014).

63 Ward, 'Sir John de Coggeshale', pp. 61–6.

64 H.L. Gray, 'Incomes from land in England in 1436', *English Historical Review*, 49 (1934), pp. 623–30, 633–4.

65 Roskell *et al.*, *The House of Commons 1386–1421*, vol. iii, pp. 690–93; *CIPM*, vol. xi, no. 296.

66 See above, pp. 65–77; N. Saul, 'Conflict and Consensus in English Local Society', in J. Taylor and W. Childs (eds), *Politics and Crisis in Fourteenth-Century England* (Gloucester, 1990), pp. 38–58.

67 Ward, 'Sir John de Coggeshale', pp. 61–2, 65; C. Starr, *Medieval Mercenary: Sir John Hawkwood of Essex* (Chelmsford, 2007), pp. 28, 49; *CIPM*, vol. 14, no. 104. John de Coggeshale's eldest son John fought in Edward III's retinue at the battle of Crécy and died during the siege of Calais.

68 *CIPM*, vol. 7, nos 452, 453.

69 *CIPM*, vol. 7, no. 450; *CIPM*, vol. 8, no. 660. John Filliol died in 1332, leaving two sons: Richard, aged 12, and John, aged seven. His lands were held jointly with his wife Margery, who died in 1346. By then the heir was their daughter Cecily; the two sons had presumably died young.

70 *CIPM*, vol. 9, no. 214; *CIPM*, vol. 10, no. 490.

71 *Oxford Dictionary of National Biography*, vol. 6, pp. 822–3, 865.

72 Roskell *et al.*, *The House of Commons 1386–1421*, vol. ii, pp. 150–52; *CIPM*, vol. 14, no. 95.

73 Joan's grandfather, John Botetourt, had held lands in Bedfordshire and Essex, and also single manors in Norfolk, Suffolk and Huntingdonshire for life. He died in 1324. *CIPM*, vol. 6, no. 587.

74 Roskell et al., *The House of Commons 1386–1421*, vol. iv, pp. 545–7; *CIPM*, vol. 15, nos 984–9.

75 William's elder brother Humphrey, earl of Hereford and Essex, played no part in warfare; he died childless and William's son Humphrey inherited his lands and titles.

76 See below, Chapter 3, pp. 53, 60; G.A. Holmes, *The Estates of the Higher Nobility in Fourteenth-Century England* (Cambridge, 1957), pp. 70, 75, 124. Nicholas Engaine served under Earl Humphrey in the Bannockburn campaign; his son John served Earl William and in 1342 was one of the four close associates to be given powers of attorney-general to lease all the earl's lands; *CIPM*, vol. 6, nos 383, 427; *CIPM*, vol. 10, no. 433.

77 Earl William's retinue at Crécy is discussed by Ayton and Preston, *The Battle of Crécy*, pp. 205–10.

78 J. Ward, 'The Wheel of Fortune and the Bohun Family in the Early Fourteenth Century', *Essex Archaeology and History*, 3rd series, 39 (2008), pp. 167–8; Ward, *Essex Gentry*, pp. 16, 18; *CIPM*, vol. 8, no. 681.

79 Ward, 'The Wheel of Fortune', pp. 167–8.

80 TNA, E101/31/15; E101/32/20.

81 Ward, 'John de Coggeshale', p. 62; TNA, C49/46/13.

82 *CIPM*, vol. 15, no. 291.

83 *CIPM*, vol. 14, no. 104.

84 *CIPM*, vol. 8, no. 681.

85 J. Ward (ed.), *Elizabeth de Burgh, Lady of Clare (1295–1360). Household and Other Records*, Suffolk Records Society lvii (Woodbridge, 2014), p. 43; TNA, E101/92/11, m. 11; E101/92/12, m. 9.

Chapter 3

The contribution of Essex gentry to the wars of Edward I and Edward II

David Simpkin

The wars of kings Edward I (1272–1307) and Edward II (1307–27) represent a watershed in English military history on a number of levels.[1] The scale and frequency of campaigns launched by the English crown increased markedly during these years. Large armies were sent into Wales in 1277, 1282–3, 1287 and 1294–5. These were followed by those sent regularly to Scotland from 1296, as well as forces deployed to defend English possessions in Gascony, mainly between 1294–8 and 1324–5. As a consequence of this the number of men involved in warfare – especially as soldiers – rose dramatically, to the extent that it would not be going too far to speak of a process of militarisation within English society. And, crucially from the point of view of the historian, these military expeditions are well documented by surviving materials, making it possible to say much more about the combatants involved than is the case for the wars of earlier reigns. This is particularly true of soldiers drawn from the ranks of the nobility and gentry, who by and large continued to perform the traditional role of men of their status, as mounted, armoured warriors. This article will consider those Essex combatants who served in these many and varied campaigns, relying primarily on contemporary lists of Essex gentry drawn up by shire officials. Some of the gentry considered in this paper also held lands in neighbouring counties, such as Suffolk or Hertfordshire, but an attempt has been made to include only those gentry who had at least a substantial interest in Essex society.

Later in the fourteenth century – during the Hundred Years War – it became common for men-at-arms (often of gentle status) and archers to be recruited together in 'mixed' retinues, with the retinue leader usually coming from the magnate class; and from the 1360s the names of thousands of both types of soldier can be found on muster rolls preserved by the Exchequer.[2] However, during the reigns of Edward I and Edward II men-at-arms and archers were still recruited separately, the former in retinues gathered by members of the aristocracy and the latter in large bodies of 20, 100 or 1,000, selected by specially appointed crown officials known as commissioners of array. In this period the names of archers are seldom available, and so this article will focus only on the military service performed by the gentry of Essex, and not on that performed by lower social groups.

It should also be borne in mind that the size of retinues varied depending on the wealth and status of the retinue leader. Later it became common for the crown to contract with retinue leaders for retinues of specified size, but under Edward I and Edward II the magnates were usually requested to gather as many men-at-arms as they could. Among the most prominent landholders in Essex were the Bohun earls of Hereford and Essex and the de Vere earls of Oxford. Below these were some prominent baronial families such as the Fitzwalters. Such men as these had the resources to recruit quite large retinues for the time, normally comprising between 10 and 100 men-at-arms, the figures varying from campaign to campaign. Retinues gathered by ordinary Essex knights (as with knights of other counties), however, would usually contain no more than two or three men-at-arms, while many other Essex knights and sergeants (usually men of gentle status who had not taken up knighthood) simply served in the retinues of men such as the Bohuns and the de Veres.

Some of the battles of these years have long since entered into popular memory and folklore, none more so than the Bruce-inspired Scottish victory against the English at Bannockburn in June 1314. One of the lasting images of that particular engagement, recounted in contemporary narratives and later paintings, is the pre-battle charge by the English knight Sir Henry de Bohun against the Scottish king, a duel that resulted in the Englishman's head being cleaved in two.[3] Such personal, chivalric encounters – and there were plenty of them during the course of these wars – made for instant legend. Yet there is no need to cease our enquiry at this arresting image, for it is possible to place brave Sir Henry into the context of the army, and in particular the military retinue, in which he served.

Sir Henry was the nephew of Humphrey de Bohun, earl of Hereford and Essex, and it was in his retinue that he served on the Bannockburn campaign.[4] The earl was constable of England and ought by right to have been constable of the army in 1314, but Edward II had controversially given that role to the young earl of Gloucester.[5] Nevertheless, Earl Humphrey sought to play a leading role in the battle, as befitted his status,[6] and it is no surprise to find that it was a member of his retinue, his nephew, who led the attack during the early stages of the engagement. His seal, with its military iconography, is illustrated in Figure 3.1.

Figure 3.1. The seal of Humphrey de Bohun, earl of Hereford and Essex, who fought at Bannockburn (1314) and was later killed in rebellion at the battle of Boroughbridge (1322). Earl Humphrey is depicted on horseback, brandishing his sword; he wears a hauberk of mail, a surcoat and a helm with a fanned plume, and his visor is down; he carries a shield with his coat of arms. On the other side is the shield with the Bohun arms (azure, a bend argent, cotised or, between six gold lioncels). The swan is depicted above the shield; this was a device inherited from the Mandevilles, earlier earls of Essex. The Mandeville arms flank the larger Bohun shield (image courtesy of J. Ward & Saffron Walden Historical Society).

What is also interesting, however, is the way that Earl Humphrey's status as a lord of the Welsh March and a major Essex landholder brought together in his retinue soldiers and officials from different parts of the realm.[7] Despite the lack of a muster roll or horse inventory for this army, we do have the names of some 38 men who took out letters of protection (legal documents postponing potential litigation against the recipient during the soldiers' absence) in April 1314 ahead of their intended service in the earl's retinue.[8] Featuring heavily alongside the earl's young kinsman Sir Henry were combatants and officials originating from both the Welsh Marcher counties and from Essex.

Among the Marcher men was none other than Master John Walwayn, a clerk made famous for being the possible author of the *Vita Edwardi Secundi* (the anonymous Life of Edward II),[9] and Sir Roger Chandos, a long-standing associate of the earl who in May 1311 had been charged with the task of raising foot soldiers from Herefordshire.[10] Yet it is the Essex gentry that really stand out as a group. We find, for example, Sir Nicholas Engaine, a man who just a couple of years earlier had been listed among the Essex gentry on the parliamentary roll of arms – an extraordinary heraldic armorial arranged, by and large, by county.[11] Also present were Roger Clifton, one of the men-at-arms to be summoned from Essex in May 1324 as part of the preparations for the war in Gascony;[12] Sir John fitz Simon, who had been summoned for military service as an Essex landholder in 1297 and 1300;[13] and Sir Bartholomew Enfield, an indentured retainer of Earl Humphrey who had been knighted at Westminster in 1306 alongside the future Edward II.[14] If we add to these few men representatives of the Essex-based (or at least Essex-associated) families of Hemenhale (Robert), Goldingham (William), Rivers (Roger) and Mereworth (John)[15] it can be seen that the Essex influence on Earl Humphrey's retinue in 1314 was strong indeed.[16]

This example perfectly illustrates how association with a prominent local magnate and the more general obligation owed by all subjects to their king could lead a group of Essex men far from their homes to a boggy and murderous patch of ground in the heart of Scotland. Moreover, it also shows how their performance of military service served both to strengthen their bonds to one another and to bring them into contact with gentry from other parts of the realm, whom otherwise they might not have met. The question is: how typical is this example? Were the Essex gentry a highly militarised group by 1314? When they gave military service, did they usually do so alongside one another in the retinues of local landholders, as in this example? And to what extent did military service broaden the horizons of the Essex gentry, opening up new opportunities and creating new allegiances?

The first two decades of the reign of Edward I were dominated, at least militarily, by the intermittent but demanding Welsh wars of 1277, 1282–3, 1287 and 1294–5. The purpose of the first of these expeditions was to punish the prince of Gwynedd, Llewellyn ap Gruffudd, for his failure to perform homage to Edward I. When this failed to dampen the ardour of the Welsh, a further expedition was launched in 1282 with the aim of conquering Gwynedd and annexing it to the English crown, something only completely achieved following two further punitive expeditions, the last of which, in 1294–5, was a major affair in its own right.

One of the chief sources of information about the armies of 1277 and 1282 are the marshal's registers recording the proffers of feudal service made by the English tenants-in-chief. As the men arrived at muster their names were written down by the marshal of the army, who also recorded the identity of the man making the proffer (he was not always present in person) and the county in which the tenant-in-chief held his lands from the king.

In the summer of 1277 twelve landholders are recorded as making proffers at Worcester for estates held in Essex,[17] but in August 1282, for the muster at Rhuddlan, the proffer roll is incomplete and the figure for Essex landholders is just seven.[18] At least some of the Essex tenants-in-chief are known to have drawn on local men to discharge their obligations. In 1277, for example, Sir Robert Fitzwalter employed the Essex knight Sir William de Wauton.[19] Essex landholders also tended to lead or send to muster members of their own families. In 1277 Ralph Perot used his son, a sergeant of the same name,[20] while five years later Sir Matthew Loveyn enlisted the services of his younger brother, Sir John Loveyn.[21] For the men of Essex, as with other parts of the country, military service in this era was often a family affair.

During the late thirteenth and early fourteenth centuries, however, feudal service was only one way in which the kings of England went about gathering their armies. In fact many armies, including those of 1287 and 1294, were recruited entirely by other means, whether by men serving for crown wages or gratuitously. Edward I and his son were also keen to create more knights to fight in their armies by forcing, via royal writ, the better-off gentry (usually those with £20 or £40 of landed income per year) to become knights or to pay fines for exemptions. The return to one such writ from 1312 is illustrated in Figure 3.2.

A writ of distraint to knighthood (as this process was known) was sent out to the shires in 1278, between the first two Welsh wars, and, fascinatingly, Essex is one of the few counties for which the returns survive.[22] Forty-three men are listed in total and, of these, some 17 (40 per cent) can be traced in the surviving records for at least one of the Welsh wars of 1277 to 1295, though not all served as knights. One distrainee was Richard Ewell, who served in the war of 1287 in the retinue of the earl of Hereford and Essex,[23] another example of the strong link between the Bohuns and the men of Essex. Also among the distrainees was Richard Cornherth of Cornard, Suffolk, who also held land in Finchingfield, Essex. He was present in the royal army in 1282–3 and 1294–5.[24]

Certain parts of the realm were, not surprisingly, more closely associated with the crown's wars than others. This was true despite the general tendency of the gentry, at least, to serve wherever they were needed, especially when the army was being led in person by the king. The real regional differences lay in regard to local defence when major armies were not in the field; it was left largely to the men of Northumberland and Cumberland, for example, to defend the Scottish March during the winter months, and to the gentry of Shropshire and Herefordshire to play a leading role in quenching any embers of Welsh unrest.

In general one might expect a southern county such as Essex to have been free from such onerous local burdens, but this changed for a few years during the mid-1290s following the outbreak of war between England and France over sovereign rights in the Plantagenet duchy of Gascony. In a rare example of Essex gentry being asked to serve together in defence of their local area, we find in December 1295 the names of 102 individuals entered on a list of men charged with the safekeeping of the Essex coastline.[25] The gentry of the neighbouring counties of Suffolk, Norfolk and Sussex were expected to perform a similar role as fears of a possible French invasion loomed.

This list of Essex gentry charged with the defence of the Essex coastline provides a wonderful snapshot of local landed society at a particular moment

Figure 3.2. List of £40 landholders in Essex and Hertfordshire who were not yet knights and were expected to become knights or pay fines. The list dates from the summer of 1312. It seems likely that one of the Crown's main aims in drawing up such lists was to increase the number of knights available for service in its armies (TNA, C47/1/7).

in time. Of the 102 men, we are informed that 11 were too weak (*impotens*) to actually perform the service being requested of them, perhaps being too old, wounded or simply war-weary, while an additional 65 men are described as being outside (*extra*) the county, by which was presumably meant either that they resided elsewhere or that they were actually away giving military service in the crown's wars.

This, then, left just 26 members of the gentry who were actually residing (*comorantes*) in the county and fit for active service. An intriguing question thus arises: were the men away from Essex in December 1295 the most bellicose members of the county, with the men residing in Essex at the time the lists were drawn up shying away from service in Gascony, where a war was currently being fought? Moreover, how many of the men described as being outside the county can actually be shown to have been away on active military service at the time?

In fact, no fewer than 28 (43 per cent) of the Essex landholders described as being away from the county in December 1295 had taken out legal safeguards (usually letters of protection or attorney) ahead of their planned service in Gascony during either 1294 or 1295.[26] This means that all of these men were almost certainly in Gascony performing military service at the time that the list was drawn up. Indeed, although the Gascon campaigns of the 1290s are poorly documented (there are no horse inventories or payrolls for the English men-at-arms), it is highly likely that most if not all of the gentry missing from Essex in December 1295 were engaged in the south-west of France. There can be few better indications than this of the degree to which Essex (like so many other counties) had become militarised by this stage of the wars, nor of the way that regional military communities were being utilised in the theatres of war that most directly concerned them. The gentry of Essex and other southern coastal communities were almost certainly over-represented in the wars on the continent, not surprisingly given the ongoing troubles in Wales and the fact that a new war was just about to break out in Scotland.

It is worth taking a look at some of the Essex gentry serving in Gascony during the mid-1290s in a little more detail. Some of the most prominent Essex landholders led retinues on the campaign, so that we find, for example: 27 individuals in 1294 and 1295 making preparations to serve in Gascony under Sir Robert Fitzwalter;[27] nine individuals taking out letters of protection for service with Sir Henry Grey;[28] and at least five men serving in the retinue of Sir Robert Pinkeney.[29] Fitzwalter, Grey and Pinkeney were each among the Essex landholders described as being outside (*extra*) the county in December 1295. Also present among the retinue leaders in Gascony were the sons of the earl of Oxford, namely Sir Robert de Vere junior and Sir Hugh de Vere.[30] Despite his title, the earl of Oxford held the bulk of his lands in Essex and other eastern counties of England.[31]

There is considerable evidence, within this sample of retinues, of Essex men serving together in Gascony and of Essex retinue leaders drawing on local recruitment pools. Taking, to begin with, the Essex knights described as being outside the county in December 1295, at least seven of these individuals served in the retinues of Essex landholders or men with strong Essex connections. Sir William Wauton and Sir William Haningfield joined the retinue of Sir Robert Fitzwalter;[32] Sir Thomas Meuse was with Sir Henry de Grey;[33] Sir John Heron served as a sub-leader under Sir Robert Pinkeney;[34] and Sir Henry Lacy, Sir Richard Weyland and Sir Guy Shenefield served in the retinue of one or other of the sons of the earl of Oxford.[35]

Moreover, if we look beyond the list of men described as being outside the county in December 1295, other Essex gentry can be found serving in these retinues. Interestingly, Sir John Praers is listed among the gentry residing in Essex in 1295, but in September 1294 he had taken out letters of protection and attorney for service in Gascony under Sir Robert de Vere junior.[36] Perhaps he had served in Gascony but returned to England by the time the sheriff's list was drawn up in the following year. The retinue of Sir Robert Fitzwalter included, among others, Thomas Filliol, a man listed on the parliamentary roll of arms for Essex some 17 years later and who would also be summoned from the county as a knight in 1324.[37]

Perhaps more interesting than this considerable body of evidence of Essex men serving together on campaign, however, is the way that military service took some Essex gentry into the social circles of prominent figures from other parts of the country. Sir John Lenham and Sir Drew Barentin, for example, found service in Gascony in the retinue of Sir Fulk fitz Warin junior, a member of the powerful Welsh Marcher family,[38] while Sir Robert Cantilupe and Sir Robert Burneville found service with the king's brother, Edmund, earl of Lancaster.[39] This reminds us that the social networks of the gentry often extended far beyond the county,[40] and that military service offered up many opportunities for advancement to the ambitious.

If the 65 Essex gentry on business away from the county in December 1295 appear to have been a most bellicose group, perhaps the 24 men still residing in Essex were, by contrast, more inclined to dabble in the affairs of the county as local administrators, keeping well away from the cut and thrust of the crown's wars. Certainly, such a division between warmongers and peace-lovers might have had some practical value. First of all, however, it is worth stressing that even if these men *were* inclined to shy away from war, Essex was still a highly militarised county, as these stay-at-homes constituted only 24 per cent of the gentry named on the sheriff's list. Moreover, far from shying away from military service, some of the gentry residing in Essex during the winter of 1295–6 were active military campaigners in their own right. In total, no fewer than 16 (67 per cent) of these men can be shown to have given military service at some stage during the wars of Edward I and Edward II.

Some of these men were possibly quite elderly by 1295, with their warring days far behind them. Sir Bartholomew Brianzon could lay claim to having taken part in the Lord Edward's crusade to the Levant during 1270–72,[41] but his last known service was as a household knight in the Welsh war of 1282–3, and it is likely that he had hung up his sword after that campaign.[42] Nevertheless, many of the gentry residing in Essex in December 1295 were still in the prime of life and took part in military expeditions during the later 1290s and 1300s.

Far from looking forward to a quiet life, no fewer than five of these men appear to have served on the opening campaign of the Scottish wars, in the spring of 1296. Sir Ralph Bigod joined the company of the earl of Hereford and Essex;[43] Sir Nicholas Wokingdon and Sir Alan Goldingham made plans for service in the retinue of the earl of Norfolk;[44] Sir Jolland of Durelm enlisted for service in the king's division;[45] and, most interestingly of all, Sir Nicholas Barentin obtained a letter of protection with the Essex and Scottish landholder Robert Bruce, earl of Carrick, father of the future King Robert I of Scotland.[46]

Other members of the Essex gentry to serve in Scotland (and probably at the battle of Dunbar) with the earl of Carrick in 1296 include the brothers William (d. 1325) and Edmund de Badewe (d. 1331) of Great Baddow.[47] The Bruce family's connections to Essex remind us that, for some Essex gentry at least, the Bruce rebellion of 1306 must have been especially shocking and potentially compromising. Personal ill-feeling arising from past acquaintance might even account for Sir Henry de Bohun's attack on King Robert I at Bannockburn, discussed at the beginning of this chapter.

It is clear that by the mid-1290s nearly all Essex gentry had some experience of war or were to gain such experience in the near future. The landholding influence in Essex of prominent families such as the Bruces, the Bohuns and the de Vere earls of Oxford meant that there would always be opportunities for military service in the retinues of great men, and this is confirmed when we find, for example, the relatively obscure Essex knight Sir John Wascul apparently serving on his one and only military campaign in the retinue of the earl of Oxford in Scotland in 1298.[48]

Wascul seems to have been one of a large number of Essex gentry serving at the battle of Falkirk on 22 July, including Sir John Lovetot (yet another knight included on the sheriff's list of 1295),[49] Sir Matthew Loveyn (a retinue leader in 1298),[50] Sir Ralph Perot[51] and William Badewe, who again appears to have served in the Bruce retinue.[52] Indeed, it is not at all surprising that at least 84 per cent of Essex knights listed on the parliamentary roll of arms of c.1312 are known to have given military service at some point in the four decades leading up to the battle of Bannockburn,[53] with participation levels in the major campaigns – such as that of 1298 – being especially high.

Having established beyond doubt that the Essex gentry, like the gentry of most counties, were heavily involved in the wars of Edward I and Edward II, we can now dwell in a little more detail on some of the personal experiences of these men during the Scottish wars of 1296 to 1328, including the range and depth of their service connections. There is no quick and easy way of summarising the range of military experience among all Essex landholders, so the focus will be on a few men whose military careers are particularly well covered by the extant documents.

It is clear that, for many Essex gentry, networks based on shared kinship or shared locality were often paramount in shaping the contours of military service. Let us take two of the knights listed under Essex on the parliamentary rolls of arms drawn up early in the reign of Edward II. We have already seen how one of these men, Sir Nicholas Engaine, served in the retinue of the earl of Hereford on the Bannockburn campaign of 1314; however, before that he had already served in Scotland in 1300 and 1303 in the retinue of his brother Sir John Engaine,[54] one of the many Essex veterans of the war in Gascony of the mid-1290s.[55] Likewise, we have seen how Sir William Haningfield served in the retinue of Sir Robert Fitzwalter during the Gascon wars, but he also went on to serve with Fitzwalter in Scotland in 1300, 1301 and the year of the Bruce rebellion, 1306.[56] This kind of service was typical of many gentry who served with the same leader from campaign to campaign.

Fortunately a number of lists of Essex gentry survive from the years of the Scottish wars, although often the men of the county were intermingled with the gentry of Hertfordshire because the two counties shared a sheriff. From 1297, 1300 and 1301 there survive sheriffs' returns of 60, 91, and 53 Essex and Hertfordshire gentry summoned for military service in Flanders (1297) and Scotland. We can add to these the 58 Essex knights named on the parliamentary roll of arms of *c*.1312 and the 68 knights and 58 men-at-arms summoned from Essex to Westminster in 1324 to give a substantial list of local landholding society.

One of the few Essex families to be represented on each and every one of these lists is the Rochefords, who derived their toponym from the vill of Rochford in the south of the county.[57] As such, a brief summary of the Rochefords' contribution to the wars of 1296–1328 offers a good opportunity to observe patterns of service and changing lordship connections among the Essex gentry.

Not surprisingly, the military service of the Rochefords predated the Scottish wars, with Sir Nicholas Rocheford, for example, being proffered at the feudal muster of 1277 by Sir Alexander Balliol of Cavers.[58] Yet it is with the outbreak of the war in Scotland that the record of their service becomes more complete, and yet again we find the usual combination of regular participation in the crown's wars combined with links to other Essex gentry.

This is manifest in the career in arms of Sir Waleran Rocheford, who was summoned from Essex as a knight (and £40 landholder) for the Caerlaverock campaign of 1300.[59] It is not, in fact, certain that he served in Edward I's army in that year, but that he most probably did is suggested by his service on other campaigns. He first appears as a *valettus* on the Scottish expedition of 1296, being knighted on 25 March.[60] Thereafter he went on to serve in Flanders in 1297 and in Scotland in 1298.[61] Particularly worthy of note, however, is that he served on each occasion in the retinue of the Essex landholder Sir John Engaine.

Nor was he the only member of the Rocheford family to have service links to other Essex landholders, for in 1300 Robert de Rocheford appeared at the feudal muster in Scotland as a sub-knightly man-at-arms on behalf of Humphrey de Bohun, earl of Hereford and Essex.[62] Later Robert served as a knight, leading his own retinue to the siege of Berwick in 1319 and taking part in the War of Saint-Sardos in Gascony during 1324–5, where he served in the retinue of Edmund, earl of Kent, half-brother of Edward II.[63] In fact he was one of a cluster of Essex gentry serving in Kent's retinue on the continent during the War of Saint-Sardos, with Walter de Colchester, Nicholas Belhous and John de Claryngg also present.[64] Belhous and Claryngg had been included on the sheriff's returns from Essex of 1324; their service in Gascony reminds us of the high levels of participation among the Essex gentry in the Gascon wars of the 1290s.

Other members of the Rocheford family who apparently served in the Scottish wars were Sir Ralph, in 1298 and 1301,[65] and Sir John, in 1308 and 1314,[66] both of whom appear on several of the Essex summons lists mentioned above. The pertinent point is that the commitment to arms of the Rocheford family was far from exceptional, and we continue to find examples of Essex men going to war in the companies of other Essex men into the 1320s. On the Scottish campaign of 1322, for example, we find three Essex men – Henry Longchamp, Martin Longchamp and Sir John Wauton – serving in the retinue of Sir Robert Fitzwalter,[67] and Robert Bousser, one of the men-at-arms summoned from Essex to Westminster in 1324, being proffered at the feudal muster on behalf of the earl of Oxford.[68]

To answer the questions posed at the beginning of this article, then, it can be said with absolute certainty that the Essex gentry was a heavily militarised group by the time of the battle of Bannockburn and that the example of Essex gentry serving together in that year was far from exceptional. The assertion made in the *Victoria County History* that 'Essex played no particular part in the larger aims and undertakings of Edward I' does not stand up to close scrutiny.[69] Certainly many more examples could have been given of Essex men serving with retinue leaders from other parts of the country, but often it is their service with fellow Essex landholders that stands out from the sources and, in this respect, it is certainly a valid conclusion that there was a vibrant military community in late thirteenth- and early fourteenth-century Essex.

Notes

1   This is a revised version of a paper first published in *Essex Journal*, 46 (2011), pp. 7–14. I should like to thank Dr Andrew Ayton for the data on the armies of 1314, 1319, 1322 and 1324–5. I should also like to thank Dr Tony Moore for his advice on the landholding backgrounds and name spellings of several of the gentry named in this paper.

2   The names of tens of thousands of soldiers from the years 1369 to 1453 can now be searched online at www.medievalsoldier.org.

3   N. Denholm-Young (ed.), *Vita Edwardi Secundi* (London, 1957), p. 51; W. Stubbs (ed.), 'Annales Londonienses', in *Chronicles of the Reigns of Edward I and Edward II*, Rolls Series, lxxvi (London, 1882–3), vol. i, p. 231. The *Scalacronica* of Sir Thomas Gray gives the identity of the slain English knight as Sir Peter de Montfort; A. King (ed.), Sir Thomas Gray, *Scalacronica, 1272–1363*, Surtees Society, vol. ccix (Woodbridge, 2005), p. 73. However, the *Vita*'s identification seems more reliable, not least because (as noted here) the possible author, John Walwayn, seems to have served in the same retinue as Sir Henry Bohun on the Bannockburn campaign. Various modern artists have taken up the theme of the Bruce–Bohun duel in their works.

4   TNA, C71/6, mm. 4, 5.

5   H.R. Luard (ed.), *Flores Historiarum*, 3 vols, Rolls Series, xcv (London, 1890), vol. iii, p. 158.

6   Denholm-Young, *Vita Edwardi Secundi*, p. 53.

7   For the estates held in chief by the earl, see *CIPM*, vol. 3, no. 552.

8   TNA, C71/6, mm. 4, 5.

9   TNA, C71/6, m. 5; Denholm-Young, *Vita Edwardi Secundi*, pp. xix–xxviii. Walwayn had also served with the earl in Scotland in 1306: TNA, C67/16, m. 9.

10   TNA, C71/6, m. 5; F. Palgrave (ed.), *Parliamentary Writs and Writs of Military Summons*, 2 vols in 4 parts (London, 1827–34), II, ii, pp. 408–9. Chandos had served with the earl at the Dunstable tournament in October 1309: A. Tomkinson, 'Retinues at the Tournament of Dunstable, 1309', *English Historical Review*, 74 (1959), p. 73.

11   TNA, C71/6, m. 5; Palgrave, *Parl. Writs*, i, p. 413.

12   TNA, C71/6, m. 5; Palgrave, *Parl. Writs*, II, ii, p. 652.

13   TNA, C71/6, m. 5; C47/1/5, m. 4; C47/1/6, m. 16.

14   TNA, C71/6, m. 5; M. Jones and S.K. Walker (eds), 'Private Indentures for Life Service in Peace and War 1278–1476', in *Camden Miscellany, Vol. XXXII*, Camden Society, 5th series, vol. 3 (Cambridge, 1994), no. 14, p. 48; C. Bullock-Davies, *Menestrellorum Multitudo: Minstrels at a Royal Feast* (Cardiff, 1978), p. 185. Enfield (Middlesex) was a Bohun manor. Sir Bartholomew held the tenth of a knight's fee in Wimbish, Essex.

15   TNA, C71/6, m. 5.

16   For further details of the links between Earl Humphrey and the gentry of Essex, see G. Jones, 'The Bohun Earls of Hereford and Essex, 1270–1322', MLitt thesis (University of Oxford, 1984), p. 76, cited in A. Ayton, 'The English Army at Crécy', in A. Ayton and P. Preston, *The Battle of Crécy, 1346* (Woodbridge, 2005), p. 213, n. 266. The Bohun family's military links to the gentry of Essex continued later in the fourteenth century under William Bohun, earl of Northampton: *ibid.*,

pp. 206, 213. See also A. Ayton, 'Edward III and the English Aristocracy at the Beginning of the Hundred Years War', in M. Strickland (ed.), *Armies, Chivalry and Warfare in Medieval Britain and France*, Harlaxton Medieval Studies, vol. vii (Stamford, 1998), pp. 174, 192 (this article is freely available online at: www.deremilitari.org/resources/articles/ayton2.htm).

17   Henry de Gaunt; the earl of Hereford; the earl of Oxford; John de Neville; Ralph Perot; Ralph de Boxtede; John fitz William; Robert Fitzwalter; John de Chauncy; Hugh Peverel; Edmund Kemesak; and Andrew Heliun: Palgrave, *Parl. Writs*, vol. i, pp. 198–208.

18   Matthew Loveyn; William Say; William Fiennes; Robert Fitzwalter; Robert fitz Roger; Robert Bruce; and Ralph Perot: *Ibid.*, vol. i, p. 232.

19   *Ibid.*, vol. i, p. 204.

20   *Ibid.*, p. 203.

21   *Ibid.*, p. 232.

22   TNA, C47/1/2, m. 21.

23   *CPR*, 1281–92, p. 272.

24   TNA, C67/8, m. 7; C67/10, m. 3.

25   Palgrave, *Parl. Writs*, vol. i, pp. 273–4.

26   The letters of protection, attorney and of respite of debts relating to the men of Essex and other counties can be found at various points within F. Michel, C. Bémont and Y. Renouard (eds), *Rôles Gascons, 1242–1307*, 5 vols (Paris, 1885–1962), vol. iii, pp. 127–327.

27   Michel *et al.*, *Rôles Gascons*, iii, pp. 120, 123, 136, 294–5, 299, 306–7, 318–20.

28   *Ibid.*, pp. 295, 308.

29   *Ibid.*, pp. 101, 131, 161, 164, 180.

30   See, for example: *ibid.*, pp. 121, 159.

31   *CIPM*, vol. 3, no. 367; vol. 7, no. 379.

32   Michel *et al.*, *Rôles Gascons*, iii, pp. 136, 295, 307.

33   *Ibid.*, p. 295.

34   *Ibid.*, p. 105.

35   *Ibid.*, pp. 121, 137, 166, 178.

36   *Ibid.*, pp. 121, 137.

37   *Ibid.*, pp. 120, 136, 295, 307; Palgrave, *Parl. Writs*, vol. i, p. 414; Palgrave, *Parl. Writs*, part II, vol. ii, p. 652. On the 1324 list, however, he is described as not having land: 'non habet terram'.

38   Michel *et al.*, *Rôles Gascons*, vol. iii, pp. 118–19, 125, 138.

39   *Ibid.*, pp. 296, 325, 326.

40   The same point has been made in J. Ward, *The Essex Gentry and the County Community in the Fourteenth Century* (Chelmsford, 1991), pp. 20, 24.

41   S. Lloyd, *English Society and the Crusade 1216–1307* (Oxford, 1988), appendix 4.

42   TNA, C47/2/3, m. 13; E101/4/8, mm. 1, 2. He was summoned to serve on the Flemish campaign of 1297–8 (TNA, C47/1/5, m. 4), but it must be considered doubtful whether he joined the army.

43   TNA, C67/11, m. 1.

44   *Ibid.*, mm. 1, 5.

45   *Ibid.*, m. 1d.

46   *Ibid.*, m. 6.

47   *Ibid.*, mm. 4, 6; *CIPM*, vol. 6, no. 598; vol. 7, no. 335. Edmund's heir was Hugh de Badewe, subject of another article in this volume, see below, pp. 65–77.

48   TNA, C67/13, m. 8.

49   *Ibid.*, m. 1.

50   H. Gough (ed.), *Scotland in 1298: Documents relating to the Campaign of Edward I in that year* (London, 1888), p. 232.

51   TNA, C67/13, m. 1.

52   On 8 June 1298 he had a letter of protection enrolled for service in Scotland with Robert Bruce, Lord of Annandale: *ibid.*, m. 6. This would again seem to have been the father of the future Robert I of Scotland, recent work suggesting that the latter did not fight on the English side at Falkirk: M. Morris, *A Great and Terrible King: Edward I and the Forging of Britain* (London, 2008), p. 313.

53   D. Simpkin, *The English Aristocracy at War: From the Welsh Wars of Edward I to the Battle of Bannockburn* (Woodbridge, 2008), p. 22.

54   TNA, E101/8/23, m. 5; C67/15, m. 9.

55   Michel *et al.*, *Rôles Gascons*, vol. iii, p. 162.

56   TNA, C67/14, mm. 4, 10; C67/16, m. 11.

57   The Rochefords held by barony tenure in Rochford, with John Rocheford being the incumbent tenant in 1303; *Inquisitions and Assessments relating to Feudal Aids, 1284–1431*, 6 vols (London, 1899–1921), ii, p. 137.

58   Palgrave, *Parl. Writs*, vol. i, p. 209.

59   TNA, C47/1/6, m. 16.

60   *Ibid.*, E101/5/23, m. 1i.

61   *Ibid.*, E101/6/37, m. 2; Gough, *Scotland in 1298*, p. 190.

62   F. Palgrave (ed.), *Documents and Records Illustrating the History of Scotland and the Transactions between the Crowns of Scotland and England* (London, 1837), vol. i, p. 209.

63   TNA, E101/378/4, fol. 28v; E101/35/2, m. 7.

64   *Ibid.*, E101/35/2, m. 7; *CPR*, 1321–4, p. 403.

65   TNA, C67/13, m. 8d; C67/14, m. 8d.

66   G.G. Simpson and J.D. Galbraith (eds), *Calendar of Documents relating to Scotland*, v (Edinburgh, 1986), p. 447; TNA, C71/6, m. 5.

67   *CPR*, 1321–4, p. 188; TNA, C47/5/10, m. 1b.

68   TNA, C47/5/10, m. 1c.

69   W. Page and J.H. Round (eds), *VCH Essex*, Vol. 2 (London, 1907), p. 212.

Chapter 4

Organised crime in fourteenth-century Essex: Hugh de Badewe, Essex soldier and gang member

Gloria Harris

Lawlessness in later medieval England is probably best represented, in the popular imagination, through the stories and images of Robin Hood and his band of accomplices. The reality behind these romantic myths, however, was very different. Throughout the later medieval period successive monarchs struggled to find effective systems to control rising levels of criminal activity, without much success. By the fourteenth century England was particularly lawless and violent and the problem of how to deal with this issue had dogged the reigns of both Edward I and Edward II. Intermittent experiments in measures for keeping the peace were attempted but these were generally in response to particular outbreaks of criminal activity. By the time Edward III assumed personal rule in 1330 criminal gangs had already taken advantage of the troubled years of his father's reign. Ormrod has described how 'bands of thugs flouted the law as they set up local protection rackets and terrorised their neighbourhoods with complete impunity'.[1] Robbery, murder, kidnapping and rape were widespread, and corruption and bribery were to be found among sheriffs, lawyers and juries.

Organised crime presented perhaps the biggest threat to public order during the later medieval period and however bad the situation had been during the first three decades of the fourteenth century it was to become much worse. Edward III's decision to go to war with France in 1337, while still engaged in conflict with Scotland, meant that the king was so preoccupied with the military matters that he 'gave no real thought to the operation of criminal law in his absence'.[2] While Edward III was actively participating in fighting overseas, many soldiers were returning home from the battlefields on leave, perhaps through injury, or at the end of their service. At this earlier stage the war was not continuous but rather a series of short campaigns, and returning home was often the result of a temporary truce, when memories of what those men had seen and done during the fighting were still fresh in their minds. With crime prevalent all over England there was a widespread belief that soldiers returning from the wars, including those of knightly status, were responsible for the increasing levels of crime and violence. Was this view justified?

The county of Essex experienced its fair share of this kind of criminal activity among the aristocracy and gentry. One such man, who was both a fighting Essex soldier in the Hundred Years War *and* a criminal gang member operating in his home county, was Hugh de Badewe. How typical was he and how close was the connection between men of the fighting military community, particularly the knights, and the incidence of criminal gang activity when they were back on home soil?

Background

Hugh de Badewe was born *c.*1315 into an established minor gentry Essex family who had held a modest estate in Great Baddow near Chelmsford for four, possibly five, generations before his birth. Since at least 1198 the land had been held as a petty serjeanty; this was a small service that was owed specifically to the king in return for the land.[3] The serjeanty involved an obligation to look after the king's palfrey, a small riding horse, for 40 days at the king's charges, when the king was in the region.[4] From 1198 the holder of the tenement, who owed the service, was always referred to as *marescallus*. In this context the term *marescallus* meant a marshal or farrier, explaining why the house and landholding became known locally as The Marshal's Tenement.[5] By definition the family were freeholders and, although their lands were not extensive, in 1279 the holding consisted of around 170 acres. This modestly sized estate afforded the de Badewes a degree of independence and elevated their social status in the local community.[6]

Little is known of Hugh de Badewe's early life. His father Edmund died in 1332, when his wife Joan was still living and Hugh was about 17 years old.[7] The Marshal's house and land lay on the east side of Great Baddow and were separated from the larger manor of Great Baddow by the width of the road leading from Great Baddow to West Hanningfield. The manor of Great Baddow had been in the possession of the wealthy and influential Bohun family since the Bruce rebellion in 1306.[8] Their family seat at Pleshey Castle, illustrated in Figure 4.1, lay just eight miles away. Throughout his life, Hugh de Badewe knew no other Great Baddow manorial lord than a Bohun.

Military experience

From the outset of the Hundred Years War, Hugh de Badewe was recruited into the retinue of William de Bohun, newly created earl of Northampton and

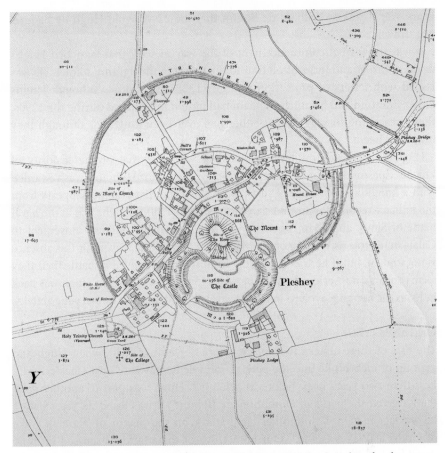

Figure 4.1. Ordnance Survey map of Pleshey Castle, the seat of the de Bohun family, showing the remains of the motte and bailey. The de Bohuns were the manorial lords of Great Baddow where Hugh de Badewe's tenancy lay (OS map 1:2,500 Essex sheet 44.9, 1921 edn; reproduced by courtesy of the Essex Record Office).

brother of Humphrey, earl of Hereford and Essex, whose seat was at Pleshey Castle.[9] It was usual at that time for newly recruited soldiers to join the retinue of the local magnate, so it would have been natural that Hugh would have joined the retinue of Humphrey, but the earl (d. 1361) was something of a recluse and never fought.[10] The Bohuns were *the* most prominent noble Essex family, with wealth and estates. Such was their influence that a significant proportion of the Essex gentry had established connections with the Bohuns and so it was natural that the county should offer a promising recruiting ground from which to boost the numbers needed in the military community generally. Recruitment also brought together men who knew each other from their locality and through family connections. So at the outset of the Hundred

Years War it was to William de Bohun that the 22-year-old Hugh de Badewe was drawn.

It was the formal commencement of the war in 1337 that launched Hugh's military career and introduced him to the world of the fighting soldier. He was issued with letters of protection in 1337, 1338 and 1340.[11] Although Hugh's father Edmund and his uncle William had fought in Scotland during the 1290s, there is nothing to suggest that either had ever been knighted, although they may have been.[12]

Hugh de Badewe's military involvement was, like that of the majority of knights, spasmodic, but his service in France with Northampton was rewarded with a knighthood in *c*.1339.[13] It is about this time that Hugh disappears from the military records for around six years, between 1340, when he was at the naval battle of Sluys, and 1346, when he was involved in the military movement to Calais in his role as Warden of the Maritime Lands.[14] The reason for this absence is not known, but if he was recovering from injuries received in battle then they were probably not serious because between 1340 and 1348, when Hugh was back in Essex, he became involved in three recorded incidents of criminal gang activity.

Organised crime

The first of these attacks took place before September 1340, when Hugh and a group of men broke into the park of John de Segrave at Great Chesterford.[15] Less than two years later, before March 1342, Hugh was part of another gang that targeted the parks of Humphrey de Bohun.[16] It was to be six years before he was again named in another gang attack on the manor of Thomas Wake of Liddel at Wakes Colne.[17] Our knowledge of the attacks (discussed in more detail below) comes from the royal issue of judicial commissions to punish the suspected culprits, copies of which were entered on the chancery's patent rolls.[18]

The gang warfare in which Hugh de Badewe seems to have participated wholeheartedly took place in the wider later medieval context of criminal activity generally and of criminal bands in particular. Lawlessness on this scale was not new and it was not confined to Essex. As Prestwich has commented, 'Medieval England was a lawless country where a quarrel over a badly cooked herring could end in a violent death, as happened in Lincoln in 1353'.[19] It was worth noting, however, that the planning of an attack on a man's park or manor required some degree of sophisticated organisation.

The size of gangs varied greatly, from two or three members to 200 or 300, depending on the type of criminal activity undertaken. In many cases the criminals themselves were often assisted by local men and women, known as receivers, who may not have been involved directly in the attacks but who helped the gangs in other ways, such as receiving stolen goods and providing food, shelter and, perhaps, valuable information based on local knowledge.

Medieval gangs often assisted one another, and individual members frequently switched between gangs. On occasion the bands would combine with similar groups with a mutual interest and would sometimes seek additional assistance.[20]

Members of such criminal gangs were often drawn from the gentry – men such as Hugh de Badewe, who were knights or esquires. Although the gentry were certainly most prominent, other gang members might be engaged in a variety of occupations.[21] Of the three attacks in which Hugh is known to have taken part, it is the first, in 1340, that is, arguably, the most interesting in terms of the numbers involved and the social composition of the group. Upwards of 34 men mounted the attack on John de Segrave's property and 'broke his park at Great Chesterford … hunted therein, carried away his goods and deer from the park, and assaulted his men and servants'.[22] In relative terms this may not have been a large number of participants, but it was clearly a major incident and the social status of the men involved was also significant. Heading the list of offenders was the magnate John, earl of Oxford, whose main residence was at Castle Hedingham in the north of Essex, about 15 miles from the target in Great Chesterford. Second on the list was John Fitzwalter, a prominent young Essex landholder who was to gain much notoriety as an Essex criminal in future years.[23] Third was Bartholomew Burghersh, whose father, also Bartholomew, was Lord Chamberlain to Edward III. These were high-profile men and, while it might be unusual to find men of noble status such as the earl of Oxford actively engaged in gang activities, Bellamy has noted that 'many criminal bands must have been founded in the halls of the nobility … for many outlaws … were members of the lord's household'. A lord might lead or plan activities and he would have not have been ignorant of his gang's strength and experience in the fourteenth century.[24]

While some gangs may well have had their origins in the halls of the nobility, the links between Hugh de Badewe and the gang members involved in the 1340 attack appear to have had more to do with their military connections than adherence to a particular magnate household, although it is often difficult to make a distinction.

While Hugh's maiden expedition to France, at the very beginning of the Hundred Years War in 1337, may well have been his first introduction to particular noblemen and knights of the military community, some of these men were already acquainted with each other following their shared experiences of active service in the wars against Scotland. John, earl of Oxford and William de Bohun, for example, were already experienced soldiers following their activities in Scotland. However, Edward III's decision to go to war with France brought many new recruits, such as Hugh de Badewe, and experienced warriors, such as Oxford and Bohun, together, although they may already have known each other through their local connections.

During the three years between the start of the wars with France in 1337 and the 1340 attack on John de Segrave's property common bonds had already been forged on the battlefield and probably strengthened by Edward's chivalric enthusiasm. These bonds of brotherhood and camaraderie appear in large part to have been transported back to the villages of Essex during breaks in the war and were likely to have been a major driving force behind collective criminal activity. The sense of brotherhood born out of adversity on the battlefields led to a transference of similar loyalties into gang warfare once back on English soil. Combined with a sense of local identity and allegiance, it must have been a powerful force behind collective criminal activity. In addition, hunting and poaching with your comrades were enjoyable pursuits.

In 1338, as part of Edward's drive to draw on untapped pools of genteel manpower, the king ordered 44 individuals to appear at Ipswich in Suffolk in December of that year equipped and ready for overseas service. According to Ayton, the list 'reads like a roll-call of colourful, gentry criminals'.[25] Of the three heading the list of offenders involved in the 1340 attack on John de Segrave, Oxford and Burghersh junior do not appear to have gone on to illustrious criminal careers. Fitzwalter, however, earned himself a considerable reputation, in the years to come, as a thug of the first order, as will be described below.[26] All three men knew each other from their military service and their common thread seems to have been the connection they had with William de Bohun, earl of Northampton.

Oxford and Northampton were particularly close. They were almost the same age, they were brothers-in-law and they campaigned together. In 1342 Oxford set out on his first major campaign in France, serving in Brittany with Northampton, who had been appointed Edward III's lieutenant there. In the following year both men were in Scotland together, and in 1345 they were back in France again.[27] Bartholomew Burghersh junior and his father were captains of their own retinues, and both were present in the Breton campaign in 1342–3.[28]

The presence of Burghersh junior in the 1340 raid must have been a great asset to the gang. According to Prestwich, the archaeological evidence shows that he was a powerful man with an unusually large physique. He was about five feet ten inches tall, broad-shouldered yet of elegant build. His bones showed none of the signs of osteoarthritis, a condition indicative of a life of heavy toil. During his military career he suffered minor injuries: cracked ribs, strained elbow joints and a twisted ankle due to a bad fall. The heavy weapons that he used in war, such as the lance and sword, had built up the muscles in his right arm and had even made it grow longer than the left.[29] Burghersh's imposing physique must have added to the fearsome nature of the warrior-led gang of which Hugh de Badewe was a member.

Furber argues that Fitzwalter's life of crime began in 1342,[30] so his involvement in the 1340 Segrave attack may have been a first taste of criminal activity that was to set him on the road to becoming probably the most feared gang member in Essex for 11 years until his career in crime was brought to an end.[31] From 1340 until 1351 Fitzwalter and his followers embarked on a reign of terror throughout Essex and a list of his crimes, including extortion, intimidation and thuggery, reads like the history of a modern racketeer, as when he besieged the town of Colchester and held the inhabitants hostage for six weeks in 1343.[32] He was born into a noble family and, following the death of his father, John, then aged 13, came into a substantial inheritance with land and possessions both inside and outside Essex. As Furber described, he went on 'to enjoy and misuse this inheritance ...'.[33] With youth, power and wealth, Fitzwalter was a 'rich kid' of his day. His youthful energy and later bloody experiences in the theatre of war must have helped fuel what seems to have been a natural appetite for aggression and intimidation.

William Tallemache, another member of the 1340 gang, also had a close connection to Northampton. Already a seasoned warrior in 1340, he had served as an esquire with Northampton, and, immediately prior to the battle of Sluys, and before the Segrave attack, had become permanently indentured – that is, a lifetime retainer – to Northampton 'in peace and war'.[34] Of the 34 men named in the Segrave attack, 10, including Hugh de Badewe, were described as knights but, although Tallemache is known to have been knighted by then, he is not titled as such on the list.

The last four named men on the list were clerks, possibly in lower orders. Men in holy orders were often to be found in indictments concerned with gang activity. They often played a passive role as receivers or maintainers, which was likely in this case.[35] Not all men in the gang with Hugh were in their youth. John Engayne of Dillington had been a soldier in his younger days and was no longer a sword-bearing retainer.[36] Some members involved in the attack on Segrave's manor were later to become casualties of war. Robert de Lacy and John de Loveyn were two who died at Calais.[37] Others would also meet as comrades in adversity as they fought the war on French soil in battles yet to come. As the years progressed, alliances would be made as men's paths crossed and recrossed in the military and social spheres.

The second attack in which Hugh was involved took place less than two years later, in 1342. On this occasion the criminal band targeted the parks of earl Humphrey de Bohun, but this group appears to have been smaller than the first, with only 11 named men involved, in addition to others who were anonymous. According to the information in the patent rolls, the men entered Bohun's parks at Great Baddow, Pleshey, Great Waltham, High Easter, Hatfield [Broad Oak], Dunmow and [Saffron] Walden. Having broken into the parks, they hunted the animals, took them away and assaulted Humphrey's men and servants at Chelmsford.[38] Although there were fewer men involved in this attack the area covered in order to carry out the deeds was geographically much wider. Whether the men operated in a single band, or whether each stayed in their own locality, with perhaps help from one or two others, is not clear. It would be a hard day's work to carry out raids on so many parks, so possibly the raids took place over a number of days or possibly weeks.

Heading the list of the 11 was Robert de Marny, an Essex knight in his mid to late 20s, who had fought alongside Northampton in Scotland and was recorded on the earl's payroll when they were together at Sluys. While he did not enjoy the high profile of John Fitzwalter, Robert de Marny was to combine a life of gentry crime in Essex with continuing regular participation in the king's war.[39] Hugh de Badewe was second on this list, immediately followed by John de Liston, John de Boys and Nicholas de Belhous. All were knights and at some time during their lives held local office, and all were part of the Essex gentry. It was common to find members of the same family belonging to one gang but this does not seem to have happened in the bands of which Hugh was a part. However, members of the same family did take part in separate attacks. John de Marny was with Hugh when Segrave's park was raided, while Robert de Marny, possibly John's brother, was part of the Bohun park attack. Nicholas de Belhous also rode with this gang, while Thomas, probably his father, was part of the criminal band that carried out the attack on Wake's property in 1348.[40]

Park raiding and breaking was common and some gang leaders may have specialised in it.[41] The theft of animals from parks was a way of securing luxury food, such as venison, making a profit on the value of the animals poached, or taking revenge on the owner – or it may just have been for the thrill of the chase. Hugh's transgression against Earl Humphrey de Bohun when he was complicit in raiding his park at Great Baddow was audacious. The perimeter of the park was just a road's width away from Hugh's land and the raid here may well have involved the connivance of Bohun's park-keeper, as keepers were notorious for their corrupt nature and criminal inclinations.[42]

Hugh de Badewe's participation in the attack on Thomas Wake's manor at Wakes Colne in 1348 was to be the last recorded and involved just six named men and others unidentified. On this occasion they 'entered his manor … broke the gates, houses, doors and windows there, carried away his goods, assaulted his men and servants and imprisoned them, whereby he lost their service for a great time', or so Wake claimed.[43] The nature of this kind of attack, where people were held hostage for a period of time, was not uncommon in Essex. It had happened five years earlier when John Fitzwalter, having by then acquired a taste for thuggery, besieged the town of Colchester from Easter to Whitsuntide, a period of six weeks, holding up market traders until bought off by the townsmen.[44] Perhaps the most notorious attack of this sort, in which Colchester was again targeted, took place in 1350, when Lionel de Bradenham besieged the town from August until October of that year.[45]

The attack on Wakes Colne was much smaller in scale, in terms of both the number of men involved and the chosen target – a manor, rather than a town – but nevertheless there were some similarities. The leading offender in the Wakes Colne raid was listed as 'Robert Maryn', but can almost certainly be identified with Robert Marny, who had led the attack on Bohun's park in 1342. It is not known for how long Hugh and the gang imprisoned Thomas Wake's men and servants, assuming that they did. When Colchester was besieged in 1350 the aggressors used the damaged doors and windows from the houses they had smashed down as shields to arm themselves in further attacks.[46] When Hugh's band attacked the gates and houses on Wake's manor they may have had a similar objective in mind, although this is the last known gang raid in which he is known to have taken part.

When Hugh de Badewe took part in the first gang attack in 1340 the belief that soldiers returning home from the wars were responsible for the increasing level of crime and violence was already widespread, and it would not perhaps be surprising if collective violent behaviour was a direct result of the corrupting influence of life on the battlefields. Many of Hugh's associates, both in war and crime, were, like him, young, energetic men, many in their 20s, who were probably still in a state of heightened exhilaration from the mayhem of battle when they embarked on a crime spree on their return to Essex. Indeed, there was much about Hugh's gangs that imitated life on the battlefields, and the military connection has already been made. The composition of the gang members mirrored a select military retinue and in some bands across England the instigators and planners of criminal activity were often given the title of captain in much the same way as they would have been on the battlefields in Scotland and France.[47]

Analysis shows that gang crime generally took place within a 40-mile radius from where the leaders originated or held property. This enabled them to capitalise on their local knowledge and gave them a greater sense of security because of their established networks with those who helped them in indirect ways.[48] Hugh de Badewe's three incidents of criminal activity took place within a radius of approximately 25 miles from his home in Great Baddow. When Hugh took part in his first known raid on John de Segrave's park in 1340 John, earl of Oxford, led the criminal band. The distance between Hedingham Castle, the earl's main residence, and Segrave's park in Great Chesterford was about 15 miles. This took the gang to the limits of the county, in its north-west corner, where the Essex boundary met those of Suffolk and Cambridge. This was ground easily covered on horseback, and made even more possible if some, or all, gang members had been overnight guests at the earl's castle.

The raids on Bohun's parks, in six parishes, covered a maximum distance of some 30 to 35 miles as the crow flies, between Great Baddow in mid-Essex to Saffron Walden in the north-west of the county. Great Waltham, High Easter and Great Dunmow are three contiguous parishes mid-way between the two extremes, and Hatfield Broad Oak was but a ride across one of the Rodings or one of the Canfields. If the park raids were co-ordinated attacks in which local men played their part in the park in their own locality, then Hugh's participation was literally on his own doorstep, with Bohun's park just across the road from Hugh's land and house. If, however, the raids took place over a number of days, and were collective acts, then all six parishes were, if not within a 40-mile radius of Layer Marney, where the leader Robert Marny's estate lay, certainly within easy riding distance. Marny also led the gang that carried out the third and final criminal act in which Hugh was involved, when the men raided Thomas Wake's manor at Wake's Colne; the distance between Layer Marney and Wake's Colne was about 10 miles.

Men banded together to commit many kinds of crime: murder, theft, poaching, extortion and kidnapping. Often money-making was the common aim, but sometimes money was sought as a means of revenge rather than for specific material gain and was perhaps seen as a means of recompense for some real or imagined wrong-doing.[49] Feuds and the desire for revenge were also common reasons why the gentry turned to crime. Fitzwalter and his criminal bands, for example, committed many crimes against the citizens of Colchester and their property, of which the 1343 case may have been a revenge attack. It is possible that Fitzwalter's career in crime may have had its origins in his quarrel with the men of Colchester. Fitzwalter held the manor of Lexden, so the dispute may have been over conflicting jurisdictional rights between neighbouring landowners and communities. Prolonged grievances may well also have been at the heart of the 1350 siege, when Lionel de Bradenham, a steward and tenant of Fitzwalter, led another attack on the town.[50]

Although men formed bands to carry out a variety of crimes, little is known about the reasons why they chose to do so and the motives for the three attacks carried out by Hugh and the other men are, unsurprisingly, unclear. The attacks on the parks of Segrave and Bohun might be considered as relatively low-level crime for the times, and perhaps the reason may have been rooted in conflicts over status within the locality. Only the very wealthy were able to create parks on their estates and so a park was a highly conspicuous statement of wealth and social standing that was a prime target for those with grievances against those lords who owned one. Although Robert Marny headed the list of offenders in the raid on Humphrey de Bohun's park, Hugh de Badewe appears to have entered wholeheartedly into the spirit of the attack. This bold and provocative act was carried out against a very wealthy and influential nobleman whose family's influence in Hugh's locality was significant. The Bohun family, as lords, had dominated the manor of Great Baddow since before Hugh was born. Such conspicuous wealth and property, especially the park, which Hugh would have been faced with whenever he left his residence, may have been a constant reminder that, as socially elevated as Hugh's family were in their own locality, they were far from equalling the nobility of the Bohuns. For Hugh and his close accomplice, Robert Marny, this act may just have been in the spirit of oneupmanship.

The attacks on Bohun's men in Chelmsford and Segrave's tenants in Great Chesterford show that the gang members were not averse to carrying out acts of violence on people, whether intentionally or in the heat of the moment, as well as causing damage to property; tenants and men may themselves have been considered as property.

Although the motives for the attacks carried out during the 1340s by Hugh and his cohorts are not known, revenge for some transgressions, real or imagined, seems the most likely explanation. The outcome of Hugh and the gangs being brought before the commissioners appointed to hear and determine the crime committed is also not known. Three isolated criminal acts across eight years in this decade, however, do not qualify Hugh as having had a career in crime. Hugh's activity was minor compared with the general level of crime in England at the time, and especially with the career of John Fitzwalter, whose activities contributed to one historian's description of the 1340s as 'a time of widespread depravity'.[51] Hugh had spent this turbulent decade experiencing and participating in violence both on and off the battlefield. After the attack on the manor of Thomas Wake in 1348 he is not known to have engaged in any further criminal activity. He had been rewarded for his war efforts with a knighthood by 1339 and he, like many other men of the gentry and of knightly status, went on to play a prominent part in local affairs of the county; many such men, indeed, were responsible for administering justice rather than engaging in criminal activity.

The arrival of the Black Death in England, which reached Essex in the spring of 1349, coincided with the last apparent instance of Hugh de Badewe's gang crime. This tumultuous event, which reduced the population of England by between a third and a half, and certainly affected Hugh's locality, may have been the reason for the change in his lifestyle.[52] Where the disease hit, few would have been unaffected by it and most of those fortunate enough to survive would have lost family, friends and workers. By this time, though, Hugh was into middle age, probably married and settled down. The years following the Black Death were to see improvements in justice both at the centre and in the counties, and Hugh was to play a prominent role in local justice and administration in Essex until a few years before his death c.1380.

Notes

1   W.M. Ormrod, *The Reign of Edward III. Crown and Political Society in England 1327–1377* (London, 1990), p. 7.

2   *Ibid.*, p. 54.

3   *Book of Fees*, vol. ii, p. 1330.

4   *Ibid.*

5   Information from the Worshipful Company of Farriers.

6   *CIPM*, vol. 2, no. 308.

7   *CIPM*, vol. 7, no. 335.

8   *Calendar of Fine Rolls*, 1272–1307, p. 535.

9   *CPR*, 1334–8, p. 531.

10   J. Ward, 'The Wheel of Fortune and the Bohun Family in the Early Fourteenth Century', *Essex Archaeology and History*, 3rd series, 39 (2008), p. 165.

11   *CPR*, 1334–8, p. 530; *Treaty Rolls, 1235–1339*, vol. ii, nos 291, 733; TNA, C76/15, m. 19; C81/1735, no. 15. I am grateful to Andrew Ayton for supplying the last two references.

12   Above, Chapter 3, pp. 51–64.

13   ERO, D/DL/T1/78.

14   T.M. Hope, 'Essex and the French Campaign of 1346–7', *Essex Review*, 51 (1942), p. 141.

15   *CPR*, 1340–3, pp. 96–7.

16   *CPR*, 1340–3, p. 446.

17   *CPR*, 1348–50, p. 79.

18   Patent rolls are discussed above, p. 15.

19   M. Prestwich, *The Three Edwards. War and State in England 1272–1377* (London, 1980), p. 231.

20   J.G. Bellamy, *Crime and Public Order in England in the Later Middle Ages* (London, 1973), pp. 70–72.

21   *Ibid.*, p. 72.

22   *CPR*, 1340–3, pp. 96–7.

23   E.C. Furber (ed.), *Essex Sessions of the Peace, 1351, 1377–9*, Essex Archaeological Society, Occasional Publication no. 3 (Colchester, 1953), pp. 61–5.

24   Bellamy, *Crime and Public Order*, p. 70.

25   A. Ayton, 'Edward III and the English Aristocracy at the beginning of the Hundred Years War', in M. Strickland (ed.), *Armies, Chivalry and Warfare in Medieval Britain and France*, Harlaxton Medieval Studies, vol. vii (Stamford, 1998), p. 16.

26   Furber, *Essex Sessions of the Peace*, pp. 61–5.

27   *Oxford Dictionary of National Biography* (Oxford, 2004), vol. 56, p. 304.

28   A. Ayton, *Knights and Warhorses: Military Service and the English Aristocracy under Edward III* (Woodbridge, 1994), pp. 263–4.

29   Prestwich, *The Three Edwards*, pp. 137–8.

30   Furber, *Essex Sessions of the Peace*, p. 61.

31   *Ibid.*, p. 64.

32   *Ibid.*, p. 62.

33   *Ibid.*, p. 61.

34   Ayton, 'Edward III and the English Aristocracy', p. 1.

35   Bellamy, *Crime and Public Order*, p. 73.

36   Ayton, 'Edward III and the English Aristocracy', p. 1.

37   Hope, 'Essex and the French Campaign of 1346–7', p. 143. Robert de Lacy died on 18 January 1347 'overseas' and John de Loveyn died on 30 January 1347: *CIPM*, vol. 9, nos 2, 24.

38   *CPR*, 1340–3, p. 446. For the locations with Essex see Figure 1.1.

39   Ayton, 'Edward III and the English Aristocracy', p. 1.

40   ERO, D/DL/T1/51 gives this relationship.
41   Bellamy, *Crime and Public Order*, p. 80.
42   *Ibid.*, p. 81.
43   *CPR*, 1348–50, p. 79.
44   W.R. Powell, 'Lionel de Bradenham and his Siege of Colchester in 1350', *Essex Archaeology and History*, 3rd series, 22 (1991), p. 69.
45   *Ibid.*
46   *Ibid.*
47   Bellamy, *Crime and Public Order*, p. 75.
48   *Ibid.*, pp. 82, 83.
49   *Ibid.*, p. 78.
50   *Ibid.*, p. 79.
51   *Ibid.*, p. 4.
52   H. Grieve, *The Sleepers and the Shadows. Chelmsford: A Town, its People and its Past*, Essex Record Office Publication no. 100, vol. i (Chelmsford, 1988), p. 29.

Chapter 5

The fighting men of Essex:
service relationships and the poll tax

Sam Gibbs

Essex in the late fourteenth century was a place of change. The Black Death was a primary cause of immense demographic dislocation and accompanying shifts in economic, social and political structures. Experiences were not uniform across England, however, and in many ways Essex stands out as atypical, which make it an interesting area for a case study of the service relationships between the men who served as archers and their retinue captains. The county had a tendency towards violent agrarian unrest (notably its involvement in the Peasants' Revolt of 1381), a high population density in some areas, an unusually developed cloth industry in both urban and rural areas, a large degree of social and economic differentiation and an inclination towards religious nonconformity.[1] Even the Black Death does not appear to have had the effects on landholding that were experienced in other areas of the country.[2] These factors make Essex different from other regions within England and its communities' experiences make it a unique area in which to study the relationships between archers and captains, and the archers' place within society.

Alongside the socio-economic and political changes that were taking place in England during the late medieval period, the English military system was also undergoing a period of flux, which saw a shift from the 'feudal'-style army that was frequently used in the late thirteenth and early fourteenth centuries to one based almost solely on contracts of indenture, a development that changed the basis of recruitment from tenurial landed obligations to contracted paid service.[3] Essex's most renowned medieval soldier, Sir John Hawkwood, is a prime example of an English soldier fighting for financial reward. From his modest background – he was born in Sible Hedingham to a tanner – he rose to become one of the premier mercenary captains in Europe, spending the majority of his lengthy career fighting on the battlefields of Italy.[4] However, his career was exceptional among English soldiers in that he spent most of it fighting as a mercenary with foreign forces, not in the English armies, and therefore his experience of medieval warfare will not be analysed as a part of this study. Instead, the focus will be upon the experience of the archers who served in the English armies, their socio-economic backgrounds and their service relationships with their social superiors, the retinue captains who recruited them.[5]

Historical research into service relationships has focused on those towards the top of the social scale, which in a military context has meant the men-at-arms. These relationships could encompass a wide variety of different interactions, ranging from the formal obligations that might tie a tenant to a landlord to the informal connections that individuals might make through shared experiences of military service.

Those of lower status are seen only in association with men of gentry rank and above, rather than as a group in their own right. This is one of the unfortunate effects of the bias of surviving sources, which has left the historian with greater volumes of evidence for those of higher socio-economic status, whose activities are better recorded. This trend is also evident when considering the military community of England. The historiography has focused on the upper echelons of society, the men who fought as men-at-arms, rather than on the archers. This study will contribute to correcting this imbalance and will focus on the county of Essex in considering the relationships between the archers and the retinue captains who made contracts, known as indentures, for service with the crown, and who were mostly drawn from the landowning class. Furthermore, the archers' 'civilian' lives will be studied: the lack of a permanent standing army suggests that these men would have needed to find non-military employment when not actively serving if they were to avoid dependence on charity or crime. As a group, the archers will be contrasted with the non-military section of Essex society to determine if there are any differences between the two groups in terms of occupational structure or (using tax paid as an indicator of wealth) economic standing.

Sources and method

There has been little investigation of the men who formed the bulk of the English armies – the archers who, over the period 1369–1417, outnumbered the men-at-arms mustered by a ratio of 2:1.[6] The archers' legendary successes in battle have focused academic attention on the technology used and the strategy and tactics employed by them and their captains. This has come at the expense of research into the men themselves, whose non-military lives have been largely ignored.[7] There are issues with the evidentiary base for a study of archers, not least that they were men of low social status without the wealth or standing to appear frequently in the surviving documents.[8] Nonetheless, there are several sources, notably the residential, occupational and economic data from the three late fourteenth-century poll tax returns and data from military sources, that can be used to undertake a wide-ranging prosopographical study. Using a clearly defined method allows this subject to be approached with confidence, and a correlation between the sources reveals the hitherto murky civilian world of the English archers.

With its focus on the archers in the Essex military community, this study contributes to an area of historiography that has developed greatly since the late twentieth century, leading to a large body of work using relational databases to assist in the analysis of large datasets connected to military service, ranging from Bell's exploration of the 1387 and 1388 English naval expeditions[9] to the comprehensive 'Soldier in Later Medieval England' database, which contains around 250,000 service records, including the muster rolls for 1369–1453.[10] The database formed the basis of an in-depth volume, *The Soldier in Later Medieval England*, which considers what this large data source can reveal about military service.[11] Other examples of the use of relational databases to undertake prosopographical analysis include the work by Ayton and Lambert on the men who served as mariners in the later fourteenth century and the ships and shipping that military expeditions required.[12] Yet, despite this increased interest, there is not yet been a full investigation of the ordinary fighting men, the archers, who have been considered 'unidentifiable' on an individual basis.[13] However, although few archers have left enough evidence to construct a complete biography after the fashion of leading military figures, a prosopographical analysis is a possibility, as demonstrated by the studies noted earlier.

Although the archers are the focus of this study, it is not directly concerned with their military activities. Instead, their motivations for undertaking military service and their socio-economic backgrounds, including their occupations, are considered. To this end, the poll tax returns of 1377, 1379 and 1381 are an ideal source and are something of a rarity for medieval historians – a large nominal dataset. Despite the vast amount of raw data contained within the returns – a total of 264,350 names – until relatively recently its potential has been largely ignored or dismissed by historians. Even studies concerned with demography, such as S.L. Thrupp's *The Merchant Class of Medieval London*, are dismissive of the returns, asserting that 'the schedule is so faulty that it cannot represent anything more than a preliminary survey; if the collectors had proceeded on this basis, they would have touched barely half their final total'.[14] This is typical of the evidentiary criticisms that have been made of the returns. A notable exception, however, is Fenwick's unpublished PhD thesis, 'The English Poll Taxes of 1377, 1379 and 1381'.[15] Of particular interest is the chapter evaluating the returns as a source, examining the weaknesses that had been highlighted by previous historians and to a great extent neutralising them.

Fenwick makes a cautious, yet comprehensive, case for the evidentiary value of the returns as a historical source. For example, a prevalent criticism of the poll tax returns was their demographic deficiencies, primarily the lack of single people, apprentices and, particularly notably, women, which were allegedly caused by corruption or incompetence on the part of the assessors. Fenwick noted that many of these people would be missing because these groups would often lack the wealth required to be liable for the tax.[16]

In addition to Fenwick's crucial analysis, a number of other published works are relevant to the present article. For example, Poos' study of Essex between the late fourteenth and early sixteenth centuries uses a sample of the extant poll tax return data to gain some insight into the demographic and occupational structure of Essex in 1381, as well as considering some of the evidentiary issues in greater depth.[17] Other publications, especially those concerned with women's history, also use the returns, as they are one of the few sources that record much detail about women of the lower social classes. There are also two case studies: the first, dealing with New Romney in Kent, examines the returns as a source for the town's social structure.[18] The second considers the demographic structure of the county of Buckinghamshire at the time of the poll taxes.[19] Of more direct relevance to this present research is Baker's study on the origins of English archers, which goes into some depth in considering the issues that surround the use of the poll tax records, particularly when identifying archers.[20] Nevertheless, despite the importance of the returns, there is no established methodology for employing them within a large relational database.[21]

As well as the poll tax returns, the muster rolls constitute an important source. These were created as a part of the indenture system which by the late fourteenth century had almost wholly replaced previous methods of raising soldiers. Instead of being based on any obligations relating to tenure of land, the indenture system in its simplest form relied on individual captains agreeing to provide a certain number of soldiers, for a certain period of time, in exchange for predetermined wages. The muster rolls are the records kept by Exchequer officials certifying that the retinue captains had indeed arrived at the start of their agreed period of service with the correct number and quality of soldiers. This step in the recruitment process has yielded vast amounts of nominal data concerning individuals who would not often appear in other sources. The musters not only contain the names of those who fought but also record how the army was divided into different retinues and how each retinue was further divided into men-at-arms and archers. They can also provide information on social status, promotions, replacements and mortality rates.[22] This information has already been used to create career profiles of individuals, including one archer, Robert de Fishlake.[23] Fishlake gave testimony in the Hastings v. Grey court of chivalry case regarding four of his incidents of service. He served in John of Gaunt's expedition to St Malo in 1378; in the ill-fated fleet commanded by Sir John d'Arundel in 1379, when the ships were scattered by a violent storm; in the earl of Buckingham's expedition to Brittany in 1380; and in Richard II's campaign to Scotland in 1385.[24] However, this testimony is exceptional; for most archers the surviving evidence is not so complete or detailed, and this is where the prosopographical approach is helpful.

Although, like the muster rolls, the poll tax returns are nominal in form, they provide a very different set of data. They are organised by residency, through county, hundred and vill, and are inconsistent between the different areas, possibly owing to different interpretation of instructions by the collectors or variations in spelling. Fenwick has suggested that the tax was an attempt to spread the financial burden onto a wider base throughout England. 'The Commons' aim in imposing the poll taxes was to ensure that all, high or low, normally exempt or not, who could pay the tax did so ... their aim was simply to relieve themselves of the main burden of tax.'[25] By shifting the basis of taxation to a per capita basis, more individuals were brought into the 'national' tax system, although the three poll taxes did vary significantly. In 1377 all persons over the age of 14 were expected to pay 4d, with exemptions for the clergy and genuine paupers. In 1379 paupers and clergy were still exempt, as were married women, and the age of liability was raised to 16. This time the charges were graduated from a base rate of 4d to a top rate of 10 marks.[26] The final collection in 1381 changed the age of liability to 15 and continued to exempt paupers and clergy, although not married women. The method of calculating liability changed again, with each vill being liable for 1s per taxable person, with a person's individual contribution varying according to their ability to pay, with a minimum liability of 4d and a maximum of 20s. The differences between the collections limit some of the demographic conclusions that can be drawn. Nevertheless, it must be remembered that the returns were never intended to be a census of the realm, and that, while caution is needed in analysing them, the data they contain is invaluable, as it is one of the few large nominal records extant for the medieval period with occupational evidence, and indirectly, indications of wealth and status.

Therefore, despite the evidentiary concerns, which include the variability of spelling, a combination of the poll taxes with the muster rolls in a relational database allows comparisons to be made between two disparate sources. In effect the database holds two main tables, keeping the data from the musters and poll tax returns distinct from each other. The soldiers in each retinue are linked to a specific retinue number, in turn linked to a captain within an army. This captain is also associated with landholdings that correspond with the vills and hundreds in the poll taxes. The main source used in this study for identifying landholdings was the inquisitions post mortem, which were the outcome of sworn inquiries by local jurors into the landholdings of a tenant in chief of the king after their death.[27] Although not a comprehensive source for late medieval landholdings, the inquisitions do provide a detailed picture, as inquiries were ordered by royal officials in each county where a feudal tenant was believed to have held property. They record not only what lands a landholder held in demesne at the time of death and land held by their vassals but also what land was held of the king and what land was held of others.[28] Although the indenture system had, on the whole, encouraged men from outside the aristocracy to lead retinues, captains were still men of property and estate. Therefore they appear in the inquisitions, which indicate where they held lands and where their estates were focused.[29]

Identifying the archers

The use of the poll taxes provided an insight into the demographic and economic structure of Essex, albeit qualified by the evidentiary issues noted above. It will also enable the identification of archers and of their links to landholding retinue captains who were resident in Essex during the collection of the three grants. A comparison of the archers to their 'civilian' counterparts within Essex will highlight any differences between the two groups. Firstly, a sample of archer service records was extracted for comparison with the Essex poll taxes. The sample forming the basis of this study is comprised of archers who served between 1367 and 1391, within 10 years of the poll taxes. This increases the potential for any identification to be correct, as the limited chronology restricts the possibility of a false positive, where a man appearing in the poll tax is linked erroneously to a similarly named but different individual, therefore making the nominal linkage more secure. This gives a sample of 18,485 unique service records. However, the number of unique individuals is lower owing to men serving on more than one occasion, and therefore having multiple service records in their name, or the repetition of common names. An example of this second issue are the 36 archers in this sample named John Clerc and 27 named John Parker. The repeat occurence of these names makes it difficult to ascertain whether any given service record should be linked to none, one, or all of the others in the sample with the same name. To assist with processing the large sample the archers have been broken down into three tiers, each tier representing a different level of probability for nominal linkage. Tier 1 comprises 10,450 names which appear once in the musters. These are the men whom it is easiest to link to a specific poll tax entry, as the names are unique and there is little chance of a false positive occurring as a result of multiple records of the same name among the archers. Tier 2, containing 1,873 names, represents names which appear on multiple occasions, within the same year, in the musters. The link between these records and the poll tax is less certain, as a false positive or indeterminate identification is more likely. The final and

Table 5.1 Nominal linkage probability between muster rolls (1367 to 1391) and poll taxes (1377 and 1381).

	Tier 1	Tier 2	Tier 3
Section 1	Strong	Potential	Good
Section 2	Potential	Weak	Weak

smallest sample, Tier 3, contains the names of 1,015 archers who appear to have served on multiple occasions and represent the more 'professional' archers, who may have been using military service as a primary occupation. These are identified by finding those names which appear on multiple occasions within the muster sample, but never more than once in a calendar year.

Once these tiers of archers were identified, the Essex sample was extracted from the returns for comparison with them. Of the 264,350 surviving nominal poll tax records, 12,965 (4.9 per cent of the whole dataset) are from locations in Essex. Unfortunately these occur only in the returns from 1377 and 1381, as none of the Essex returns for 1379 survive. As this study focuses on those individuals who may have seen service as archers and have the potential for nominal linkage to the muster rolls, the Essex sample from the poll tax returns was reduced to contain only those entries with full or partial names that can be positively identified as male, giving a total of 6,853 men.[30] This was then further divided into Section 1, containing 4,901 names that appear only once in the returns; and Section 2, containing 1,952 entries that represent the 654 unique names that appear on more than one occasion in the same tax year. Unlike repeat muster roll entries, which can indicate multiple incidents of service, each poll tax record theoretically represents a unique individual, as no one should have been taxed in more than one location. Therefore Section 2 does not provide very secure nominal linkage, as it is impossible to identify which of two or more Essex residents could be linked to a muster entry. Table 5.1 provides a representation of the strength of the links between the various sub-groups between the two samples.

These probability groups highlight the points where the nominal linkage is strongest, and also where the intersection between the samples is least likely to represent a significant relationship. It is highly unlikely that the matches between Section 2 and Tier 2, both of which represent multiple occurrences of the same name, could be linked with any certainty, so these matches cannot necessarily be deemed to be the same individual and therefore are not of use for this study. Cross referencing in this manner breaks down the samples into broad probability groups which can be seen in Table 5.2.

Table 5.2 Matches between archers and Essex poll tax returns.

	Tier 1	Tier 2	Tier 3	Unmatched Essex Residents	% Essex population sample matched to archers
Section 1	276	155	116	4359	11.2%
Section 2	86	106	61	n/a	n/a

Table 5.2 makes it apparent that Essex men appearing as archers in the 1369–91 sample are in a minority, indicating that military service was not a common occupation. However, this should be qualified by noting the percentage of the population recorded in the poll tax returns as labourers or farm labourers, which at 10 per cent is close to the apparent Essex service rate of 11 per cent, suggesting that military service was as prevalent as labouring among the wider population.[31] However, when considered on its own, this does not reveal much about potential motivations that may have encouraged Essex men to fight as archers. To this end, those identified as archers who lived in Essex have been compared against the retinues of the captains who held land in the county. The details of these Essex retinues are shown in Table 5.3. This comparison has been made to determine whether landlords were recruiting heavily from their areas of landed influence or, instead, relying on a 'military service market' arising from the contract-based system of recruitment. Table 5.4 shows the matches between captains' retinues mustered for service between 1367 and 1417 and persons resident in their Essex lands. Here the sample range of archers has been expanded to provide a larger sample, while still representing a reasonable age for a soldier to be in active service. For example, if a man had been the minimum taxable age of 15 in 1381, he would have been 51 by 1417. Although this may seem old for the period, there are several examples of soldiers serving at greater ages than this – notably Sir Andrew Luterell, who appears to have been serving at arms for at least 50 years, so continuing past the age of 70.[32]

Table 5.4 has been constructed by comparing the retinue captains from the muster rolls to the inquisitions post mortem that note their landholdings at death. Not all the vills in Essex have been included in this comparison, as only 70 can be linked to retinue captains and of these only 55 have extant nominal lists for 1377 or 1381. This means that 3,052 named archers from 30 retinues are being compared to 3,396 men extracted from the original Essex poll tax sample where the vill taxed matches a landholding of a retinue captain.

As Table 5.4 shows, the level of recruitment from a captain's landholdings is very low, with only Sir William Bourchier recruiting more than 2 per cent of

Table 5.3 Retinues of Essex captains, 1370 to 1417.

Retine captain	Type of service	Year	Total retinue size	Number of archers	Reference
Edmund, Earl of Stafford	Expedition	1400	328	179	E101/42/16
Edward Sakvyle	Expedition	1417	6	4	E101/51/2
Humphrey, Earl of Hereford	Naval	1371	198	120	E101/31/15
Humphrey, Earl of Hereford	Naval	1372	679	384	E101/32/20
John Coggeshale	Garrison	1370	2	1	E101/30/38
John Coggeshale	Garrison	1371	1	0	E101/31/18
John Driver	Expedition	1415	2	1	E101/45/4
John Sutton	Standing army	1403	6	4	E101/43/21
John Sutton	Expedition	1415	9	6	E101/45/4
Lord Henry Ferrers	Expedition	1415	5	0	BL/Harley/782
Lord John Cobham	Naval	1377	227	112	E101/36/29
Lord Walter Fitzwalter	Expedition	1370	80	40 (not named)	E101/30/25
Lord Walter Fitzwalter	Standing army	1384	188	124	E101/39/38
Richard Beamond	Expedition	1415	13	9	E101/45/13
Sir Edward Burnell	Expedition	1415	33	24	E101/45/4
Sir Henry le Scrope	Naval	1372	42	25	E101/31/34
Sir Henry le Scrope	Standing army	1403	30	24	E101/43/21
Sir John Bohun	Naval	1388	71	41	E101/41/5
Sir John Bourchier	Expedition	1370	400	200 (not named)	E101/30/25
Sir John Neville	Standing army	1395	406	320	E101/41/39
Sir John Neville	Expedition	1417	166	122	E101/51/2
Sir Walter atte Lee	Expedition	1370	20	10 (not named)	E101/30/25
Sir William Bourchier	Expedition	1415	25	unknown	BL/Harley/782
Sir William Bourchier	Expedition	1417	163	123	E101/51/2
Sir William Marny	Naval	1404	85	52	E101/43/32
Thomas Holand	Naval	1387	2	2	E101/40/34
Thomas, Earl of Arundel	Expedition	1415	90	68	E101/50/26
Thomas, Earl of Arundel	Expedition	1415	470	356	E101/47/1
Thomas, Earl of Nottingham	Naval	1388	237	135	E101/41/5
Thomas, Earl of Nottingham	Standing army	1389	1229	748	E101/41/17

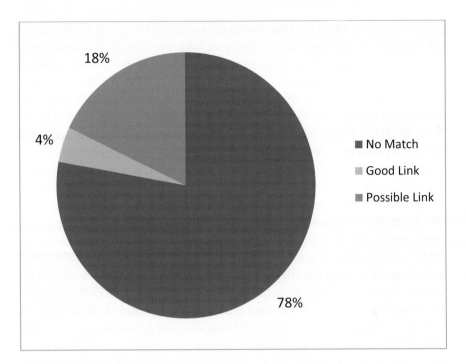

Figure 5.1. Essex men in retinues outside Essex.

his archers from within his own landholdings. There do appear to have been greater levels of recruitment from Essex as a whole, with more matches between retinue archers and the Essex poll taxes. The amounts vary from 7.3 per cent up to 30 per cent in the case of John Sutton's retinue. On average, archers in Essex captains' retinues can be found in the county around 10 per cent of the time, an average similar to that mentioned in relation to Table 5.2. There are several potential causes of this low match rate. Firstly, as previously mentioned, it is possible that landowners saw these men as crucial to the productivity of their estates. Secondly, it is possible that captains wanted to recruit men willing to go, rather than imposing pressure on those unwilling, a hypothesis that is strengthened by considering the contract system that was employed to obtain soldiers for the English armies, as discussed earlier. Furthermore, although population density across the county was not especially high for England, when viewed locally the central and northern areas were heavily populated. In these areas density of population is likely to have produced a large stratum of landless labourers and surplus craftsmen throughout the later medieval period, even following the Black Death.[33] This, in turn, could have encouraged men to undertake military service as an alternative to civilian occupations, as the wages of 6d a day for a mounted archer compared favourably to those of a skilled builder, at 5d, in the later fourteenth century.[34] Of course, there was the risk of death at the hands of the enemy or from the rigours of campaigning, disease, or starvation, but the higher wages may still have made military service an attractive alternative to the life of a landless labourer. There was also the possibility of plunder and ransoms to boost incomes. Roger Mill, an archer serving in France in the early fifteenth century, sold a sword he had won for 7s 6d, roughly 15 days' pay,[35] and there may have been pensions, or assistance with legal problems, including pardons for any crimes committed.[36]

After looking at the relationships between Essex captains and their local populations, it is also possible to consider the case of Essex men serving 'abroad' with retinues whose captains did not hold land in Essex. Of course, this drastically increases the sample size extracted from the muster rolls, as it covers the 16,789 men who were not in the retinues of the captains listed in Table 5.4. Therefore the results must be treated with caution. Nonetheless, they provide an interesting counter-point to the results discussed above. As can be seen in Figure 5.1, a large majority of Essex men cannot be found serving in the military at all, with 78 per cent of names from Section 1 of the poll tax (the unique names in the returns) not being matched to the non-Essex retinue archers. Where a good link – between a unique Essex poll tax name (Section 1) and a unique archer name (Tier 1) – exists the percentage of matches is lower than the 9.7 per cent matched between retinues and poll tax returns of Essex. However, when the other possible matches are included the combined match rate rises to 22 per cent, noticeably higher than the Section 1 names matched to the Essex retinues. Although this could be attributed to the larger sample size, it also could indicate that an Essex man who engaged in military service was more likely to have served with a captain who hailed from outside the county than with one who held lands within it. This supports the idea that there was a military 'service market', as men were not necessarily limited to serving those who could have claimed to exercise some form of official or unofficial tenurial influence over them. Instead they had at least some freedom to offer their service where good opportunities arose.

Although this study focuses on service relationships and archers' civilian lives, there is an opportunity to consider whether the Essex archers demonstrated a different pattern of service in contrast to the archer sample as a whole. This has been achieved by looking at the numbers of archers from the muster rolls and the type of service for which they were recruited (Table 5.5). The breakdown reveals that there was little difference between the different tiers of archers, and that the Essex men who can be identified as serving only once – the Tier 1 Essex archers – were not too dissimilar from their more professional colleagues in Tier 3. There is a slight increase in the number of Tier 3 archers serving in expeditionary or standing armies and a

Table 5.4 Retinue archers present on captains' landholdings in Essex, 1370 to 1417.

Essex captains	No. retinue archers	No. of male poll tax residents	No. retinue archers matched to Essex landholdings	No. retinue archers matched to Essex county wide	% retinue archers matched to Essex landholdings	% retinue archers matched to Essex county wide
Edmund, Earl of Stafford	179	163	0	13	0.0%	7.3%
Edward Sakvyle	4	49	0	0	0.0%	0.0%
Humphrey, Earl of Hereford	504	84	4	53	0.8%	10.5%
John Coggeshale	1	60	0	0	0.0%	0.0%
John Driver	1	27	0	0	0.0%	0.0%
John Sutton	10	12	0	3	0.0%	30.0%
Lord John Cobham	112	39	1	15	0.9%	13.4%
Lord Walter Fitzwalter	124	77	0	19	0.0%	15.3%
Richard Beamond	9	256	0	1	0.0%	11.1%
Sir Edward Burnell	24	50	0	2	0.0%	8.3%
Sir Henry le Scrope	49	1434	1	6	2.0%	12.2%
Sir John Bourchier	200 (but no names)	406	n/a	n/a	n/a	n/a
Sir John Bohun	41	42	0	3	0.0%	7.3%
Sir John Neville	442	166	2	24	0.5%	5.4%
Sir Walter atte Lee	10 (but no names)	17	n/a	n/a	n/a	n/a
Sir William Bourchier	123	210	3	24	2.4%	19.5%
Sir William Marny	52	134	1	9	1.9%	17.3%
Thomas Holland	2	116	0	0	0.0%	0.0%
Thomas, Earl of Arundel	492	46	2	39	0.4%	7.9%
Thomas, Earl of Nottingham	883	20	0	77	0.0%	8.7%

Table 5.5 Types of service, 1367 to 1391.

Service type	Archers 1367–1391		Essex archers Tier 1		Essex archers Tier 3	
Expeditionary	2,840	15%	17	6%	38	12%
Garrison	1,423	8%	23	8%	26	8%
Standing army	4,639	25%	34	12%	45	14%
Escort	166	1%	6	2%	4	1%
Unknown	721	4%	12	4%	10	3%
Naval	8,696	47%	184	67%	191	61%
	18,485	100%	276	100%	314	100%

slight decrease in the proportion engaged in naval service. Of course, the difference between the various types of service can be hard to distinguish: for example, an expeditionary army recruited for service in France would have had to be transported by sea. However, if the objective of the force at the time of recruitment is considered, then the category of standing or expeditionary army includes those forces closest to a professional army in a modern or early modern sense. That the Essex archers who engaged in multiple incidents of service have a higher rate of service in these armies is perhaps indicative of the type of service involved, usually to English possessions abroad, including Ireland and Gascony, as well as the marcher areas of Scotland. Although service in standing armies in Scotland and Ireland may not have had the potential high rewards that came from service in wealthier France, for those who felt that military service was their best prospect service in these armies would have represented gainful military employment, employment that they were willing to undertake. Equally, when opportunities arose for service in France, the more professional archers may have been in a better position to respond, using their previous military experience and relationships with other soldiers and recruiting captains to enlist more quickly than their 'civilian' peers. In essence, the career soldiers were willing to undertake service opportunities where they arose, rather than waiting for certain types of service. This practical approach is supported by further analysis. Table 5.6, which shows the 12 names from Essex that are unique across the entire poll tax and appear among the Tier 3 career soldiers, indicates that a majority of incidents of service were naval, in line with the majority shown in Table 5.5. John Maldon of Navestock in Essex appears to have made naval service something of a speciality, with five of his eight campaigns taking place at sea. Of the sample contained in Table 5.6, 52 per cent of the service is naval. Clearly the more 'professional' archers were engaging in service regularly, as and when it was available, with little consideration for the location or type of service.

Table 5.6 Unique poll tax names in Essex as career soldiers.

Name	Expeditionary	Garrison	Standing army	Escort	Naval
John Bode	1415, 1417				1374, 1387
John Fryth	1380		1384		1388
John Maldon	1415		1374, 1375		1371, 1372, 1378, 1385, 1388
John Neweton			1389		1372
John Sompter		1369, 1404		1370	
John Wytton		1403	1389		1377
Richard Colne					1387, 1388
Richard Holde					1371, 1372
Richard Tanner			1389		1388
Thomas Bury	1373				1372, 1378
Thomas Chaumbre			1374, 1375		
William Somerton					1371, 1372

Table 5.7 Locations of service, 1367 to 1391.

Service location	Archers 1367–1391		Essex archers Tier 1		Essex archers Tier 3	
England	452	3%	14	7%	10	5%
England/France	268	2%	12	6%	6	3%
France	6,770	49%	116	61%	121	61%
Gascony	411	3%	2	1%	7	4%
Ireland	3,236	24%	12	6%	24	12%
Scotland	2,422	18%	34	18%	28	14%
Wales	120	1%	0	0%	2	1%
	13,679	100%	190	100%	198	100%

This pattern of behaviour is also suggested by Table 5.7, which breaks down each service entry for archers between 1367 and 1391 by the location in which the retinue served. A majority of the Tier 1 archers appear to have served primarily in France. This might be expected: after all, France was the closest theatre of war to Essex that saw regular fighting by English soldiers in the later fourteenth century, and it offered theoretically richer rewards than the other regions. The Tier 3 service records show a more even spread, with fewer archers engaged in service in England and greater numbers serving in the potentially poorer or more remote areas, such as Ireland, Gascony and Wales. Interestingly, there is a higher rate of service in Scotland among Tier 1 archers. This could

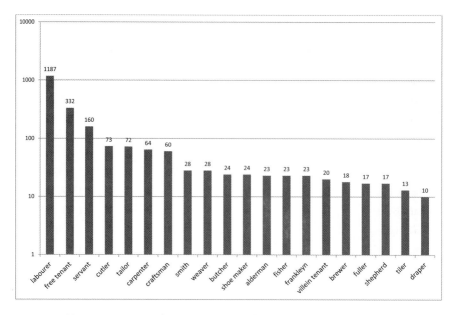

Figure 5.2. Top 20 occupations from 1381 Essex poll tax returns.

be caused by the relative ease of access to Scotland provided by proximity to the North Sea, which was commonly used to move men and supplies to the Scottish theatre. In summary, however, this supports the hypothesis that these career soldiers were willing to serve wherever they had the opportunity, and that they were willing to serve in the standing armies which may not have presented them with opportunities for personal gain beyond wages.

After considering the service relationships between Essex captains and their archers it is also worth studying the poll tax evidence itself in more detail to see what can be learnt about the socio-economic status of archers in comparison with their non-military civilian counterparts. Poos has already considered this matter, analysing the 70 vills of the hundreds of Chelmsford, Dunmow and Hinckford that contain occupational data in the 1381 returns. This analysis, which shows that 52 per cent of heads of households were wage labourers,[37] agrees with other research that has recognised that Essex had unusually high proportions of wage labourers in comparison with other areas of England.[38] Poos' analysis also supports the theory that Essex had a large cloth industry, as his figures indicate that cloth workers formed the largest group of occupations recorded.[39] This is supported by the breakdown shown in Figure 5.2, which draws its data from the poll tax database assembled by the author. This, again, shows that a large proportion of people – 50 per cent – were classed as labourers, rather than craftsmen or agriculturists. It also supports the

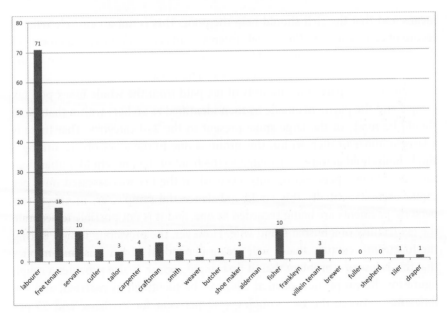

Figure 5.3. Essex archers in top 20 Essex occupations.

importance of the cloth industry, as, of the 20 occupations shown in Figure 5.2, four (tailors, weavers, fullers and drapers) were involved in the textile trade and represent 26 per cent of persons with a recorded artisanal occupation.

These percentages do change when the sample of men who can be identified as potential archers (matches between Tiers 1 and 3, and Section 1) is extracted and analysed independently. The exact numbers are shown in Figure 5.3. The most noticeable change is in the cloth-related occupations, with the archer sample comprising only 15 per cent of the artisans, a significant drop. The other significant difference can be seen among 'fishers', where 6.4 per cent of archers can be found against 0.9 per cent of 'civilians'. Yet, despite these variations, the overall profile remains broadly similar and, given the relative sample sizes, the differences cannot be seen as especially significant, and it must be concluded that those men who served as archers came from the same occupational and social backgrounds as their 'civilian' counterparts.

The occupational data is not the only information that can be extracted from the returns: the levels of tax paid are also of interest. As previously noted, Essex does not have surviving returns for 1379, which is particularly disappointing in this context as this tax followed a schedule that associated socio-economic rank with a level of tax liability. However, the basis of the 1381 returns was a form of income assessment that set the amount payable at 12d per person resident within a vill, but instructed that everyone should be charged according to their means and that the rich should help the poor. This is not an entirely reliable record of economic standing, as self-interest could corrupt the calculations and the amounts recorded, but the 1381 returns should provide a glimpse of the gradations of economic standing in Essex in that year.

Figure 5.4 compares the amounts of tax paid from the whole Essex poll tax sample and the payments made by men identified as archers within that. Note should be made of the large spike present in the 24d category. That there is a large number of men within this group is due to the assessors' recording a single household amount, attributed to the head of the household, rather than each individual's personal liability, even when the tax was assessed on a per capita basis. Potentially this could unbalance the sample, as, in effect, two persons' payments are being recorded as one, and it is not possible to separate the tax liability of a husband and wife. However, the prevailing notion during the fourteenth century that a wife was a dependant of her husband implies that this is less of a problem than it first might appear. It also provides a rough figure for the proportion of men who can be identified as married, and the difference between the two samples – 43 per cent for 'civilians' and 35 per cent for archers – suggests that the latter group were less likely to be married. The close proportional matches between the two series continue throughout the chart, with little difference between the two. There is a slight trend for the archers to appear in proportionally higher numbers in the lower tax brackets, and in lower numbers, or not at all, in the higher brackets. Indeed, archers are not found in the highest four tax brackets. Furthermore, the average amount paid by a possible Essex archer was only 6½d, some 1½d less than the 8d paid

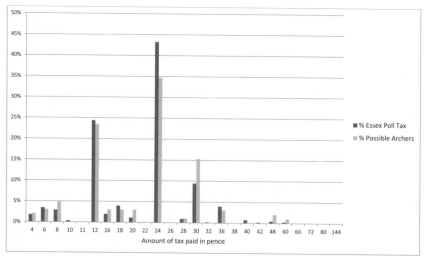

Figure 5.4. Comparison of tax paid in 1381 between Essex population and Essex archers.

on average by the whole Essex poll tax sample. Of course, the financial evidence from the poll tax returns must be qualified with some of the issues noted with their source data. The prevalence of 12d and 24d assessments could reflect the self-interest of the more wealthy members of society, who were reluctant to pay extra to subsidise their poorer neighbours or to pay a large increase in taxation over the previous poll taxes, and the impact of these variables is difficult to quantify. Nonetheless, the data does suggest that archers were likely to come from the lower sections of society but that they could be found across a wide range of economic statuses, not just the poorest.

Conclusions

Overall, the poll tax data does provide some insight into the Essex men who served as archers. They appear to be relatively unremarkable, with no particularly strong trends to mark them out as distinct from those individuals who did not undertake military service. The slightly higher numbers at the bottom of the taxation scale and a corresponding decline at the top suggest that men of lower economic status were more likely to serve as archers than those of greater wealth. This theory fits with the demographic structure of Essex, characterised by relatively high population density and income inequality compared with other regions of England, perhaps providing stimulus for military service.

The county of Essex in the later fourteenth century was an interesting place, at once a part of the wider realm of England, but with enough variation to make this case study unique. It is apparent that the links between tenurial obligation and military service were limited in Essex, with few men appearing to serve as a result of their residency on their captain's lands. This, then, raises the question of why they served at all. In the case of Essex it is evident that demographic pressures encouraged military service, as it provided a useful source of alternative and relatively well-remunerated employment for the county's pool of men whose landholdings were small or non-existent. This theory is further supported by the evidence taken from the poll tax returns, which indicates that archers were more likely than non-archers to be of lower economic status, appearing less frequently at the top end of the tax scale and paying less on average than the non-archers. Sweeping conclusions are often inaccurate, and the close proportional correlation between the two samples means that it cannot be suggested that there is an 'archer profile' which marks a man out as different from his fellows. However, it can be argued that the military revolution that had seen widespread change in the composition and abilities of English armies affected Essex, as it encouraged the development of a military service market that enabled Essex men to seek opportunities for military service both with retinue captains who held lands within the county and with those who did not.

Notes

1 L.R. Poos, *A Rural Society after the Black Death. Essex 1350–1525* (Cambridge, 1991), p. 4.

2 *Ibid.*, p. 9.

3 A.E. Prince, 'The Indenture System under Edward III', in J.G. Edwards, V.H. Galbraith and E.F. Jacob (eds), *Historical Essays in Honour of James Tait* (Manchester, 1933), pp. 283–97, was the first study of this change to a contract-based army. This has influenced a great deal of later research into the military community, which is discussed in more detail below.

4 C. Starr, *Medieval Mercenary: Sir John Hawkwood of Essex* (Chelmsford, 2007), pp. 13–17.

5 M.J. Bennett, *Community, Class and Careerism: Cheshire and Lancashire Society in the Age of 'Sir Gawain and the Green Knight'* (Cambridge, 1983); S.K. Walker, *The Lancastrian Affinity 1361–1399* (Oxford, 1990).

6 There are 51,692 archers recorded on musters in the period 1369–1417, and 28,235 men-at-arms.

7 M. Strickland and R. Hardy, *The Great Warbow: From Hastings to the Mary Rose* (Stroud, 2005) and R. Wadge, *Arrowstorm* (Stroud, 2009) do discuss archers as a body, outside of their purely military function, although this has focused on their military lives rather than the cross over with the 'civilian' world.

8 Examples are A. Ayton, *Knights and Warhorses: Military Service and the English Aristocracy under Edward III* (Woodbridge, 1999) and A. Curry, *Agincourt: A New History* (Stroud, 2005), which both focus on the men-at-arms.

9 A. Bell, *War and the Soldier in the Fourteenth Century* (Woodbridge, 2004).

10 A. Bell, A. Curry, A. King, D. Simpkin and A. Chapman, 'Protections/ Letters of Attorney/ Musters', *The Soldier in Later Medieval England* <http://www.medievalsoldier.org>, accessed 30 September 2009.

11 A. Bell, A, Curry, A. King and D. Simpkin, *The Soldier in Later Medieval England* (Oxford, 2013).

12 A. Ayton and C. Lambert, 'Shipping, Mariners and Port Communities in Fourteenth-century England', *ESRC Data Store*, <http://store.dataarchive.ac.uk/store/viewItemPage.jsp?collectionPID=archive%3A665&itemPID=archive%3A772&data=&tabbedContext=collCollection>, accessed 20 Febuary 2013.

13 Ayton, *Knights and Warhorses*, p. 2: 'The great majority of fighting men, the infantry and horse archers, will probably prove to be unidentifiable. We may often be able to ascertain their numbers, but rarely more than a small proportion of their names.'

14 S.L. Thrupp, *The Merchant Class of Medieval London 1300–1500* (Chicago, IL, 1948; reprinted with updated introduction, 1989), p. 49. Other critical authors include N. Bartlett, *The Lay Poll Tax Returns for the City of York in 1381* (Hull, 1953).

15 C.C. Fenwick, 'The English Poll Taxes of 1377, 1379 and 1381: A Critical Examination of the Returns', PhD thesis (London School of Economics, 1983).

16 'The form of each poll tax was quite different. In 1379, married women were excluded ... the effects of this were, at the time, and have been since, seriously underestimated. No two poll taxes were levied from the same age range. Thus, those who paid as fourteen year olds in 1377 paid again as sixteen year olds in 1379, but those who were twelve in 1377 did not pay in 1379 when the exemption level was raised by two years ... . It is not surprising that the number of tax-payers recorded was quite different for each tax. Thus, some of the discrepancies we seem to find are the result of a careless reading of the rules laid down for the taxes...Single people and single women in particular were much more likely to be poor than married couples and the rolls of all three poll taxes reflect this fact ... . [This was] due far more to the fact that they were legally exempt from the taxes than to the fact that they evaded payment.' Fenwick, 'The English Poll Taxes of 1377, 1379 and 1381', pp. 167–8.

17 Poos, *A Rural Society after the Black Death*, pp. 21–7, 294–9.

18 S. Sweetinburgh, 'The Social Structure of New Romney as revealed in the 1381 Poll Tax Returns', *Archaeologia Cantiana*, 131 (2011), pp. 1–22.

19   K. Bailey, 'Buckinghamshire Poll Tax Records 1377–79', *Records of Buckinghamshire*, 49 (2009), pp. 173–87.

20   G. Baker, 'Investigating the Socio-Economic Origins of English Archers in the Second Half of the Fourteenth Century', *Journal of Medieval Military History*, 12 (2014), pp. 186–91.

21   S. Gibbs and A. Bell, 'Fighting Merchants', in M. Allen and M. Davies (eds), *Medieval Merchants and Money: Essays in Honour of James L. Bolton* (London, 2016), pp. 93–113, provides a more detailed discussion of the historiography of these areas of study.

22   Bell, *War and the Soldier*, p. 34.

23   D. Simpkin, 'Robert de Fishlake: Soldier Profile', in *The Soldier in Later Medieval England*, <http://www.icmacentre.ac.uk/soldier/database/February2008.php>, accessed 9 September 2008.

24   College of Arms, *Processus in Curia Marescalli*, i, p. 429. Cited in Simpkin, 'Robert de Fishlake: Soldier Profile'.

25   Fenwick, 'The English Poll Taxes of 1377, 1379 and 1381', p. 24.

26   This was a nominal unit of account which had no corresponding coinage. One mark was equal to 13s 4d. However, this top rate was payable only by the duke of Lancaster.

27   M. Hicks, 'Introduction: What were Inquisitions Post Mortem?' in M. Hicks (ed.), *The Fifteenth-Century Inquisitions Post Mortem: A Companion* (Woodbridge, 2012), p. 1.

28   *Ibid.*, p. 3.

29   Gibbs and Bell, 'Fighting Merchants', provides a more detailed explanation of both methodological concerns and database construction.

30   This is a large reduction, and represents the 5,963 poll tax entries that can be identified as female. The remaining 149 entries do not have names recorded.

31   S. Gibbs, 'The Service Patterns and Social-economic Status of English Archers, 1367–1417: The Evidence of the Muster Rolls and Poll Tax Returns', PhD thesis (University of Reading, 2016).

32   Bell *et al.*, *The Soldier in Later Medieval England*, p. 88.

33   Poos, *A Rural Society after the Black Death*, p. 24.

34   S. Penn and C. Dyer, 'Wages and Earnings in Late Medieval England: Evidence from the Enforcement of the Labour Laws', *Economic History Review*, 2nd series, 43 (1990), p. 356.

35   Wadge, *Arrowstorm*, p. 113.

36   *Ibid.*, pp. 118–20.

37   Poos, *A Rural Society after the Black Death*, p. 24.

38   R.H. Hilton, *Bond Men Made Free: Medieval Peasant Movements and the English Rising of 1381* (London, 1973), pp. 171–5.

39   Poos, *A Rural Society after the Black Death*, pp. 24–5.

Chapter 6

Shipping the troops and fighting at sea:
Essex ports and mariners in England's wars, 1337–89
Andrew Ayton and Craig Lambert

In June 1372 Edward III and his council commissioned a census of mariners residing in Essex.[1] It is likely that neither those tasked with drawing up the lists nor those enumerated were particularly surprised by the survey,[2] for the crown had for some time been showing a particular interest in mariners as an occupational group, being concerned on the one hand to prevent abuses that might alienate them, such as extortion by those recruiting seamen for the king's ships,[3] while on the other endeavouring to prevent those who had been selected for naval service from 'withdrawing ... in order to fish and for diverse other causes'.[4] Managing the pool of indigenous mariners was a crucial component of the English war effort as it had developed after the recommencement of the Anglo-French conflict in 1369. English strategy and operations during the years of attritional warfare of the 1370s and 1380s became focused on the sea to a far greater degree than they had been during the first phase of the war (1337–60). In part this was to counter French and Castilian coastal raiding and commercial predation on the high seas, in part to sustain land-based operations – and especially England's 'barbican' strongholds on the French coast, which were designed to keep the war confined to France.[5] In financial terms, the war at sea was not the most demanding branch of the war effort: naval expeditions accounted for approximately 23 per cent of the crown's total war expenditure from 1369 to 1380.[6] But the manpower demands were particularly heavy. During this period more than 40,000 mariners were employed in transportation fleets or 'fighting' naval operations, while the latter also required about 27,000 soldiers (serving as 'marines'), almost as many as were enlisted for land campaigns.[7] An important recruiting area for these naval soldiers was the 'coastal zone', which, in addition to supplying the great majority of mariners, had to find men for defence of the maritime land. Indeed,

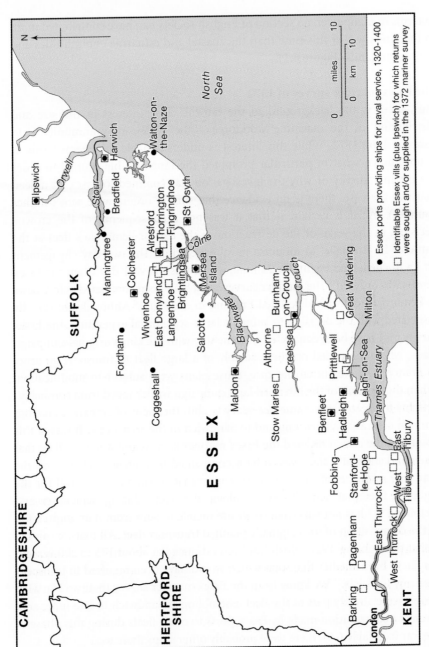

Figure 6.1. Sources of fourteenth-century Essex ships and mariners.

in terms of manpower, no section of English society can have contributed more to the king's war at this time than the coastal and estuarine communities and their hinterlands (Figure 6.1).

The Essex mariner survey of 1372

This, then, is the background to the crown's close interest in the size and distribution of the maritime workforce – the shipboard community – in Essex in June 1372. While this interest is understandable in general terms, it is not known what in particular prompted the king and his council to order the mariner survey or why the investigation was confined to Essex (if indeed that was the case: there is no evidence that similar orders were sent to other counties). What is certain is that it was not a consequence of the crown's decision, in the wake of the destruction of the earl of Pembroke's fleet at the battle of La Rochelle, to mount a naval expedition. The two-day engagement off La Rochelle had begun on 22 June, which was the very day when the Essex census was ordered.[8] The mariner survey must have been completed before news of Pembroke's defeat had reached England in early July.[9] Although not directly associated with the decision to launch a large-scale naval expedition, the Essex survey may have been connected in some way with the king's original campaign plans, which depended on the assembly of a large fleet to transport an army to France.[10] As was often the case, those plans were subject to modification. When the location of the intended land campaign was changed from (probably) Brittany to Picardy, it became necessary to shift the focus of embarkation from ports in central-southern England to Sandwich in the south-east. It was at this point that the crown ordered the Essex mariner survey, and it may well be that disembarkation at Calais was to be accompanied by a greater reliance on the maritime resources of the east coast. Unfortunately, the naval pay roll for the 'fighting' fleet that actually served, albeit abortively, during September and October 1372 has not survived, so we are unable to gain from it an impression of the composition of the originally planned transport fleet. All that we can say is that the 'fighting' fleet, which has been estimated at about 175 to 200 vessels, may have been smaller than that which would have been required to transport the army to Calais.[11] We know from the Essex mariner survey that two Harwich vessels were already part of the fleet assembling at Sandwich in late June, and, given the contribution made by Essex ports to other fleets during this phase of the war (see Table 6.6), there were probably other ships there too.

A closer look at the surviving documents connected with the mariner survey may cast some light on why it was undertaken, as well as highlighting their potential as sources for the shipboard community of Essex. Orders dated 22 June were sent to the constables of 20 vills (mostly in Essex), plus Dengie hundred, instructing them to draw up lists of the names of all mariners resident within their constabularies, whether at home, at sea or away for other reasons. Meanwhile, on the same day, the sheriff of Essex, William Baud, was ordered to undertake his own parallel investigation.[12] All of the lists of mariners were to be brought to king's council on the next Sunday (27 June). This was a tight schedule, especially for the sheriff, and yet he was able to make a more than respectable return that, in addition to the dorse of the king's writ, occupied two separate pieces of parchment.[13] On one are listed the names of mariners resident in Colchester, Mersea, Harwich, St Osyth and the vills of Dengie hundred,[14] while on a second are the mariners of Fobbing, Stanford-le-Hope, Benfleet, East Tilbury, West Thurrock, Dagenham and Barking.[15] These two documents probably reflect the way the information gathering was undertaken, with separate 'rides' being made north and south of the river Crouch. On the dorse of the king's writ the sheriff noted that: (i) he could make no return for the five vills within the liberty of Rochford hundred because he had not received a response from the bailiff, Geoffrey de la Rokele;[16] (ii) no return had been made for Ipswich and Stepney because they were not in Essex; and (iii) there were no mariners in the vills of West Tilbury or East Thurrock.

Overall, the sheriff submitted the names of 291 mariners from 17 vills. It is unfortunate that about 10 per cent of the names are now partially or wholly illegible,[17] but the sheriff can no more be blamed for that than he can for failing to survey each and every coastal and estuarine community in Essex. He implemented his orders to the letter; it was the government that had not provided a comprehensive list of maritime vills. Judging by the ships contributed to royal fleets during the fourteenth century, the most significant omission was Brightlingsea, but there must also have been mariners resident at Manningtree, Bradfield, Salcott, Walton-on-the-Naze and Tollesbury, among other places. Indeed, the 1381 poll tax returns reveal that over a quarter of the 60 or so households at Tollesbury were dependent on waterborne occupations.[18] Nevertheless, none of these shortcomings significantly affects what is perhaps the most striking feature of the sheriff's return: namely, the large number of mariners who were resident in smaller coastal and estuarine communities. While Colchester and Harwich were by far the most important sources of shipping for royal fleets (see Table 6.3), between them supplying 60 per cent of all separately identifiable ships, according to the sheriff's return these two ports were home to only a little over a quarter of the county's mariners (in all, 77 men).[19] As important for the provision of seafarers were Fobbing (48) and Stanford-le-Hope (44).

Just how complete and thorough the sheriff's work was can be explored further by comparing his returns with those drawn up by the constables of those vills who had been sent direct orders by the crown. Only three of the constables' returns have survived. That one of them is from Ipswich is particularly helpful to

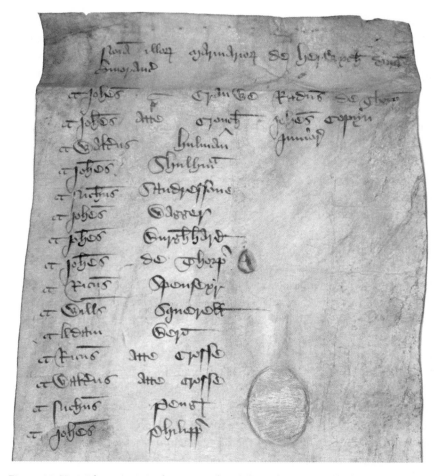

Figure 6.2. Harwich mariners in the survey of 1372 (TNA, C47/2/46, no. 7).

us, because the sheriff had declined to visit the town on jurisdictional grounds, and it is a revealing document. And that the two returns that can be compared with the sheriff's are those from Colchester and Harwich, the two most important port towns in Essex, is also fortunate. What is immediately striking is that while the sheriff returned a simple list of names for each town, the constables, in responding to their instructions in different ways, distinguished sub-groups within the mariner populations. The constable of Colchester's return separated the 59 mariners residing at home within the liberty of the town from the 37 at home outside the liberty, assigning the latter to six vills clustered around the estuary of the river Colne.[20] However, no attempt appears to have been made to list the mariners who were at sea at the time of the survey.

Approaching his task differently, the constable of Harwich distinguished three groups: 17 mariners who were at home, 10 who were serving in the 'comitiva' of the earl of Pembroke and 10 who were currently employed in two Harwich-based ships (the *Edmund* and the *Gaynepayn*) in the king's service at Sandwich (Figure 6.2).[21] The constable of Ipswich's return takes a similar form, distinguishing 14 of the town's mariners who were there from others who were at sea: 19 on unidentified vessels and 27 on Ipswich ships (20 on the *Trinite*; seven on the *George*).[22] While apparently drawn up according to the same principles, these two returns are actually different in an important respect. Whereas the Harwich constable confined his attention to local men, and thus listed only part of the crews of the *Edmund* and *Gaynepayn*, his Ipswich counterpart recorded what look like complete crew lists for the *Trinite* and the much smaller *George*, even though some of the mariners – notably a certain Piers Dansk – may not have been true Ipswich men.[23] Even allowing for the Ipswich constable's inclusion of outsiders, what his survey and the Harwich return highlight with particular force is the proportion of resident mariners – over half – who were actually at sea at the time of the survey. But the other perspective on the data is equally interesting: that, at a time of heavy naval demand, there were still significant numbers of mariners in these two busy port towns who were at home and apparently available for recruitment.

Comparison of the sheriff's and constables' returns, with particular reference to the overlap between them, casts further light on the thoroughness of the mariner survey. The incompleteness of the sheriff's return for Colchester (35 mariners) is highlighted by the fact that the constable found about three times as many men: nearly twice as many within the liberty of the town itself and another 37 in smaller, neighbouring settlements. That only one of these 37 mariners was noticed by the sheriff may well be indicative of the limitations of his survey as a whole: that he had insufficient time to visit all of the coastal and estuarine communities in Essex. However, comparison of the sheriff's and constable's returns for Harwich offers a different perspective on the former's work, perhaps suggesting that the incompleteness of his Colchester survey was not typical. Correlation of the Harwich returns is hampered to some extent by the illegibility of part of the sheriff's list, and that may explain the comparatively small overlap between the returns: only 10 names appear on both (roughly a quarter of each). But these 10 mariners are interesting. Six were at home, two were with the earl of Pembroke and two at Sandwich. This is of particular importance because it shows that the sheriff's survey *did* include both 'at home' and 'away' mariners, even though he was not explicit on this point. This key conclusion should perhaps inform our interpretation of the rest of his work. Indeed, to return to Colchester: it may well be that the 13 mariners on the sheriff's return who do not appear on the constable's much longer list were actually at sea. This would make sense because, as we have noted, the constable at Colchester confined his attention to mariners who were at home.

To the names of the 291 mariners (including illegible ones) from 17 vills supplied by the sheriff can be added 101 additional names from the constables' returns for Colchester (74) and Harwich (27), plus 60 from the list for Ipswich, making a grand total of 452. As we have seen, there are good reasons for thinking that the coverage of the Essex mariner survey should not be regarded as comprehensive. A number of coastal and estuarine communities likely to have been home to mariners were not surveyed, either because the crown failed to target them or because the sheriff had insufficient time or resources to investigate them. Of those vills that were surveyed, comparison with the number of taxpayers recorded in 1377 suggests that the investigation was not consistently probing (see Table 6.7). Under-recording is particularly evident in the case of Colchester, where the constable, while listing many more mariners than the sheriff, concerned himself only with those who were 'at home'. Indeed, it was perhaps inevitable that some, perhaps many, of those who were 'at sea' would be missed, particularly by the sheriff. It is only through the constables' returns for Harwich and Ipswich that we are offered an apparently reliable impression of the whole mariner workforce, at home and away. That said, while 60 or so mariners is probably about right for Harwich, which had 222 taxpayers in 1377, we might expect a port of Ipswich's size (1,507 taxpayers) to have considerably more.[24]

Although evidently incomplete, the mariner survey offers a revealing snapshot of the shipboard community of Essex at a time when this socio-economic group was playing a leading part in the kingdom's affairs.[25] As such, and because few comparable documents exist for other counties, the Essex survey should be considered a record of national as well as regional significance. We shall return to it regularly throughout the remainder of this chapter, exploiting its two distinctive features. The first of these is that the mariners are named and geographically located in large numbers, which means that what is probably a significant proportion of the county's maritime workforce is both quantifiable at a local level and potentially 'identifiable' through linkage with other documents. The implications and potential of these features of the survey will be explored later in this chapter. Second, because some at least of the returns distinguished between those mariners who were at home on the day of the survey and those who were at sea, with additional detail thrown in, light is cast on the dynamics of maritime recruitment. These features of the survey would make this an important corpus of records at any time during the Middle Ages; but the circumstances of the early 1370s confer upon them a particular significance and even a degree of poignancy. The intensive naval operations of this decade and the next meant that, in terms of manpower, the coastal and estuarine communities of Essex, along with those of the other maritime counties of England, would make a leading contribution to the king's war effort. The accustomed maritime commercial life was to be interrupted and, for some men, largely displaced by a fighting naval role. The poignancy arises from the realisation that most of the 10 Harwich-based mariners who are listed on the constable's return as serving with the earl of Pembroke were probably already dead by the time their names were written down.

The richness of detail that the Essex survey provides on the mariner workforce – its distribution among coastal and estuarine communities large and small, and the extent to which it was actually at sea at a single moment (and, thus, the amount of spare capacity there was) – combined with the fact that it appears to be a unique collection of documents that have left no imprint on other records, may offer clues as to the origins and purpose of the crown's information-gathering initiative of June 1372. As we have seen, the survey was perhaps connected in some way with the raising of a large transport fleet that was intended to convey the king's army from Sandwich to Calais. Alternatively, or additionally, it was possibly triggered by anxieties concerning the vulnerability of the coast and maritime commerce to French, Castilian and Flemish raiders.[26] However, given the nature of the crown's instructions and the documentation drawn up in response to them, a case can be made for connecting this fact-finding exercise not only with the crown's new focus on naval warfare but also with a marked shift in naval requisitioning policy that for some time had meant less reliance on the shipping of the larger ports and more on the resources of the numerous smaller coastal and estuarine communities. Interpreted in this way, the survey looks like an attempt by government, aware of the relative abundance of potential mariners (many of them part-time 'fisher-farmers') in the smaller communities of the coastal zone, to gather precise information about them. Moreover, it has the appearance of a pilot study conducted speedily in the maritime county nearest to the capital. As we have seen, although it was undoubtedly incomplete, the Essex survey yielded the information that the government had been seeking. We might speculate further that the results of this trial run might then have informed the terms of reference for an investigation applied to the coastal zone of the entire kingdom. That this never happened was probably because the initiative was overtaken by events. The Essex returns could hardly have been digested before news of the La Rochelle debacle arrived in England, and from that point on the king became wholly preoccupied with mounting a large-scale naval expedition. Interpreting the Essex survey as a pilot exercise that was never taken further would explain why it has left so modest a documentary footprint and why such documentation exists for Essex alone.

The nature and role of naval operations

The English king's wars during the fourteenth century necessitated three types of naval deployment.[27] First, soldiers and horses had to be transported to various theatres of land-based operations, most obviously in France and the

Low Countries but also in Ireland and, on occasion, Scotland as well. Second, the provision of supplies – foodstuffs, munitions and money – to field forces and garrisons was often most efficiently achieved by means of seaborne transport. Third, in addition to these logistical tasks, it was often necessary to organise defensive and offensive naval operations tasked with the interception of coastal raiders or armed commercial convoys, with the relief of blockaded ports and with the mounting of amphibious operations. In the absence of a permanent, professional navy, each of these forms of naval deployment was dependent on fleets of privately owned vessels requisitioned in accordance with the crown's prerogative rights, with stiffening provided by hired vessels, the king's specialised warships and, on occasion, purpose-built oared craft. During the Anglo-Scottish wars of Edward I and Edward II it was often necessary to make provision for both logistics and patrolling – as, for example, in 1322, when a fleet of nearly 300 ships was mobilised to supply the English army in Scotland and patrol the coastal shipping lanes.[28] During the first phase of the French war, up to the Treaty of Brétigny in 1360, it was the logistical tasks that provided most work for the requisitioned fleets. In 1338 Edward III assembled about 400 ships from over 70 ports to transport his army to Flanders.[29] However, transport fleets could have a dual purpose. During the Brittany campaign of 1342–3 more than 200 ships were ordered to remain with the king while he campaigned on land. Given that the Genoese, allies of the French, were active around the coast of Brittany, and to reduce the risk of isolation in this corner of France, Edward needed naval support to keep open his lines of communication and supply with England while also preventing seaborne supplies reaching his enemy in Brittany, Charles de Blois. Unfortunately for Edward, in October and November the fleet deserted from Brest and left his forces in a potentially vulnerable position, from which the truce agreed at Malestroit provided a welcome escape.[30]

Ships assembled for use in an offensive capacity might operate individually or in war fleets. In 1337–8 the crown hired the *Gracedieu* of King's Lynn, manned by 40 men-at-arms, 40 archers and 50 mariners, to make a series of patrols that ranged from the Firth of Tay to the coasts of Brittany and Calais, and from the Channel Islands to Bordeaux. The French coast was raided and a ship carrying 260 tuns of wine was seized on the high seas.[31] During this long period of duty the King's Lynn vessel was joined at one point by one of the king's ships, the *All Hallows Cog*, and at another by two ships owned by the earl of Salisbury, but the *Gracedieu* itself had been put to sea by the merchant and shipowner John Weasenham. The crown often relied in this way on the maritime resources of the commercial community. From 1337 to 1340 the burgesses of Newcastle launched a heavily armed flotilla to protect English supply ships as they sailed to Scotland. The level of organisation for this fleet is evidenced by the associated expenses account, in which the burgesses claimed the cost of red cloth to make caps for the mariners as well as equipment purchased from a Cologne arms dealer.[32] Similarly, in the summer of 1346, Edward III commissioned the wealthy King's Lynn merchant Thomas Melcheburn to provide two ships to carry supplies to Edward's forces in Normandy, to patrol the French coast and to attack enemy shipping.[33] A reliance on such men as Weasenham and Melcheburn made sense. Lacking the resources to maintain a permanent Channel fleet and aware of the practical limits of its naval 'reach', the crown recognised that the people who best understood how to defend the coast, and who had the keenest incentive to do so, were the local communities who worked on the sea. By drawing on these maritime resources the crown acquired a tactical flexibility that the traditional mechanisms of fleet assembly could not provide.

A notable feature of French naval operations, involving their own and their allies' galley fleets, was coastal raiding. In 1338 Portsmouth and Southampton were attacked, as was Winchelsea in 1360,[34] and the coastal raids were particularly frequent and intense during the later 1370s, with a serious threat of invasion during the mid-1380s.[35] Defence against such raids involved local levies, stiffened by fixed fortifications and small paid garrisons,[36] combined with naval patrols. During the 1330s and 1340s there was greater reliance on land-based defence, but, as we have seen, during the 1370s and 1380s naval operations became much more important – a switch in strategic emphasis that is easily illustrated by examples.[37] In August 1371 a war fleet commanded by the earl of Hereford won a notable victory against a Flemish fleet in the Bay of Bourgneuf.[38] In 1373 the earl of Salisbury conducted a series of naval operations around the coast of Brittany in support of English land-based operations.[39] And in 1387 and 1388 the earl of Arundel led two naval campaigns in the Channel, the first of which was notably successful.[40]

The shipping and shipboard community of Essex took an active role in these intensively pursued naval operations (see Table 6.6). Take, for example, the period immediately preceding and following the mariner survey of June 1372. In May 1371 John Airmyn, master of the *Seintemariecog Leget*, and William Hull were appointed to take 90 mariners in the city of London and the counties of Kent, Sussex, Essex and Suffolk and put them on this ship 'to go at the king's wages where the king shall be pleased to order'.[41] We know that this ship, the crew of which included in all likelihood some Essex men, took part in Hereford's expedition to the Bay of Bourgneuf, followed by another naval expedition during the winter of 1371-2.[42] Then, on 6 November 1372, during a spell of defensive 'sea-keeping' directed by the king's esquire Helming Leget, his ship *Seintemariecog Leget* was 'broken' at Harwich. Having apparently transferred his company of men-at-arms and archers from the wrecked ship to the *James* of Colchester and the *Seynt Marieschip* of Coggeshall, Leget put to sea again, his flotilla also including the *Barge Leget* and another 'petite Barge', the *Margerye*.[43] In the meantime, as we have seen, 10 mariners from Harwich had been serving with the small fleet that came to grief at La Rochelle, and 10 more were employed in the abortive naval expedition from Sandwich.[44] Thus, during the course of a year and a half, Essex mariners participated in operations that represented all facets of the maritime war effort: army transport, defensive patrolling and offensive cruising.

Assembling a fleet and manning the ships

Lacking a royal navy that could transport armies, freight victuals, patrol the seas and attack enemy shipping, the English crown had by necessity to rely on requisitioned merchantmen to meet its naval requirements, which were indeed great. English armies raised during the first phase of the Hundred Years War (1337–60) were sometimes large by the standards of the period, but even an army of as few as 5,000 men (including horses and supplies) would require a fleet of several hundred ships to transport it to France or the Low Countries. In 1346, for example, it took over 700 ships manned by close to 16,000 mariners to carry an army of 14,000 combatants to St Vaast La Hougue in Normandy.[45] While this was the largest fleet to be assembled for a single expedition, it was but one of several large armadas raised during this phase of the war. Just four years previously the king had mobilised a fleet of over 450 ships to transport his army to Brittany.[46] And these transport fleets do not represent the full story of maritime operations for, while they were at sea, other ships were also needed to take supplies to English garrisons in Scotland, burn enemy ports and patrol the Channel.

Assembling a fleet could be achieved in a variety of ways.[47] The crown could call on the traditional service of the Cinque Ports, which required the five head ports to provide the crown with 57 ships each manned by 21 mariners for 15 days. Pardons could be offered to shipowners, shipmasters and full crews, in return for which the recipients would provide ships or service for two months at their own expense. The government also concluded agreements with shipowners who would provide ships for naval operations in return for tax exemptions and other favours. While such methods were useful for supplementing fleets, they could not in themselves yield enough ships for the crown's needs. In order to meet its major logistical and naval requirements, the crown turned to its ancient right of requisition. Because of the dispersed nature of the merchant fleet this process was administratively complex, but the requisition clerks' task was made easier by the fact that, for the most of the fourteenth century, the coastline of England was divided into two admiralties. The admiral of the north was responsible for the ports located on the east coast from the north bank of the Thames to Berwick and the admiral of the west for those situated from the south bank of the Thames around the Channel and Welsh coasts right up to Skinburness in Westmorland.[48] So, as well as being located on the estuary that led to the kingdom's political and economic capital, the ports of Essex were also near the jurisdictional boundary between the two admiralties. As we shall see, we would do well to bear in mind the geopolitical issues that conditioned not only the nature of the maritime contributions that Essex made to the king's war but also the impact that those contributions had on the county's coastal and estuarine communities.

At the start of the French war in 1337 the crown had at its disposal a skilled and experienced team of clerks, sheriffs and admirals who were tasked with raising the naval forces required.[49] The results of their work are preserved in the fleet payrolls. Here we can see the range of ports called upon to supply shipping, and also that the scale of contribution varied a good deal from place to place (with reference to Essex ports, this can be seen in Tables 6.1 and 6.3). How are these individual contributions to be interpreted? The evidence that we have suggests that requisitioning policy involved a selective approach informed by a knowledge of local shipping capacity. We know that the crown ordered surveys of available shipping to be undertaken,[50] and a variety of documents that were generated by these investigations have survived, such as the list of Norfolk and Suffolk shipowners grouped by port drawn up by the sheriff, Robert Causton, in about 1340.[51] Moreover, close inspection of the shipping of three ports (Great Yarmouth, Dover and Exeter) suggests that the crown's officers usually aimed to requisition no more than a modest proportion – say a third – of a port's ships, though its proximity to the intended theatre of war might, on occasion, prompt a higher level of impressment.[52] It seems that these limits were set so as not to interfere too much with maritime trade and the collection of taxes generated by it. At the same time, the policy placated shipowners and shipmasters, whose continued acquiescence in the requisitioning process was essential.

Understanding how the crown manned the vessels that had been requisitioned for service as army transports or warships is essential if we are to assess the impact of naval recruitment, not only on a section of society whose primary purpose was trade or fishing rather than war, but also on the cohesion and operational effectiveness of ships' crews. Three issues require attention. Assuming a degree of stability in a ship's normal, 'commercial' crew, to what extent did this group of men accompany the vessel when it was taken into royal service? Were ships more heavily manned when they operated in a naval capacity than when they were engaged in commerce? If crews were enlarged, how was this achieved? To start with the second question: the problem here is how we are to determine the 'normal' manning requirements of fourteenth-century ships when most of the evidence for crew size is to be found in the naval pay records. We can but make the most of the data that are available. It is estimated that the Bremen cog, a ship of 140 tons, required a crew of 20 mariners (ton:man ratio of 7:1) to operate it.[53] In 1336 a ship of 160 tons engaged in a commercial capacity had a crew of 27 men (6:1).[54] Compare these manning levels with an order issued in 1324 stipulating that a 240-ton vessel arrested for naval service should have 60 mariners on board (4:1) and it seems logical to argue that when requisitioned for naval service ships were likely to be manned more heavily than when engaged in commerce.[55] It may well be that men brought along to fight, who would later be termed 'marines', were included among the mariners in naval pay records, thereby inflating the size of crews.[56] Indeed, the records generated by the recruitment and payment of naval manpower often make explicit reference to mixed crews of mariners and soldiers (men-at-arms, armed men, archers). However, supplementation of the normal crew with fighting men appears to have been more usual with ships intended as escorts for transport fleets or commercial convoys or as warships in offensive or defensive naval operations.[57] The crews of horse or troop transports would normally be kept at optimal operational level in order to maximise carrying capacity. Only when a clear threat to the security of a fleet had been identified was it likely that the crews of transports would be supplemented – as, for example, occurred with the fleet that sailed from Southampton to Aquitaine in 1324.[58] Nicholas Huggate's exceptionally detailed naval accounts reveal that additions were made to the crews of 29 ships (in all, a further 250 mariners) after it had become known that the French had assembled a large fleet to disrupt English naval preparations.[59] For example, the *Godyer* (200 tons) of Dartmouth was initially manned by 28 men (a ratio of 7:1),[60] which reflected normal commercial manning levels, but after it had served for 14 days a further 14 men were added to the crew.

There are good reasons for thinking that the men who sailed a requisitioned ship from its home port to the embarkation anchorage would have been accustomed to working together on the vessel. A master's association with a particular ship, often longstanding, would commonly involve alternating between trade and war. For example, William Tye's work at the helm of the *James* of Colchester in 1371–3 included at least two commercial voyages and two tours of naval duty.[61] As far as the ordinary mariner is concerned, family ties and shared locational roots are evident from surviving crew lists for ships in royal service – characteristics that are certainly discernible in the list of William Tye's crew on the *James* in 1372.[62] In addition to being a natural consequence of recruitment dynamics, a cohesive crew was in the shipowner's – and indeed the crown's – best interests, maximising the likelihood that the vessel would be brought home safely. But if we may reasonably conclude that the bulk of the ships in a transport fleet would have benefited from settled crews, what of those requisitioned vessels that were to have a 'fighting' role, as fleet escorts or in prowling war fleets? How would the original crew be supplemented? Royal officials could add mariners and soldiers to ships that were to be employed in a fighting capacity before they set out from their home ports. Alternatively, once requisitioned vessels had arrived at the port of embarkation extra men could be gathered by impressment from within the 'maritime land' (of variable size: usually extending six leagues inland, sometimes 12) or further afield.[63] The Essex mariner survey of 1372 lists the kind of settlements the crown searched in these circumstances: places such as Burnham-on-Crouch, Fingringhoe, Fobbing and Stanford-le-Hope, which were situated near the coast or estuary shore. In this coastal zone dwelled both mariners who engaged in deep-sea commerce and also men known to historians as 'fisher-farmers', because they combined fishing and other relatively short coastal voyages with the farming of smallholdings.[64] Some indication of their overall numbers in the county is provided by the 17 men designated either 'fisher' or 'dragger' in the 1381 poll tax return for a single little village, Tollesbury, on the north shore of the Blackwater estuary.[65]

Naval commanders would sometimes take on additional manpower as and when necessary during a tour of duty. Take, for example, Helming Leget, who had to replace the *Seintemariecog Leget* after it was wrecked at Harwich in early November 1372. Retaining the services of the *Barge Leget*, he engaged three additional ships.[66] Crew lists reveal that he divided his men-at-arms and archers between the *James* of Colchester and the *Seynt Marieschip* of Coggeshall, which appear to have retained their existing 'local' crews of mariners.[67] Very few of the soldiers can be traced in the 1372 Essex survey,[68] whereas at least half a dozen of the mariners on each ship had been recorded as Colchester residents, with others having been listed in the smaller coastal or estuarine settlements. That two of the *Barge Leget*'s crew had been 'at home' at Harwich in the mariner survey suggests that they were taken on while Leget's flotilla was being reorganised in that port. The fourth vessel for which a crew list exists is the *Margerye*, a little barge manned by 12 mariners, including the master, Robert Waltham. It is not accounted for separately on the pay roll and (whatever its origins) may have been employed as a lighter, serving the larger vessels.[69] So, after the loss of the *Seintemariecog Leget*, the rebuilding of Helming Leget's flotilla necessitated the supplementation and mixing of personnel. However much a ship's commercial crew was stable in composition and, in terms of locational origins, homogeneous, participation in naval operations meant that their now crowded wooden world may have been more prone to rivalries and conflict. It is small wonder that many ships performing a naval role had a 'constable' on board, an officer apparently responsible for maintaining discipline.[70]

The increased frequency of naval operations in the last three decades of the fourteenth century meant that the crown needed more men to sail and fight aboard ships. This prompted two key changes in military recruitment and combatant experience. The first was that the traditional military community

Figure 6.3. The fourteenth-century common seal of Maldon, showing a medieval warship with fighting towers. The seal continued to be used and this specimen, in better condition than earlier surviving examples, dates from 1600.

– the nobility and gentry on the one hand, and the section of the peasantry that supplied archers on the other – began to fight more frequently at sea. The earl of Hereford's naval expedition of 1371 that culminated in the defeat of the Flemings in the Bay of Bourgneuf was an early example: the fleet carried 420 men-at-arms and 460 archers in the retinues of the earl and the two admirals, Lords Brian and Neville.[71] The second change was that inhabitants of the coastal zone were now liable to be recruited in significant numbers to fight aboard ships as men-at-arms, armed men or archers. Thus, for example, when the 1,724 mariners manning the 42 vessels in Hereford's fleet were backed up by 243 armed men and 279 archers,[72] we can safely assume that the king's recruiting agents searched the coastal and estuarine communities in the first instance.[73] There were two issues here. First, the rural population as a whole was still supplying manpower for land campaigns. For example, in July 1370 67 *armati* and 100 archers recruited in Essex were marched from Tilbury to Rye, where they joined Robert Knolles's ill-fated expedition to France.[74] Second, the communities of the coastal zone could yield precisely the kind of men who would quickly adapt to life at sea: it was, after all, where most of the kingdom's mariners lived. So, as a result of the changing demands of naval recruitment, men for whom seafaring was their principal or part-time occupation could now find themselves serving as 'marines' as well.

This dual role, seafarer and soldier, is demonstrable when crew lists of mariners can be compared with muster rolls of shipboard men-at-arms, armed men and archers. In the case of Essex, the mariner survey of 1372 provides a similar opportunity for comparison. In the late spring of 1374 Geoffrey Starling was at sea on a defensive patrol in command of the *Maudeleyn* of Ipswich.[75] Starling was accompanied by 29 armed men, 30 archers and 50 mariners (including the master and constable), all of whom are listed on a nominal roll. An undated document notes that Starling had a commission to raise these numbers of mariners and soldiers in Suffolk and Essex,[76] but, since he had served with the *Maudeleyn* as a wine convoy escort in 1372–3 with precisely the same numbers of soldiers and seafarers, we cannot be sure that the commission relates to the naval service of 1374. What the records for the spell of convoy duty make clear is that the *Maudeleyn* was a 150-ton ship that was normally crewed by a master and 20 mariners.[77] So, in addition to carrying soldiers, the ship was to have a much expanded crew (*duplex eskippamentum*) in 1374. It is not surprising, therefore, that only seven of the mariners in 1374 can be found on the 1372 Ipswich list (several more can probably be identified as men resident in Essex); but what is of particular note is that six of the armed men in 1374 appear on the 1372 list of Ipswich mariners.[78] Given that eight of the *Maudeleyn*'s enlarged crew in 1374 (four mariners, four armed men) had probably been serving at sea together when the 1372 mariner survey was undertaken, it can be seen that the process of crew supplementation, necessary for naval voyages, was likely to involve not simply mariners sometimes serving as soldiers but also altered roles within a settled ship's company.

This was not a wholly new development, but the increased frequency of naval operations in the 1370s and 1380s must have resulted in many more mariners serving at sea as soldiers. And this shift in recruitment dynamics affected not only the lower ranks of seamen; several shipowners/masters were employed as retinue captains in the naval expeditions of the late fourteenth century.[79] Indeed, more frequent naval operations naturally led to increased demands being made on other members of the wider maritime community, including those whose skills were required to maintain ships. On one occasion, for example, the king summoned to London 11 carpenters from Maldon, Hadleigh, Chadwell, Prittlewell, Tilbury, Wakering, Bromley and Brightlingsea to work on a barge belonging to Sir John Ipres.[80] As we shall see, the intensification of naval service and the new recruitment dynamics that accompanied it provides the context within which the impact of naval recruitment on port towns and smaller coastal and estuarine communities should be understood.

The contribution of Essex shipping to naval operations

The system employed by the crown to record the payment of wages to serving mariners has bequeathed to us an invaluable collection of source material. From the historian's point of view, the significance of the naval records derives

Table 6.1 Naval ship-voyages undertaken from Essex ports, 1320–1400.

Port	Number of ship-voyages	Number of mariners
Alresford	1	—
Benfleet	5	158
Bradfield	2	31
Brightlingsea	33	403
Burnham-on-Crouch	15	127
Coggeshall	1	34
Colchester	96	2,204
Fobbing	11	246
Fordham	2	23
Hadleigh	2	20
Harwich	79	2,055
Maldon	20	275
Manningtree	8	91
Mersea	4	38
St Osyth	3	94
Salcott	5	59
Walton-on-the-Naze	6	53
Total	293	5,911

Sources: BL, Additional MS 7967, fo. 99r.; BL, Stowe MS 553, fos, 77r.–77v.; BL, Harleian MS 3968, fo. 133r.; BL, Additional MS 37494, fos, 19r.–19v.; TNA, E36/204, pp. 229, 232, 233; E101/16/40; E101/17/3; E101/18/3; E101/18/31; E101/19/16; E101/20/1; E101/21/7; E101/21/10; E101/21/12; E101/24/9b; E101/25/9; E101/25/24; E101/26/18; E101/26/38; E101/27/22; E101/27/24; E101/27/25; E101/27/37; E101/28/23; E101/28/24; E101/29/1; E101/29/35; E101/32/1; E101/33/27; E101/33/31; E101/34/25; E101/36/14; E101/36/20; E101/37/7; E101/37/13; E101/37/14; E101/37/15; E101/37/17; E101/37/18; E101/37/25; E101/38/18; E101/38/30; E101/39/2; E101/40/8; E101/40/9; E101/40/19; E101/40/20; E101/40/36; E101/40/40; E101/41/26; E101/42/21; E101/42/22; E101/612/40; E101/612/41; E101/612/44; E101/612/48; C47/2/11; *CCR, 1343–46*, pp. 128–32, 359; *CCR, 1369–74*, p. 227; *CCR, 1377–81*, p. 263; *CPR, 1361–64*, p. 515; *CFR*, 22 vols (London, 1911–62), *1337–47*, pp. 4, 151; M. Lyon *et al.* (eds), *The Wardrobe Book of William de Norwell, 12 July 1338 to 27 May 1340* (Brussels, 1983), pp. 378, 382-3.

from two key characteristics. The first is consistency of documentary format: for each ship, the fleet payrolls usually supply its name and home port, the master's name and crew numbers, and the period of its service. The second notable characteristic of the naval records – their bulk – is the consequence of the large size of many of the fleets documented. This, combined with the high survival rate of the records, means that we have an abundance of data on the shipping contributed to naval operations by individual ports and, indeed, by whole counties and regions: data that can be supplemented by reference to other sources, perhaps most notably the enrolments and miscellanea of the Exchequer and Chancery (including the 1372 mariner survey) and the records generated by the taxation of maritime commerce.[81]

Our purpose in what follows is to investigate the shipping and manpower contributed to the king's maritime war effort during the fourteenth century by the coastal and estuarine communities of Essex; or, to put it another way, to assess the impact of the crown's naval demands on those communities. With the quantitative and qualitative data supplied by the pay rolls of army transport and war fleets as our starting point, we shall proceed by correlating these data with the information contained in other sources, including the 1372 mariner survey and taxation records. Throughout it should be borne in mind that by no means all fleet payrolls survive, and that some are incomplete or difficult to interpret.[82] This means that collectively the naval records – and the tables of data that have been compiled from them – offer an indication of the numbers of ships and mariners provided by Essex ports rather than a comprehensive picture.

Aggregating all of the known naval contributions by 17 Essex ports during the period 1320–1400 results in the totals shown in Table 6.1. All told, nearly 300 ships were manned by a little under 6,000 mariners. It is important to recognise that these ship totals represent 'ship-voyages' rather than separately identifiable vessels. As an indication of the number of occasions when ships were taken into royal service this is a valid measure of naval impact, albeit an absolute minimum, given the incompleteness of the records. But what of the numbers of separate ships and mariners performing this service? For this, we need to distinguish individual vessels from ship-voyages, identifying and reconstructing the 'service careers' of ships that were employed on more than one expedition. Generating reliable ship totals depends upon a method that minimises the likelihood that the same vessel is counted more than once ('double-counting') – which, if left uncorrected, would lead to an inflated estimate of overall ship numbers – while at the same time avoiding the conflation of ships of the same name – which, if not prevented, would result in an underestimation of the number of separate vessels involved.

Our method of distinguishing individual ships makes use of three key pieces of information, or 'identifiers', as provided by the sources: the ship's name,

Table 6.2 Number of voyages with named masters undertaken in the *James* of Colchester.

Master	Year[s] of service	Number of voyages
John Aleyn	1338	1
Nicholas Belche	1329	1
John Broun	1342	1
Geoffrey Dawe	1369	1
John Estman	1357	1
William Fey	1373	1
John Ketel	1342	1
Richard Nicholas	1378	1
William Tye	1369, 1371, 1372, 1373, 1377, 1378 (2 voyages), 1379, 1383, 1385, 1386, 1387	12
Richard Wright	1363	1
Richard Wyser	1355, 1359, 1377	3

Sources: Lyon *et al.* (eds), *Wardrobe Book of William de Norwell*, p. 382 (Aleyn); TNA, E101/78/4a, m. 4 (Belche); E36/204, p. 232 (Broun); E101/29/35 (Dawe); E101/173/4, fo. 73v. (Estman); E101/602/3, fo. 41r. (Fey); *CCR, 1343–46*, p.132 (Ketel); E101/37/25, m. 4 (Nicholas); BL Additional MS 37494, fo. 19v. (Tye); TNA, E101/32/1 (Tye); E101/34/25, m. 4 (Tye); E101/36/14, m. 4 (Tye); E101/37/25, m. 13 (Tye); E101/38/18, m. 1 (Tye); E122/158/25 (Tye); E101/40/8, m. 1 (Tye); E101/40/9, m. 3 (Tye); E101/40/19, m. 5 (Tye); E101/40/36, m. 2 (Tye); E101/179/10, fo. 51v. (Tye); E101/29/1, m. 3 (Wright); E101/26/38, m. 2 (Wyser); E101/27/24, m. 3 (Wyser); E101/36/20, p. 4 (Wyser). The last of these accounts offers details of the shipment of troops to Gascony, but the document is imperfect and while much of the ship service was in 1377, it is possible that some relates to the 1360s.

the home port and the master's name.[83] Within a 20-year time-frame, records of ships that are identical according to these three identifiers are deemed to be referring to the same vessel; otherwise, they are counted as different ships. Record linkage can sometimes be confirmed by reference to the ship's tonnage, but inconsistent recording of this information prevents it from qualifying as a fourth identifier.[84] No nominal record linkage method can produce perfect results, and it is important to recognise the limitations of our approach to distinguishing individual ships. There would have been vessels that operated with more than one master, just as there were no doubt masters who during their careers took to sea more than one ship with the same name. But to some extent such cases will cancel out, especially when the data are aggregated for large ports or whole counties. (Linkage errors are likely to be relatively more disruptive with ports that were home to small numbers of vessels.) While the certainty of linkage at the level of individual ships is necessarily variable, it is our belief that the 'three identifiers' approach offers the best available method of identifying

Table 6.3 Estimate of separate ships contributed by Essex ports to naval operations, 1320–1400.

Port	Number of ships	Number of mariners	Tonnage (number of ships with recorded tonnage)
Alresford	1	—	21 (1)
Benfleet	1	40	140 (1)
Bradfield	2	31	100 (1)
Brightlingsea	11	129	145 (3)
Burnham-on-Crouch	11	76	183 (7)
Coggeshall	1	34	—
Colchester	55	1,058	2,193 (32)
Fobbing	6	125	354 (4)
Fordham	2	23	70 (2)
Hadleigh	1	20	—
Harwich	40	1,065	1,593 (18)
Maldon	12	186	312 (6)
Manningtree	4	52	90 (2)
Mersea	2	23	40 (2)
St Osyth	2	50	140 (1)
Salcott	5	59	—
Walton-on-the-Naze	2	27	90 (2)
Total	158	2,998	5,471
			Average: 66

individual ships within a large corpus of records as the necessary first step in the compilation of ship statistics at local, regional and national levels.

The three identifiers method and how successfully it can hope to avoid the potential pitfalls of double-counting and conflation is best demonstrated with a specific example. The most popular ship name associated with Colchester was the *James*, for which 24 voyages can be found in the records (Table 6.2). Application of the three identifiers method suggests that these 24 voyages were undertaken by 11 separate vessels called *James*, a total that is unlikely to be far wide of the mark. The 12 voyages that William Tye mastered from 1369 to 1387, assigned here to a single ship, may conceivably have involved a couple of vessels with the same name, but hardly more than that. The same applies to Richard Wyser's three voyages. Elsewhere in the table there is unlikely to be much, if any, double-counting. The fact that in 1342, 1373, 1377 and 1378 the naval records show that there were simultaneously at least two Colchester ships called *James* makes the total of 11 for the whole period all the more plausible.

As Table 6.3 shows, application of the 'separate ship' methodology to the 293 naval ship-voyages made by ships from Essex ports in the period 1320–1400 suggests that 158 separate vessels were employed in a variety of naval operations, requiring all told about 3,000 mariners to man them. (For vessels serving more than once, the largest crew is included in the total.) The data presented in this table do not, of course, show the full extent of Essex's naval contribution. There are several large fleets for which no payrolls exist, and the data that we have for the largest of all, which conveyed the English army to Normandy in 1346, have been excluded because we cannot identify individual ships.[85] Moreover, because we lack a comprehensive collection of crew lists we will never know how many individual Essex-based mariners served on these naval expeditions (an issue to which we shall return below). However, some conclusions can safely be drawn. Of the 17 Essex 'ports', many of which were really no more than villages, Colchester and Harwich stand out as by far the most important, with Brightlingsea, Burnham-on-Crouch and Maldon being of moderate significance. But in terms of a simple count of ships and mariners, Essex's contribution to naval operations was smaller than those of its immediate neighbours, Suffolk and Kent, especially the latter, which supplied about twice as many vessels and men.[86] Indeed, the relatively modest scale of Essex's naval contribution is thrown into still sharper relief when it is compared with those of the most heavily exploited ports, such as Great Yarmouth, which provided 61 ships to a single transport fleet in 1338,[87] or Dartmouth and Bristol, which became particularly important during the later decades of the fourteenth century.[88]

How should we interpret Essex's standing as very much a second-rank supplier of shipping? It was argued earlier that the crown's approach to requisitioning was essentially selective, informed by knowledge of local shipping capacity. Indeed, it seems likely that the mariner survey of June 1372 was in some way related to the review and recalibration of royal requisitioning demands. When compared with its immediate neighbours, Essex's county-level naval contribution does seem to be broadly proportionate to the size of its merchant and fishing fleet. That Kent was home to several of the Cinque Ports was certainly a factor in that county's prominence as a supplier of shipping: it is notable that these ports provided over 80 per cent of Kentish vessels in royal service.[89] But the biggest difference between Essex and its immediate neighbours lay in the fact that it lacked a port of the importance of Sandwich or Ipswich, both of which supplied two or three times more ships than Colchester, whose contribution was on a par with those of Dover and Gosford Haven. Although a large town of perhaps 6,000 souls in 1377, Colchester was a river

Table 6.4 Estimate of separate ships contributed by Essex ports to naval operations, 1320–54.

Port	Number of ships	Number of mariners	Tonnage (number of ships with recorded tonnage)
Brightlingsea	11	129	145 (3)
Burnham-on-Crouch	3	19	—
Colchester	26	526	470 (7)
Hadleigh	1	20	—
Harwich	23	689	266 (3)
Maldon	3	43	—
Manningtree	1	12	—
Mersea	2	23	40 (2)
St Osyth	1	—	—
Salcott	5	59	—
Walton-on-the-Naze	2	27	90 (2)
Total	78	1547	1011
			Average: 59

Table 6.5 Estimate of separate ships contributed by Essex ports to naval operations, 1355–1400.

Port	Number of ships	Number of mariners	Tonnage (number of ships with recorded tonnage)
Alresford	1	—	21 (1)
Benfleet	1	40	140 (1)
Bradfield	2	31	100 (1)
Burnham-on-Crouch	8	57	183 (7)
Coggeshall	1	34	—
Colchester	29	532	1723 (25)
Fobbing	6	125	354 (4)
Fordham	2	23	70 (2)
Harwich	17	376	1327 (15)
Maldon	9	143	312 (6)
Manningtree	3	40	90 (2)
St Osyth	1	50	140 (1)
Total	80	1451	4460
			Average: 68

port and largely reliant on the 'restricted mooring facilities' downstream at Hythe, where there was 'a detached settlement of seafarers and fishermen'.[90]

Of greater interest than how Essex's naval contribution compared with neighbouring counties is how in detail it changed over time – changes that are highlighted if the port-level totals for separate ships are divided into two periods: up to 1354 (Table 6.4) and from 1355 (Table 6.5). Examining the numbers of Essex-based ships serving in a selection of the larger fleets before and after the mid-1350s adds a valuable 'snap-shot' perspective to our investigation (Table 6.6). The first point to make is that, taking the county's contribution as a whole, very similar numbers of ships were drawn into royal service before and after the mid-1350s watershed. This is a point that is disguised if we focus on individual fleets. At least two dozen Essex-based ships participated in each of the huge army transport armadas of 1338 (24), 1342 (25) and 1346 (26), while only a handful served in those of the 1370s. But whereas the largest fleets of the later fourteenth century were smaller than before, with corresponding much reduced contributions by individual ports, there was now a greater intensity of naval operations and so the overall number of ships provided by Essex ports held up.

The other area of change that is detectable in the data after the mid-1350s concerns the ports that were supplying ships for royal service. The smaller coastal and estuarine communities had always contributed a few ships to the large transport fleets of the early years of the French war. In 1338–9, for example, the *Nicholas* of Hadleigh, a ship belonging to a royal household knight, Sir John le Sturmy, was deployed.[91] But such occasional contributions were overshadowed by the ships supplied by Colchester and Harwich, which, combined, provided nearly two-thirds of identifiable Essex-based vessels during the period up to 1354. This proportion rises to over three-quarters when Brightlingsea's important second-rank role (14 per cent of ships) is added. From the mid-1350s a selection of the smaller ports took on a relatively more prominent role in naval operations. While the combined contribution of Colchester and Harwich dropped to 58 per cent, Brightlingsea stopped providing ships altogether, as did Salcott, Mersea and Walton-on-the-Naze.

The most enigmatic of these changes is the disappearance of Brightlingsea's ships from the naval records in the early 1350s,[92] only to reappear in 1423, when two vessels formed part of the transport fleet shipping Thomas Beaufort to France.[93] What is particularly striking about this is that Brightlingsea's ships also disappear from the documents recording custom charges on the wine trade: the *Jonette* in 1343 is the last one until 1410, when the *Marie*, with Richard Lament as master, is recorded in the Bordeaux accounts.[94] Moreover, it will be recalled that Brightlingsea was also one of the more notable omissions from the Essex mariner survey of 1372. It is not easy to explain this sudden disappearance

Table 6.6 Contribution of Essex ports to a selection of naval operations.

Campaign	Ports	Number of ships	Number of mariners
1324 and 1325 Fleet size: 237 ships with 3,906 mariners.	Brightlingsea	6	79
	Burnham	1	14
	Colchester	1	—
	Harwich	1	—
	Salcott	3	30
	St Osyth	1	—
1338 Fleet size: 391 ships with 13,346 mariners.	Brightlingsea	4	100
	Colchester	8	221
	Hadleigh	1	20
	Harwich	9	319
	Mersea	2	23
1342 Fleet size: 487 ships with 8,397 mariners.	Brightlingsea	4	61
	Burnham	2	19
	Colchester	5	120
	Harwich	10	213
	Maldon	2	44
	Mersea	1	8
	Salcott	1	28
1346 Fleet size: 747 ships with 15,917 mariners.	Brightlingsea	5	61
	Colchester	5	90
	Harwich	14	383
	Maldon	2	32
1359 Fleet size: 446 ships with 6,149 mariners.	Burnham	7	57
	Colchester	7	107
	Harwich	1	25
	Maldon	4	24
	Manningtree	1	15
1369 Fleet size: 250 ships with 5000 mariners.	Colchester	4	104
1373 Fleet size: 220 ships with [1,600+] mariners.	Colchester	3	57
	Fobbing	1	33
	Harwich	3	95
1377 Fleet size: 172 ships with 4,000 mariners.	Bradfield	1	8
	Colchester	1	24
	Harwich	3	58
	Manningtree	1	13

Sources: 1324–5: BL, Additional MS 7967, fos 99r., 99v.; TNA, E101/16/40; E101/17/3. 1338: Lyon *et al.* (eds), *Wardrobe Book of William de Norwell*, pp. 378, 382–3; TNA, E101/21/7, m. 2; E101/21/10, m. 3. 1342: E36/204, pp. 221–40; E101/24/9b; *CCR 1343–46*, pp. 128–32. 1346: BL, Harleian MS 3968, fos, 132r.–133v. 1359: TNA, E101/27/22; E101/27/23; E101/27/24; E101/27/25. 1369: E101/29/33; E101/29/35; E101/29/36; E122/7/12. 1373: BL, Additional MS 37494, fos 17v.–23v. 1377: TNA, E101/36/14; E101/36/15; E101/34/25; E101/37/3; E101/37/7; E101/37/8; E101/37/13; E101/37/14; E101/37/15; E101/37/16; E101/37/17; E101/37/18; E101/37/20.

from the records. Brightlingsea may have experienced some form of economic decline, perhaps as a result of the Black Death.[95] Alternatively, its absence from the records may have been connected in some way with its status as a limb of Sandwich, an association that can be dated to *c*.1360.[96] It is possible that clerks drawing up the naval records henceforward recorded Brightlingsea's ships with those of its head-port.

As Brightlingsea's ships disappeared from the naval records, some coastal and estuarine communities emerged for the first time as suppliers of ships for royal fleets: notably Fobbing, from 1355, but also Alresford, Benfleet, Bradfield, Coggeshall and Fordham, while others – Burnham-on-Crouch, Maldon and Manningtree – expanded their role. The combined contribution of these small to middling maritime communities to naval operations during the post-1354 period comprised over 40 per cent of the recorded ships from Essex. Bearing in mind the numbers of mariners enumerated by the 1372 survey, the only communities of this status that did not make an independent contribution to the naval war effort at this time were Stanford-le-Hope and Mersea.

In experiencing a relative shift in the burden of naval service from the larger ports to their second- or third-rank neighbours, Essex was not exceptional. During the later decades of the fourteenth century and throughout the fifteenth the crown showed a greater inclination to requisition ships from smaller fishing and estuarine ports, while simultaneously hiring larger numbers of foreign ships. There has been a tendency to explain this trend in terms of a putative decline in the merchant fleet, which – so the argument goes – had been seriously degraded during the war by damage to maritime infrastructure and commerce.[97] As the stock of available shipping shrank it was necessary for those assembling royal fleets to look further afield, beyond the kingdom's front-rank ports. Although undoubtedly exaggerated by some historians, the deleterious effects of war cannot be ignored; rather, they should be assessed within a more sophisticated conceptual framework that also takes account of the socio-economic consequences of the Black Death and the variations of experience that occurred at local and regional levels. Moreover, a more nuanced interpretation of the partial shift in the focus of requisitioning should also give due weight to two interrelated political developments. The first was the increased influence of merchants and shipowners, which during the 1370s found expression in a spate of parliamentary complaints about ship requisition and from 1381 in demands that English merchandise should be transported in English ships, the rationale for the latter being that it would contribute to the health of the merchant fleet, which was crucial to the crown's naval operations.[98] The second was the pressing need to protect shrinking commercial taxation revenues as raw wool exports declined and, owing to vested interests in parliament, the crown was unable to tax growing cloth exports as heavily.[99]

One way of achieving such protection was to requisition fewer ships from the major ports that were exporters of wool, thereby minimising interference with taxable trade.

What the consequences were of spreading the burden of naval requisitioning among smaller ports has yet to be researched. The impact of the crown's shipping demands on the socio-economic life of coastal communities has usually been investigated from the perspective of large port towns, as exemplified by Anthony Saul's influential study of Great Yarmouth; and the conclusions reached by such investigations have been by no means uniform.[100] In evaluating the impact of more diversified requisitioning we need to remember that it was accompanied, during the 1370s and 1380s, by a greater focus on *viages de guerre* by war fleets, which, compared with the continuing need for logistical operations, could be more burdensome for the shipowners and maritime communities involved. We shall shortly consider how these developments affected the potential pool of manpower in the coastal zone. As far as the ships are concerned, we have seen already that, in total, as many were needed during this phase of the Anglo-French war as during its early decades. It is likely that requisitioning one or two vessels from a village had a proportionately greater impact on that community than taking a dozen from a large port would have had during the 1330s and 1340s. This is perhaps how best to interpret the four naval voyages that, from surviving documentation, we know were undertaken by Fobbing ships during the 1370s.[101] We should also bear in mind that *viages de guerre* and tours of escort duty could be more time-consuming and hazardous than army transport operations. The *Seintmarieshipp* of Coggeshall, taken into royal service at Harwich in early November 1372, was employed on sea-keeping patrols for nearly two months.[102] But that was a modest spell of duty by comparison with the seven months in 1374–5 endured by the owner and crew of the 100-ton *Seintemariebot* of Bradfield, most of it spent in idleness in port waiting to carry troops to Brittany.[103]

Naval service and the shipboard community of Essex

What impact did naval recruitment have on the pool of potential manpower in the coastal and estuarine communities of Essex? As we have seen, application of the 'three identifiers' methodology suggests that at least 158 ships from Essex ports performed naval service during the period 1320–1400, some of them on several occasions. At the helm of these requisitioned vessels were over 100 separately identifiable masters. What is altogether less clear is how many individual mariners served on these ships. The paucity of crew lists means that only a small proportion of mariners can be identified – a deficiency of the evidence that serves only to underline the importance of the 1372 mariner survey. Simply aggregating the number of mariners serving on about 300 naval voyages made by Essex ships produces a total of about 6,000 men (see Table 6.1), but, given that many would have served more than once, there must be much double-counting of individuals in this total. Another estimate of mariner numbers – about 3,000 – can be arrived at by aggregating the largest crew for each of the 158 separately identifiable Essex ships. Again, this total may well conceal the double-counting of individuals, as some mariners would certainly have served on more than one ship during the course of their working lives. But, on the other hand, as noted earlier, the incompleteness of the records means that a significant proportion of the naval service actually performed is invisible to us and so not included in our totals of voyages, ships and mariners.

The real significance of this somewhat notional total of 3,000 mariners is, like the 300 documented naval voyages undertaken by Essex-based ships, to emphasise the long-term impact of the crown's maritime demands. Indeed, given that this service was spread over an 80-year period, it is clear that only a fraction of our 3,000 mariners would have been available for naval service at any single moment. For a more authentic view of the shipboard community as it actually existed and worked we should return to Table 6.6, which offers a series of snapshots of naval service. The largest number of mariners to serve simultaneously on Essex-based ships did so in 1338: 683 of them in 24 vessels, with high levels of naval recruitment also registered in 1346 (566 in 26) and 1342 (493 in 25). Such figures offer a county-level impression of the scale of the manpower demands made by the maritime dimension of the war effort. But, as a comparison of Tables 6.3 and 6.6 makes clear, even the most demanding of naval operations would tap the resources of only a proportion of the county's ports. In other words, while it is likely that the great majority of mariners serving aboard Essex ships were recruited from within the coastal zone of the county,[104] the impact of naval recruitment was localised, rather than general, within that zone. We should avoid the assumption, usually unfounded, that a ship's crew would be drawn exclusively from the residents of its home port; but the fact that 319 men served in Harwich-based vessels in 1338, 221 in those from Colchester/Hythe and 100 in those from Brightlingsea does surely point to three localities within Essex that had made a heavy manpower contribution to that transport fleet. Indeed, given that all but one of the Essex-based ships in 1338 were provided by ports located north of the river Blackwater, and that neighbouring Ipswich sent 17 ships manned by 532 mariners,[105] it would seem that over 1,000 mariners were drawn from, say, a 20- to 30-mile stretch of the coastal zone.

To what extent can we contextualise naval recruitment by reconstructing the pool of potential manpower in the coastal zone? The most promising sources for doing this are the records generated by the poll taxes of 1377–81. Everyone from their mid-teens was included, with the exception of clerics and the poor. Modern scholarship has argued for the essential reliability of the 1377 poll tax returns in particular;[106] and had they survived in their entirety for Essex we would have been able to calculate with a fair degree of accuracy the number of men resident in the vills throughout the coastal zone in the late 1370s. Unfortunately the returns are far from complete. The names of taxpayers are known only for Colchester, but even more disruptive is the fact that vill-level taxpayer totals can be established for only a proportion of the coastal hundreds of Essex.[107] In these circumstances the best we can do is offer a very rough and ready estimate. Given that the total number of taxpayers in the county was 47,962,[108] we can deduce that perhaps 20,000 were men of suitable age, with (excluding Colchester) several thousand resident in the coastal zone. But where vill-level totals of taxpayers are available we can at least examine the demographic context of naval recruitment at local level, an exercise that is brought into sharper focus by the availability of the mariner survey of 1372. The naval service of the 1370s was, as we have seen, less 'concentrated' than during the first phase of the war. The largest transport fleets were now smaller, but, because there was a greater emphasis on *viages de guerre*, more fleets were raised. Although the largest known simultaneous naval contribution by Essex-based ships – 185 mariners serving in seven vessels in 1373[109] – is indicative of less heavy manpower demands at local level, understanding the local impact of naval service becomes particularly important in the 1370s because the crown was now drawing more heavily on the shipping of smaller coastal and estuarine communities.

The vill-level data from the mariner survey of 1372 provide an invaluable means of assessing that local impact (see Table 6.7). It is instructive to begin with a comparison of the numbers of mariners listed at vill level in the 1372 census with the poll taxpayers recorded in those vills five years later. As we have seen, the 1372 survey cannot be considered comprehensive. Some vills that would surely have been home to seafarers were not surveyed, and it is unlikely that the sheriff and his staff were consistently thorough in those that were visited. That they missed some potential mariners is suggested not only by comparison of their returns with those of the constables of Colchester and Harwich but also perhaps by the nil returns that were made for West Tilbury and East Thurrock and by the small number of mariners found in St Osyth, a vill that occasionally contributed ships to royal fleets. On the other hand, when reflecting on the degree of prominence of mariners within the vills that were surveyed, we need to remember that some, perhaps many, of them would have been married with children, and that there would also have been other relatives who were now too old to go sea or who went only intermittently. The demographic footprint of mariner families was therefore larger than is suggested by a simple count of names in the 1372 survey.

While allowing for these caveats, it is possible to draw some conclusions from Table 6.7. Given that approximately half of the 1377 taxpayers were men, those

Table 6.7 Mariners recorded in the 1372 survey compared with poll taxpayers in 1377.

Vill	Number of mariners	Number of poll taxpayers in 1377	Mariners as % of taxpayers
Alresford	7	65	11
Althorne	7	—	—
Creeksea	4	—	—
Barking	9	—	—
Benfleet (North and South)	12	180	7
Burnham-on-Crouch	21	214	10
Colchester	72	2,955	2
Dagenham	5	—	—
East Donyland and Wivenhoe	13	167	8
East Tilbury	7	161	4
Fingringhoe	12	—	—
Fobbing	48	225	21
Harwich	69	222	31
Langenhoe	2	—	—
Maldon (Magna and Parva)	16	542	3
Mersea	21	—	—
St Osyth	5	362	1
Stanford-le-Hope	44	251	18
Stow Maries	9	86	11
Thorrington	3	77	4
West Thurrock	2	155	1
'Wolne' (Dengie Hundred)	4	—	—

Notes: Vill totals of 1377 poll taxpayers: Fenwick (ed.), Poll Taxes, vol. 1, pp. 173–80. Blanks denote missing data. In 1377 the vills of Althorne and Creeksea were probably taxed with Southminster (380 taxpayers), as they had been in 1327.

vills with mariners at around the 20 per cent level or higher should be seen as heavily committed to seafaring.[110] The density of mariners within the coastal and estuarine vills surveyed appears to have varied a great deal. To some extent this was the consequence of differences in the size and territorial extent of these 'vills', and of the patterns of settlement and economic activity within them. For example, that there were apparently few mariners within the extensive vill of St Osyth may have been because, away from the principal settlement near the creek, there was little engagement with the maritime life, though we should not discount the possibility that the dispersed nature of the population may in itself have contributed to under-recording by the sheriff. The situation of mariners in Colchester was rather different. More were recorded there than anywhere else, and yet they represented only a very small proportion of the population of what was the largest settlement in the coastal zone.[111] Rather like Exeter, Colchester's river site and diverse economy made it something of an anomaly. The greatest concentrations of mariners relative to population were to be found in vills of middling size in terms of taxpayer numbers (200–300): Burnham-on-Crouch, Harwich, Fobbing and Stanford-le-Hope.[112] Indeed, 46 per cent of the Essex mariners recorded by name in the 1372 survey (that is, excluding Ipswich) were resident in these four vills. For the king's agents, finding suitable manpower for naval impressment may well have been much easier in such places than in the more complex societies of the larger port towns.

An understanding of the distribution of mariners in 1370s Essex casts light on the shift in naval requisitioning policy that, during the later fourteenth century, resulted in a greater participatory role for small to middling coastal and estuarine communities. The impact of requisitioning on local seafaring populations – how intensive it was and the likely spread of impact – can be assessed by looking at specific cases. Take, for example, the service performed in 1374 by the 100-ton *Seintemarieship* of Fobbing, with John Burgeys at the helm, accompanied by a constable and 30 mariners.[113] Did Burgeys rely exclusively on Fobbing men to crew this ship, or was it necessary for him to look further afield? Given that we lack lists of either the crew or taxpayers for this part of Essex, any answer must be tentative. And the fact that the normal commercial crew may have been supplemented for naval service does complicate matters. What we can say is that, according to the 1372 survey, there were 48 mariners resident in Fobbing in 1372, including John Burgeys and John Burgeys junior.[114] And since there were 225 taxpayers in this vill in 1377 and the 1372 census was probably incomplete, we might reasonably conclude that half of the male workforce of the vill were seafarers.[115] The *Seintemarieship* could, therefore, have been manned exclusively from Fobbing manpower, but this is, on balance, unlikely. First, there were other ships operating out of Fobbing during the 1370s. The naval records show that the *James*, whose master was William May, and the *George*, with John Burgeys at the helm, were in royal service at the same time in 1377.[116] Second, according to the 1372 survey there were 63 mariners resident in neighbouring vills: principally Stanford-le-Hope (44), but also Benfleet (12) and East Tilbury (seven).[117] Third, the crews that we have examined thus far – the Harwich and Ipswich vessels that feature in the 1372 mariner survey and the *Maudeleyn* of Ipswich, for which a crew list survives (1374) – all consisted of a mix of home-port residents and men from neighbouring vills or further afield. The whole corpus of surviving crew lists has yet to be subjected to close analysis, but for the moment we would propose a model of recruitment, whether for commercial voyages or naval operations,

Table 6.8 Mariner family groups suggested by the 1372 survey.

Vill	Number of mariners	Number of family groups (total number of men in family groups)	Men in family groups as % of mariner population
Alresford	7	—	—
Althorne	7	—	—
Barking	9	2 (4)	44
Benfleet	12	3 (6)	50
Burnham-on-Crouch	21	—	—
Colchester	72	12 (27)	38
Creeksea	4	—	—
Dagenham	5	—	—
East Donyland	8	1 (2)	25
East Tilbury	7	—	—
Fingringhoe	12	1 (2)	17
Fobbing	48	7 (16)	33
Harwich	69	12 (26)	38
Ipswich	60	5 (11)	18
Langenhoe	2	1(2)	100
Maldon	16	2 (4)	25
Mersea	21	3 (6)	29
St Osyth	5	—	—
Stanford-le-Hope	44	4 (9)	20
Stow Maries	9	1(2)	22
Thorrington	3	—	—
Wivenhoe	5	2 (4)	80
'Wolne' (Dengie Hundred)	4	1 (2)	50

that assumes reliance where possible on local men but also on the mobility of mariners, the nature of the 'mix' within a particular ship being dependent on, among other things, the size and location of the home port.[118]

There can be no doubt that, for a small vill such as Fobbing, contributing as few as one or two ships to a royal fleet would require the services of a significant proportion of the local mariner workforce, from Fobbing itself and from neighbouring vills. One aspect of that workforce that would affect crew dynamics when ships were sent to war is nicely highlighted by the names listed in the 1372 mariner returns: for there, within the vill lists, we find men with shared surnames, a phenomenon suggestive of family ties. As can be seen in Table 6.8, 'family groups' represented a significant proportion of the recorded mariners for many of the vills surveyed. What this suggests is that mariner communities should be viewed as interlocking family networks that shaped employment experience and career advancement as experienced seafarers mentored sons, nephews and cousins: the next generation. When transferred to the social world of an operational crew, familial ties can only have had a settling, cohesive effect. But were a ship to be lost with all hands, the existence of family groups within its crew would make the impact of loss all the more devastating for relatives at home. For example, the 10 Harwich mariners who, according to the constable, had sailed with the earl of Pembroke and so would fight at the battle of La Rochelle included John Feld senior and John Feld junior – clearly father and son.[119] The likelihood is that most of the Harwich 10 were killed, given the merciless nature of sea combat, particularly for ordinary mariners and soldiers who could hardly hope to be held for ransom. And yet on this occasion we know that a John Feld continued to serve after 1372, suggesting that at least one of the two escaped the battle.[120]

Essex mariners, the Great Rising and the fortunes of war

When considering the impact of naval service on the lives of individuals, families and communities, the potential for disruption and, on occasion, permanent damage is easily demonstrated. Mariners and ships that would have been engaged in trade or fishing were diverted, perhaps in a heavy-handed fashion, to service the king's war at sea, a distraction that, as well as being potentially hazardous, might last months. Men's lives and their family's livelihoods were placed at risk, and there was clearly potential for serious discontent. Given that we have been examining these and a range of interrelated issues with specific reference to Essex during the second half of the fourteenth century, we are naturally drawn to asking how far the war at sea contributed to tensions and pressures that culminated in the explosion of the Great Rising of 1381. More specifically, can it be demonstrated that the shipboard community played a part in the rebellion that was motivated by circumstances particular to its predicament?

There is a little evidence – mostly circumstantial, some of it more clear-cut – that there were indeed mariners among the rebels. As two contemporary chroniclers make clear, the rebellion began among the residents of a cluster of coastal communities in Essex, starting with Fobbing and soon spreading to neighbouring Corringham and Stanford-le-Hope.[121] We cannot be certain whether the Thomas Baker who, according to Henry Knighton, 'began to exhort and gather together' the men of Fobbing was in some way related to the Richard Baker who, in 1372, had been recorded as a mariner residing in the town.[122] But some of the 48 Fobbing mariners listed by the sheriff were surely among 'toutz les gentz de Fobbame' who confronted John Bampton at Brentwood on 30 May, refusing either to pay or be arrested.[123] In judicial proceedings at Chelmsford on 2 July no fewer than 28 Fobbing men, including Thomas Baker, were named as ringleaders of the Essex rising: 'an astonishing number for a tiny village at the world's end out on the marshes'.[124] At least two of them – Richard Fraunceys and Robert Knyght – had been recorded as mariners in that vill in 1372. Records of their seized property show that Fraunceys, who was hanged, had been in possession of a messuage and an acre of land worth 12d per annum, while Knyght lost his boat and its gear, valued at 20s.[125]

In the days that followed the Brentwood incident, the rising spread eastwards along the coastal zone of Essex to the estuary of the river Crouch. This is clearly shown by mapping the localities mentioned in judicial indictments: that is, the places where revolt was proclaimed and from where those inciting it came.[126] Looking north of the river Blackwater, it is intriguing to find that Wat Tyler, said to be 'of Maidstone' by the author of the Anonimalle chronicle, was assigned to Colchester by 'the indicting jury of Maidstone hundred'.[127] Although Richard Britnell was not at all convinced that Colchester was a 'hotbed of rebellion',[128] some men from the town might have joined a contingent from Manningtree on their way to Mile End.[129] Otherwise, there are but a few fragments of circumstantial evidence. A rather well-heeled rebel from St Osyth, who was executed, had his property confiscated.[130] Four Brightlingsea men forced their way into St John's Abbey, Colchester, and stole the manorial court roll.[131] The names of two of the attackers – William Pache and John Ford – are suggestive of a relationship with local maritime families.[132]

That there is so little hard evidence of mariner involvement in the Great Rising is not altogether surprising. It may well be that, once the rebellion had begun in earnest, its leaders discouraged the maritime community from active participation. The Anonimalle chronicle records that, in early June, the Kentish rebels decided that residents of the maritime land should not join the descent upon London but should stay put to defend the coast against French attacks.[133] Something similar may have happened in Essex. However, it should not be forgotten that historians have not hitherto been looking for the shipboard community among the rebels. The ease with which the present authors traced two Fobbing mariners in sources on the rising that have been in print for over a century suggests that a more systematic comparison of maritime and judicial records would be worthwhile as part of the 'painstaking work of tracing [the] local background' of the 'nearly 1,000 Essex rebels' that are now known by name.[134]

Whatever may be concluded from the limited evidence currently available concerning mariners' participation in the revolt, there is a second issue to consider: namely, whether the conditions experienced by the residents of the coastal zone, especially the maritime community, set it apart from the rest of England, and, if so, whether circumstances particular to the maritime sphere of the war were sufficient to drive men to rebellion. An aspect of coastal life that did set it apart from the wartime experience of much of the rest of England was its direct exposure to enemy action. On the one hand, there were coastal raids. The period of attacks that began in June 1377 was particularly sustained and damaging.[135] While the south coast was most vulnerable to these amphibious landings, the coastal and estuarine communities of Essex were by no means safe. In the late summer of 1380 an audacious Castilian raid into the Thames estuary, little noticed by the English chroniclers, burned Gravesend and attacked shore-side settlements in Essex and Kent, seizing ships, cargoes of wool and prisoners for ransom.[136] It is hardly surprising that Sir Richard Waldegrave, commons Speaker in the parliament of November 1381, considered the coastal raids, 'against which no defence has ever been, nor is yet, provided', to be one of the 'outrages' that drove the 'poor commons' to rise up and wreak havoc.[137] He was no doubt also thinking of the damage inflicted by the enemy's 'barges, galleys and other vessels' at sea. This was often small-scale in nature and indistinguishable from private enterprise predation, a fact of maritime life, and so its overall, cumulative impact is difficult to gauge. What can perhaps be appreciated more easily is the impact of losses at a local level, though it is not always clear whether the 'lachrymose complaint' by a beleaguered coastal community should be taken at face value.[138]

An event that gave rise to particularly rich documentation was the attack, on 10 August 1375, by a squadron of Castilian galleys on an English commercial convoy collecting salt in the Bay of Bourgneuf. Thirty-six ships were taken and burned, a disaster that the Anonimalle chronicle considered to be 'the greatest loss of ships that England suffered at sea' during this period of the war.[139] Overall, Essex ports were not hard hit, losing only one ship, while Ipswich lost three and Great Yarmouth six.[140] But the home port of the 100-ton Essex ship, the Seintemariebot, was Bradfield, a small village on the estuary of the river Stour, in which resided only 79 poll taxpayers in 1377.[141] So, while the destruction of the ship and its cargo, valued at £220, was no doubt a serious blow for its Colchester-based owner, John Aleyn,[142] Bradfield's loss could conceivably have amounted to as many as 20 of its menfolk, since few if any of the crew would have survived the encounter with the Castilians.[143]

The other respect in which the wartime predicament of the coastal zone was distinctive concerns its direct contribution to the war, about which much has been said already. As we have seen, manpower demands were particularly heavy during the 1370s. Intensively pursued naval operations – offensive and defensive patrolling, as well as in support of land campaigns and garrisons – depended on the regular requisitioning of shipping and crews and the impressment of additional manpower to serve on the king's vessels or as shipboard soldiers. Although requisitioning was by no means new, the recruitment of 'marines' in such numbers was, as was the scope of the orders to selected towns to build warships: 70 barges in 1372 and 32 balingers in 1378.[144] It has been noted already how smaller coastal and estuarine communities were more heavily targeted by the crown's requisitioning agents during the second half of the century. Implementation of the orders to construct barges and balingers had similar effects. Colchester and Ipswich, jointly responsible for building a barge in 1372, managed to transfer part of the cost to Hadleigh (Suffolk), which in 1377 had about a quarter of Colchester's population.[145] In 1378 the men of the 'coastal village' of Bawdsey, who only the previous year had contributed three ships to a transport fleet,[146] petitioned against having to join forces with Ipswich, Sudbury and Hadleigh in the building of a balinger. 'The men of Bawdsey resented their inclusion in such wealthy company', notes Christopher Dyer, who adds that 'it is not surprising to find that [they were] involved in the rising'.[147] The same applies to Essex: it should occasion no surprise that small communities such as Fobbing were more militant than Colchester.

What are we to conclude from all this? We should not discount the likely effect of the Castilian raid of 1380 on the estuarine villages whose menfolk were rebellious at Brentwood the following year. As was argued by Searle and Burghart, 'war was ... central to the growing self-awareness and radical questioning' of such men; and they, having been trained in arms, were ultimately 'reduced to insecurity, fear, and at last to fury', when defensive arrangements proved inadequate.[148] We would add to this the point that, as the mainstay of naval operations, the communities of the coastal zone had also been making a disproportionately heavy contribution to the war effort. Whether the maritime communities of Essex felt the impact of the war at sea more keenly than those of other coastal counties can hardly be demonstrated, given the nature of the evidence. But several issues specific to Essex are worthy of consideration. The easy accessibility of that county from the realm's capital must have contributed to the burden that it bore. It was, for example, all too easy for the crown to order the impressment of mariners residing along the Thames estuary – as happened in March 1375, when five London shipmasters were licensed to select over 100 of the 'better and stronger mariners' from Essex and Kent,[149] and in 1377–8, when one of the king's sergeants at arms was ordered to enlist 170 mariners in Essex and bring them to London.[150] The 1372 survey was also symptomatic of this close governmental interest. Whatever conclusions were drawn from it at the time, the data deliver a clear message to us, especially when mariner and poll taxpayer numbers at vill level are compared.

Essex was a county without a populous town that functioned as a major port. This meant, firstly, that the burden of naval recruitment – ships and men – was borne by smaller communities, most of which were home to hundreds rather than thousands of people; and, secondly, that this burden was often relatively heavy, because in vills that were dependent on seafaring in its various forms, mariners represented a higher percentage of the adult male workforce than would be the case in a larger town with a more complex and diversified economy. The vulnerability of such communities to the deleterious effects of requisitioning and impressment can have only increased during the 1370s, as the overall burden of naval service grew and to a degree shifted from the major ports to middling and small coastal and estuarine villages. Seen from this perspective, it is hardly surprising that the menfolk of Fobbing were among the instigators of the rising in 1381. For such men as these, whose communities had been under great strain from wartime burdens not experienced by settlements inland nor even by the large ports, the imposition of the three-groat poll tax in November 1380, combined with the aggressive fashion with which it was administered, would have been merely the last straw. And, as the rising gathered pace, mariner and 'inland' peasant would have shared other resentments.[151] It is widely accepted that the expectations of the peasantry at large rose as living conditions improved during the decades following the first plague visitation, and that it was a sense of thwarted expectations, combined with recognition that social bonds had loosened, that influenced the judgement of many who resorted to rebellion during the early summer of 1381. The maritime community would no doubt have shared such views, especially those who, like the mariner–tenants of St John's Abbey, Colchester, were obliged to perform humiliating labour services tied to their smallholdings.[152]

It is our contention, therefore, that the role of mariners in the Great Rising, prompted by conditions particular to their lives and circumstances, as well as by the issues that affected the population at large, deserve to receive more attention from historians. That said, and by way of contextualisation, it is important to stress the complexity – and no doubt ambivalence – at the heart of how seafarers would have viewed the prospect of naval service at the king's command and pay. We might know little about the thoughts and fortunes of most individual Essex mariners – a deficiency that can too easily be compensated for by speculation – but what is demonstrable is how intermingled naval and 'civilian' seafaring was for many of them. The 'mixed' careers of John Shipman of Brightlingsea and Thomas Crosse of Colchester, as wine shippers and transporters of soldiers, have been written about elsewhere, for example.[153] And in assessing those mixed careers we should avoid the easy assumption that misfortune flowed exclusively from the crown's naval impositions. As examples of this, let us consider two men from Fobbing who occupied opposite ends of the socio-economic spectrum. On the one hand there was John Burgeys, whom we glimpsed earlier at the helm of the *Seintemarieship* of Fobbing in 1374. Listed among the 48 mariners in that vill in 1372, Burgeys was a shipowner and active trader who also participated in numerous naval expeditions.[154] But it was apparently commercial rivalries or personal enmities, rather than the work of the king's enemies, which led to the loss of his ship, the *Marie* of Fobbing and its cargo, valued at 2,000 marks, when it foundered on the rocks in Brittany in 1375.[155] At the other end of the spectrum was John Henry, who, according to a later investigation, had 'a messuage in the vill of Fobbing which is worth 6d after expenses'. When Henry's name was added to that vill's list of mariners in 1372[156] he was seriously in debt, owing two London fishmongers £26 7s 6d.[157] He may well have participated in the war at sea, but his default on the debt, flight from the bailiwick and loss of his messuage is suggestive of straightforward business misfortune.

To set against such casualties of life, it is not difficult to find others named in the 1372 mariner survey who appear to have prospered. Indeed, in the cases of men such as William Thorp and Roger Clerk of Harwich, both of whom were at sea at the time of the survey, probably as ordinary mariners,[158] naval service may well have contributed to career advancement. As master of the *Edmond* of Harwich, Thorp was involved in a series of naval expeditions from 1374 to 1378, continuing with other vessels during the 1380s,[159] which is when Clerk appears as master.[160] The highlight of Roger Clerk's career at sea, and probably the most lucrative episode, was his involvement, at the helm of the *Eleyne*, in the earl of Arundel's *viage de guerre* of 1387. The climax of that voyage was the battle of Margate/Cadzand: a great confrontation with a Franco-Flemish fleet that resulted in the capture of about 40 ships laden with 5,000 tuns of wine.[161] And there were others who had been returned as mariners in 1372 who were in command of ships in Arundel's fleet. For William Tye of Fingringhoe[162] the battle of Margate/Cadzand came at the end of nearly 20 years as master of the *James* (one of four Colchester ships at the battle), while the career of Henry Fyn of Ipswich, master of the *George* in 1387, stretched back to the early 1370s.[163] Neither man is seen again in the maritime records. Perhaps their prize money permitted them to retire from active seafaring.[164]

Not only was the war at sea in its various facets an influential part of the lives of many Essex mariners but it could be argued that their lives had prepared them well for the challenges and rigours of maritime warfare. Chaucer's Shipman is typical of men of this stamp, their lives at sea demanding resourcefulness, hardiness and a willingness to resort to sharp practice and violence. Apart from the scale of the operations, the practicalities of warfare sanctioned by the crown were little different from those required for private commercial predation, which was an everyday hazard – or opportunity – for those who spent their working lives at sea – that 'lawless space separating nations, beyond the "King's peace"'.[165] Viewing the mariners listed in the Essex survey in this light makes it easy to see why the crown considered the coastal zone an ideal recruiting ground for shipboard 'soldiers'. This is not, of course, to argue that spells of naval service were invariably welcomed. Cases of resistance to impressment and desertion offer ample evidence that naval commitments were often resented as a distraction from commercial activity or simply because they represented too 'controlled' an environment for those accustomed to more opportunistic, private enterprise predation. But, like the lure of ransoms for soldiers fighting on land, the ships and cargoes seized at such sea battles as Sluys (1340), the Bay of Flemings (1371) and Margate/Cadzand (1387), as well as at countless smaller encounters, were a constant reminder to mariners of the potential gains to be made from prize money. For those in paid royal service, shipowners had a right to a quarter share of the value of prizes, with half going to the master and crew.[166]

It is not only the implied character of Chaucer's Shipman that is relevant to our understanding of the Essex mariner but also his life experience: the years of voyaging that had taken him from Hull to Cartagena on the Mediterranean coast of Spain and from the Baltic to Cape Finisterre on the Atlantic coast of Iberia, and which had left him with an intimate knowledge of 'every cryke in Britaigne and in Spayne'.[167] One aspect of naval service that it is important to recognise is the potential that it offered for the widening of our mariners' horizons, taking them beyond the trading routes or fishing grounds with which they were familiar. This must have been the case with our old friend William Tye of Fingringhoe, for whom at least 18 years at the helm of the *James*, out of Colchester, can be documented. We catch but a glimpse or two of his trading voyages,[168] but it is in the naval sphere that the range of his seafaring can be seen. For example, in July 1386, less than a year before fighting in Arundel's fleet at the battle of Margate/Cadzand, Tye had joined the transport fleet that took John of Gaunt's army to Corunna in Galicia, stopping off at Brest on the way to break up the French siege.[169]

We might wonder whether the adventurous lives and accompanying expectations of seafaring men who had seen the world were a source of volatility as well as vitality within coastal and estuarine communities: a further ingredient in the mix of tensions that proved explosive in 1381. What we may be sure of is that it was during the era of the Hundred Years War that the foundations were laid in Essex, as elsewhere in England, for the Elizabethan age of discovery. Indeed, it is fitting that, in June 1553, the prelude to Richard Chancellor and Sir Hugh Willoughby's epic journey to the White Sea was spent on the Essex coast, sailing from Tilbury to St Osyth and Walton-on-the-Naze and finally docking at Harwich for over two weeks.[170] This seems to have cemented a place for Harwich in the operations of the newly founded Muscovy Company.[171] Then, in 1562, Benjamin Gonson, Treasurer of the Royal Navy and based at Seabright Hall near Chelmsford, funded the voyage of John Hawkins from Guinea to the West Indies and married his daughter to the famous Elizabethan adventurer and pirate.[172] When the achievements of these remarkable sixteenth-century seafarers are celebrated, we should spare a thought for their forebears – men like that old salt William Tye, whose trading and naval voyages had given Essex mariners an experience of the wider ocean and perhaps an understanding of the possibilities that lay beyond.

Notes

1 This chapter draws on data collected during the course of projects funded at Hull (Ayton and Lambert) by the ESRC (RES-000-22-4127) and at Southampton (Lambert) by the AHRC (AH/L004062/1).

2 TNA, C47/2/46, nos 6, 8, 11, 14 (orders), 7, 8d, 9, 10, 12, 13 (returns).

3 E.g., *CCR, 1369–74*, p. 439.

4 E.g., *CCR, 1369–74*, p. 371.

5 J.J.N. Palmer, *England, France and Christendom, 1377–99* (London, 1972), pp. 7–8.

6 J.W. Sherborne, 'The Cost of English Warfare with France in the Later Fourteenth Century', in A. Tuck (ed.), *War, Politics and Culture in Fourteenth-Century England* (London and Rio Grande, 1994), pp. 59–60, 66–7, 69.

7 J.W. Sherborne, 'The English Navy: Shipping and Manpower, 1369–89', in Tuck (ed.), *War, Politics and Culture*, pp. 35–9.

8 J.W. Sherborne, 'The Battle of La Rochelle and the War at Sea, 1372–75', in Tuck (ed.), *War, Politics and Culture*, pp. 41–53.

9 *Ibid.*, p. 47.

10 *Ibid.*, pp. 46–7.

11 Sherborne, 'English Navy', p. 36.

12 The vills that were to receive direct orders are listed in the orders sent to the sheriff.

13 TNA, C47/2/46, nos 8d, 9, 10.

14 TNA, C47/2/46, no. 10. The vills in Dengie Hundred are: Maldon, Burnham [on Crouch], Stow [Maries], Creeksea, Althorne and 'Wolne'.

15 TNA, C47/2/46, no. 9.

16 TNA, C47/2/46, no. 8d. The vills being Great Wakering, Prittlewell, Hadleigh, Leigh [on Sea] and Milton.

17 Damage to the document particularly affects the list of Harwich names, about a third of which are difficult or impossible to read. The constables' returns are affected far less by legibility problems.

18 One seafarer, two fishers, 14 draggers and two fowlers. C.C. Fenwick (ed.), *The Poll Taxes of 1377, 1379 and 1381*, British Academy Records of Social and Economic History, new series, vol. xxvii, 3 vols (Oxford, 1998–2005), vol. i, p. 247.

19 When the constables' returns are included, and Ipswich excluded, the contribution rises to 36 per cent.

20 TNA, C47/2/46, no. 13.

21 TNA, C47/2/46, no. 7.

22 TNA, C47/2/46, no. 12.

23 Contemporary evidence suggests that the first name on each list was the master; crew size is appropriate for the known tonnages of these vessels. TNA, C47/2/46, nos 7, 12.

24   Fenwick, *Poll Taxes*, vol. i, p. 179; vol. ii, p. 500.
25   For an examination of the records available for the study of the shipboard community, together with appropriate methodologies, see C. Lambert and A. Ayton, 'The Mariner in Fourteenth-Century England', in W.M. Ormrod (ed.), *Fourteenth-Century England VII* (Woodbridge, 2012), pp. 153–76.
26   Sherborne, 'Battle of La Rochelle', pp. 45–6.
27   For a wide-ranging examination of naval operations during the Hundred Years War, including their strategic purpose and resource implications, see A. Ayton and C. Lambert, 'Navies and Maritime Warfare', in A. Curry (ed.), *The Hundred Years War. Problems in Focus Revisited* (London, forthcoming). See also C. Richmond, 'The War at Sea', in K. Fowler (ed.), *The Hundred Years War* (London, 1971), pp. 96–121, and several of James Sherborne's papers collected in A. Tuck (ed.), *War, Politics and Culture in Fourteenth-Century England* (London and Rio Grande, 1994).
28   C.L. Lambert, *Shipping the Medieval Military: English Maritime Logistics in the Fourteenth Century* (Woodbridge, 2011), p. 65.
29   *Ibid.*, pp. 114–19.
30   *CPR*, 1343–5, p. 92; TNA, E101/23/35; Lambert, *Shipping the Medieval Military*, pp. 128–36.
31   TNA, E101/20/28; E101/20/27, m. 2; *CCR*, 1337–9, pp. 557, 561–2; *CCR*, 1339–41, pp. 27–8.
32   TNA, E101/20/34.
33   TNA, E101/25/12.
34   M. Hughes, 'The Fourteenth-Century French Raids on Hampshire and the Isle of Wight', in A. Curry and M. Hughes (eds), *Arms, Armies and Fortifications in the Hundred Years War* (Woodbridge, 1994), pp. 121–44; C. Given-Wilson and C. Scott-Stokes (ed. and trans.), *Chronicon Anonymi Cantuariensis: The Chronicle of Anonymous of Canterbury, 1346–1365* (Oxford, 2008), pp. 58–61.
35   E. Searle and R. Burghart, 'The Defense of England and the Peasants' Revolt', *Viator*, 3 (1972), pp. 380–83.
36   J.R. Alban, 'English Coastal Defence: Some Fourteenth-Century Modifications within the System', in R.A. Griffiths (ed.), *Patronage, the Crown and the Provinces in Later Medieval England* (Gloucester, 1981), pp. 57–78.
37   Sherborne, 'English Navy'; Sherborne, 'Battle of La Rochelle'.
38   V.H. Galbraith (ed.), *The Anonimalle Chronicle, 1333–1381* (Manchester, 1927), pp. 68–9, 177; Ayton and Lambert, 'Navies and Maritime Warfare'.
39   J. Sumption, *Divided Houses. The Hundred Years War, vol. III* (London, 2009), pp. 181, 185–6.
40   T.K. Moore, 'The Cost-Benefit Analysis of a Fourteenth-Century Naval Campaign: Margate/Cadzand, 1387', in R. Gorski (ed.), *Roles of the Sea in Medieval England* (Woodbridge, 2012), pp. 103–24.
41   *CPR*, 1370–4, p. 91.
42   TNA, E101/31/23, mm. 2, 3; E101/31/22, m. 2.
43   TNA, E101/32/1.
44   TNA, C47/2/46, no. 7.
45   Lambert, *Shipping the Medieval Military*, pp. 136–40.
46   *Ibid.*, pp. 128–36.
47   *Ibid.*, chapter 1.
48   For practical purposes the admiral of the west drew most of his ships and mariners from the coastal communities of south-east and south-west England, from Kent to Somerset.
49   Lambert, *Shipping the Medieval Military*, pp. 25–33.
50   E.g., in 1353: *CPR*, 1350–54, pp. 419–20.
51   TNA, C47/2/32. Cf. C47/2/46, m. 18.
52   Lambert, *Shipping the Medieval Military*, pp. 174–7.

53   C. Tipping, 'Cargo Handling and the Medieval Cog', *The Mariner's Mirror*, 80 (1994), pp. 3–15. Cf. J.H. Parry, *The Age of Reconnaissance: Discovery, Exploration and Settlement* (London, 1963), p. 61, which suggests that a 250-ton squared rigged ship needed only 20 to 26 men to sail it (12.5 tons per man).

54   *Calendar of Inquisitions Miscellaneous Preserved in the Public Record Office, vol. 2, 1307–49* (London, 1916), p. 367. See also the 'peacetime' ton:man ratios for ships employed as escorts of the 1372–3 wine convoy: references in n. 57.

55   *CPR*, 1321–24, p. 417.

56   S. Rose, 'Maritime Logistics and Edward I's Military Campaigns: What can be Learnt from the Surviving Documents', *The Mariner's Mirror*, 99 (2013), pp. 392–3.

57   For example, the pay records for the ships escorting the wine convoy during the winter of 1372–3 state how much manpower had been added to the normal 'peacetime' commercial crews: TNA, E101/32/3, 4, 7, 9, 10, 11 and 28.

58   BL, Additional MS 7967, fos 94r–99v. For this fleet, see Lambert, *Shipping the Medieval Military*, pp. 109–11.

59   TNA, C61/36, m. 29. As the French threat increased, orders were issued to ports to assemble ships with extra men before they set out: C61/36, m. 25d.

60   BL, Additional MS 7967, fo. 94r.

61   Commerce: TNA, E122/158/25 (1371–2); E101/179/10, fo. 51v. (1373). War: E101/32/1 (1372); BL, Additional MS 37494, fo. 19v. (1373).

62   TNA, E101/32/1, m. 3d. On crew lists, see Lambert and Ayton, 'Mariner in Fourteenth-Century England', pp. 161–2, but note that many more have come to light since that article was written. On family and locational ties within crews, see M. Kowaleski, 'Working at Sea: Maritime Recruitment and Remuneration in Medieval England', in S. Cavaciocchi (ed.), *Ricchezza del mare, ricchezza dal mare, secoli XIII–XVIII* (Florence, 2006), pp. 909–13.

63   Alban, 'English Coastal Defence', p. 69–70. For impressments, see Lambert and Ayton, 'Mariner in Fourteenth-Century England', p. 161 and notes.

64   Kowaleski, 'Working at Sea', pp. 915–16.

65   Fenwick, *Poll Taxes*, vol. i, p. 247.

66   TNA, E101/32/1.

67   TNA, E101/32/1, mm. 2, 3.

68   It is striking that two of the eight 'armed' archers who joined Leget's company at Harwich in November can be linked with Essex mariners recorded earlier in the year.

69   In 1373 Robert Waltham is recorded at the helm of the *Trinity*, a Hull ship of similar size (BL, Additional MS 37494, fo. 17r.). The surnames of two of the *Margerye*'s crew ('Hedon') reinforce this possible Humberside connection.

70   Lambert, *Shipping the Medieval Military*, pp. 203–5.

71   TNA, E101/31/11, 12, 15 and 27.

72   TNA, E101/30/13, m. 5; E101/30/15, m. 3; E101/31/10; E101/31/12, m. 1; E101/31/14 and 23; E364/5, rot. 31d. (a).

73   1371: *CPR*, 1370–74, p. 88; *CCR*, 1369–74, p. 229; TNA, E101/31/11, m. 7 (Guy Brian's recruiting itinerary).

74   TNA, E101/557/15, mm. 6, 7, 8 (muster roll), 9.

75   TNA, E101/32/29.

76   TNA, SC 8/299/14911.

77   TNA, E101/32/28.

78   TNA, C47/2/46, no. 12.

79   For example, Geoffrey Starlyng and Benedict Botenshall were shipowners and masters who also served as men-at-arms and retinue captains: Starlyng, TNA, E101/32/29; Botenshall, BL, Additional MS 37494, fo. 37v.; TNA, E101/30/21, m. 1; E101/32/6; E101/33/17, m. 2; E101/39/17, m. 2.

80 TNA, C81/1759, no. 37. The document is not dated, but the career of John Ipres suggests that it dates from the 1370s or 1380s (TNA, E101/396/11; E122/16/14). Cf. royal orders for the taking on of carpenters for work on barges in November 1372: *CPR, 1370–4*, p. 219.

81 For an assessment of the value of the commercial taxation records, see Lambert and Ayton, 'Mariner in Fourteenth-Century England', pp. 156–7.

82 Interpretative issues: identification of the home port is sometimes not altogether clear, a problem that in the case of Essex affects 'Burnham' and 'Hythe' in particular.

83 The crown clearly recognised the value of the three identifiers of shipmaster, home port and ship name. They were used to track down ships if necessary, as during the years 1337–40, when over 300 requisitioned ships refused to go on the king's service. TNA, C47/2/30. See also *CCR, 1343–46*, pp. 128–33, where we see Edward III's officials using the three identifiers to hunt down over 200 ships' crews which had deserted his army in Brittany.

84 The naval records do not always specify the tonnage of ships, particularly during the first half of the fourteenth century. Additionally, it is evident that the tonnage assigned to particular vessels might vary from one set of records to the next.

85 But note that the ship totals for each port in the 1346 fleet have been included in Table 6.1, which is simply counting voyages.

86 A. Ayton and C. Lambert, 'A Maritime Community in War and Peace: Kentish Ports, Ships and Mariners, 1320–1400', *Archaeologia Cantiana*, 134 (2014), pp. 67–103.

87 M. Lyon *et al.* (eds), *The Wardrobe Book of William de Norwell, 12 July 1338 to 27 May 1340* (Brussels, 1983), pp. 379–82; Lambert, *Shipping the Medieval Military*, pp. 175–6.

88 M. Kowaleski, 'Port Towns: England and Wales 1300–1540', in D. Palliser (ed.), *The Cambridge Urban History of Britain, vol. 1: 600–1540* (Cambridge, 2000), pp. 467–94 (Table 19.5, p. 488); M. Kowaleski, *Local Markets and Regional Trade in Medieval Exeter* (Cambridge, 1995), pp. 29–30; C. Liddy, *War, Politics and Finance in Late Medieval English Towns. Bristol, York and the Crown, 1359–1400* (Woodbridge, 2005), pp. 45–6.

89 Ayton and Lambert, 'Maritime Community in War and Peace: Kentish Ports'; C. Lambert, 'The Contribution of the Cinque Ports to the Wars of Edward II and Edward III: New Methodologies and Estimates', in R. Gorski (ed.), *Roles of the Sea in Medieval England* (Woodbridge, 2012), pp. 59–78.

90 R.H. Britnell, *Growth and Decline in Colchester, 1300–1525* (Cambridge, 1986), pp. 11, 23, 93–5. Most of the ships listed in the naval records with 'Colchester' as their home port were therefore probably from Hythe.

91 Lyon *et al.* (eds), *Wardrobe Book of William de Norwell*, p. 378; *CPR, 1338–40*, p. 329; *CCR, 1339–41*, p. 207.

92 The last documented Brightlingsea contribution to the naval war was John Shipman's voyage at the helm of the *Swallow* in 1351: TNA, E101/612/40; E101/26/18, m. 1.

93 Two crayers: the *Crayer*, master John Barre, and the *Katerine*, master John Jacob. TNA, E101/51/7, m. 1.

94 TNA, E101/79/10, m. 1; E101/184/19, fo. 63v.

95 See, for example, E.P. Dickin, *A History of the Town of Brightlingsea, a Member of the Cinque Ports* (Colchester, 1913), p. 147.

96 C. Dove, *The Liberty of Brightlingsea* (Brightlingsea, repr., 1996), pp. 23–31, 73. Note, however, that clerks continued to list the naval service of other towns linked to the Cinque Ports separately.

97 See, for example, N.A.M. Rodger, *The Safeguard of the Sea: A Naval History of Great Britain, vol. 1: 660–1649* (London, 1997), pp. 124–5; Sumption, *Divided Houses*, pp. 132–5, 377–9; G. Cushway, *Edward III and the War at Sea* (Woodbridge, 2011), chapter 20.

98 *PROME*, vol. vi, pp. 262–3; discussion in M. Kowaleski, 'Warfare, Shipping and Crown Patronage: the Impact of the Hundred Years War on the Port Towns of England', in L. Armstrong, I. Elbl and M. Elbl (eds), *Money, Markets and Trade in Late Medieval Europe* (Leiden, 2005), pp. 240–43.

99 W.M. Ormrod, 'The Domestic Response to the Hundred Years War', in A. Curry and M. Hughes (eds), *Arms, Armies and Fortifications in the Hundred Years War* (Woodbridge, 1994), pp. 92–4.

100 A. Saul, 'Great Yarmouth and the Hundred Years War in the Fourteenth Century', *Bulletin of the Institute of Historical Research*, 52 (1979), pp. 105–15. Cf. Kowaleski, 'Warfare, Shipping and Crown Patronage', for a more positive view of the impact of war on port towns.

101 BL, Additional MS 37494, fo. 19v.; TNA, E101/33/27; E101/36/20, p. 4.

102 TNA, E101/32/1, m. 1.

103 TNA, E101/33/31, m. 6.

104 Cf. Kowaleski, 'Working at Sea', pp. 911–13; I. Friel, 'How Much Did the Sea Matter in Medieval England (c.1200–c.1500)?', in R. Gorski (ed.), *Roles of the Sea in Medieval England* (Woodbridge, 2012), p. 184.

105 Lyon *et al.* (eds), *Wardrobe Book of William de Norwell*, pp. 378–9; TNA, E101/21/7, m. 2.

106 See L.R. Poos, *A Rural Society after the Black Death: Essex 1350–1525* (Cambridge, 1991), Appendix A, pp. 294–9, for a valuable discussion.

107 For a map, see Poos, *Rural Society*, p. 33 (Figure 2.1). The most significant gaps in the returns concern the area to the west of Tilbury, and the stretches of coast from Canvey Island to the Crouch and between the Blackwater and the Colne.

108 Fenwick, *Poll Taxes*, vol. i, p. 173.

109 BL, Additional MS 37494, fos 19r–19v.

110 This sits comfortably with the single Essex vill among the patchily surviving 1381 poll tax returns, Tollesbury, which the occupational designations suggest was truly 'maritime'. Fenwick (ed.), *Poll Taxes*, vol. i, p. 247. Cf. examples, notably Dartmouth, discussed in M. Kowaleski, 'The Demography of Maritime Communities in Late Medieval England', in M. Bailey and S.H. Rigby (eds), *England in the Age of the Black Death. Essays in Honour of John Hatcher* (Turnhout, 2012), pp. 74–97.

111 Note also Ipswich: 60 mariners (4%) and 1,507 poll tax payers. Fenwick, *Poll Taxes*, vol. ii, p. 500.

112 Harwich in particular stands out, though this may well be attributable to the availability of the constable's, as well as the sheriff's, return, and to the partial illegibility of the latter.

113 TNA, E101/33/27.

114 TNA, C47/2/46, no. 9. The sheriff did not distinguish between mariners at home and at sea.

115 Fenwick, *Poll Taxes*, vol. i, 173.

116 TNA, E101/36/20, p. 4. The combined crew was 36. It may have been the *Seintemarieship* that foundered on the Breton coast a couple of years earlier while engaged in trade: *CPR, 1374–77*, p. 156.

117 TNA, C47/2/46, no. 9. There is evidence of naval service by single ships from Benfleet and Stanford during the late 1370s.

118 Cf. Kowaleski, 'Working at Sea', pp. 911–13 and table 1, where the contrast between the crews of 'Exmouth' and Dartmouth ships is particularly instructive; and Liddy, *War, Politics and Finance*, p. 48, on the 40-man crew of the barge that York built in 1373, of which only a quarter were from the home port.

119 TNA, C47/2/46, no. 7.

120 In 1378 John Feld served at the helm of the *Marie* (120 tons) of Harwich: TNA, E101/37/25, m. 5.

121 The most detailed account, naming these three vills, is Galbraith, *Anonimalle Chronicle*, pp. 134–5. For Fobbing, see also G.H. Martin (ed. and trans.), *Knighton's Chronicle, 1337–1396* (Oxford, 1995), pp. 208–9. For critical evaluation of the chroniclers' testimony, drawing on judicial records, see N. Brooks, 'The Organisation and Achievements of the Peasants of Kent and Essex in 1381', in H. Mayr-Harting and R.I. Moore (eds), *Studies in Medieval History Presented to R.H.C. Davis* (London and Ronceverte, 1985), pp. 250–51.

122 TNA, C47/2/46, no. 9.

123 Galbraith, *Anonimalle Chronicle*, p. 134.

124 H.E.P. Grieve, 'The Rebellion and the County Town', in W.H. Liddell and R.G. Wood (eds), *Essex and the Great Revolt of 1381*, Essex Record Office Publication 84 (Chelmsford, 1982), p. 50.

125 A. Réville, *Le soulèvement des travailleurs d'Angleterre en 1381* (Paris, 1898), pp. 226–7. For critical evaluation of the records of forfeiture, see A.J. Prescott, 'Judicial Records of the Rising of 1381', PhD thesis (London University, 1984), pp. 339–49.

126 Brooks, 'Organisation and Achievements', pp. 255, 257 (Map 7).

127 *Ibid.*, p. 258.

128 Britnell, *Growth and Decline in Colchester*, pp. 124–5. For the predominant reluctance of Colchester residents to join the rebels, see J. Taylor, W.R. Childs and L. Watkiss (eds), *The St Albans Chronicle. The Chronica Maiora of Thomas Walsingham. I (1376–1394)* (Oxford, 2003), pp. 516–17.

129 Réville, *Soulèvement*, pp. 216–17 (from confessions). But note Prescott, 'Judicial Records', pp. 293–9, which reconstructs the movements of the Manningtree band, one of three from Essex to move on London, from a more reliable indictment (TNA, KB145/3/5/1), which specifies Chelmsford rather than Colchester.

130 Property worth £4 4s. 2d. Réville, *Soulèvement*, p. 226.

131 Dove, *Liberty of Brightlingsea*, pp. 29–30, where the labour services owed by the men to the abbey are examined. The court rolls were burned by the rebels in nearby Wivenhoe: C. Dyer, 'The Social and Economic Background to the Rural Revolt of 1381', in C. Dyer, *Everyday Life in Medieval England* (London and New York, 2000), p. 218.

132 John Ford may have been related to William Ford of Brightlingsea, who sailed to Gascony in 1324 and 1325: see BL, Additional MS 7967, fo. 99r.; TNA, E101/16/40, main roll, m. 1. For the maritime interests of the Pache family, see Lambert and Ayton, 'Mariner in Fourteenth-Century England', p. 167.

133 Galbraith, *Anonimalle Chronicle*, p. 136.

134 Poos, *Rural Society*, p. 234, acknowledging the important work of Dr Andrew Prescott.

135 On the impact of the raids and other wartime pressures on coastal communities (though not those of Essex), see Searle and Burghart, 'Defense of England'.

136 T. Hog (ed.), *Adami Murimuthensis Chronica* (London, 1846), p. 241 (continuation of Murimuth's chronicle to 1380); H. Ph. Terrier de Loray, *Jean de Vienne, amiral de France, 1341–96* (Paris, 1877), Pièces Justificatives, no. 71 (pp. lxii–lxiii).

137 *PROME*, vol. vi, p. 217.

138 As with Budleigh's claim, in November 1347, to have lost three ships, twelve boats and 141 men 'captured by the French upon the sea' in a matter of months: *CPR*, 1345–8, pp. 467–8.

139 Galbraith, *The Anonimalle Chronicle*, pp. 77, 79, 180.

140 TNA, C47/30/8, no. 14, printed in N.H. Nicolas, *A History of the Royal Navy* (London, 1847), vol. ii, pp. 510–14; *PROME*, vol. v, pp. 351–2.

141 Fenwick, *Poll Taxes*, vol. i, 179.

142 Aleyn: Britnell, *Growth and Decline in Colchester*, pp. 18–19. Aleyn had sent a ship of this name to the Bay of Bourgneuf in 1364: *CPR*, 1361–4, p. 507.

143 The crew of this ship when serving as a troop transport in April 1375 was the master, a constable, 19 mariners and two cabin boys. TNA, E101/33/31, m. 6.

144 Sherborne, 'English Navy', pp. 33–4; J.W. Sherborne, 'English Barges and Balingers of the Late Fourteenth Century', in Tuck (ed.), *War, Politics and Culture*, pp. 71–6; Liddy, *War, Politics and Finance*, pp. 44, 46–8, 53–4.

145 Britnell, *Growth and Decline in Colchester*, pp. 82–3.

146 TNA, E101/36/20, p. 3.

147 C. Dyer, 'The Rising of 1381 in Suffolk: Its Origins and Participants', in C. Dyer, *Everyday Life in Medieval England* (London and New York, 2000), p. 232.

148 Searle and Burghart, 'Defense of England', p. 366.

149 TNA, C61/88, mm. 7, 8. Via the website of the Gascon Rolls Project (1317–1468): <www.gasconrolls.org>, accessed 8 November 2016.

150 Warrant to pay the sergeant at arms for his work: TNA, E43/662. Essex mariners had long been arrested against their will (e.g. St Osyth, 1311: TNA, SC8/194/9654), and it continued after the Great Rising (e.g. 1386: TNA, SC8/306/15282).

151 See C. Dyer, 'The Causes of the Revolt in Rural Essex', in W.H. Liddell and R.G. Wood (eds), *Essex and the Great Revolt of 1381*, Essex Record Office Publication 84 (Chelmsford, 1982), pp. 21–36.

152 Dove, *Liberty of Brightlingsea*, pp. 21–3.

153 Lambert and Ayton, 'Mariner in Fourteenth-Century England', pp. 166–7.

154 The mariner survey of 1372 includes four men called John Bogeys/Burgeys. The sheriff returned three men of that name, two (including 'junior', who heads the list) from Fobbing and one from Burnham-on-Crouch (TNA, C47/2/46, nos 9, 10). The constable of Colchester noted a fourth as 'at home' in that town (note, however, that no John Burgeys is recorded in the 1377 poll tax returns for Colchester: Fenwick, *Poll Taxes*, vol. i, pp. 194–205). A John Burgeys appears at the helm of a Fobbing ship in 1355 (TNA, E101/26/38, m. 2), and – in addition to 1374 – does so again in 1377 (E101/33/27; E101/36/20, p. 4). A man of that name, who commanded ships from London and Queenborough (E101/29/39, m. 5; E101/36/14, m. 2; E101/37/13; E101/37/14, m. 1; E101/37/18; E101/38/19, m. 2; E101/38/30, m. 3), can be linked to Burgeys, father or son, of Fobbing: *CPR*, 1374–7, p. 156.

155 The ship was in Brest harbour when it was rammed and its anchor cable 'maliciously cut' by William Baker, shipmaster from Yarmouth, and John Covenant, merchant of the Humber: TNA, SC8/303/15124; *CPR*, 1374–7, p. 156.

156 TNA, C47/2/46, no. 9.

157 TNA, C131/45/9; C131/45/17; C131/211/16; C 241/184/5.

158 TNA, C47/2/46, no. 7d.

159 TNA, E101/33/31, m. 6; E101/37/13; E101/37/15, m. 2; E101/37/7, 17, 18; E101/38/18; E101/39/2, m. 1; E101/40/9, m. 4.

160 TNA, E101/39/2, m. 7; E101/40/21, m. 5.

161 TNA, E101/40/36, m. 1; Moore, 'Cost–Benefit Analysis'.

162 TNA, C47/2/46, no. 13.

163 TNA, C47/2/46, no. 12; BL Additional MS 37494, fo. 19v. (1373); TNA, E101/40/9, m. 3; E101/40/21, mm. 2, 4, 5; E101/40/36, m. 2 (1387).

164 For the prize money, see Moore, 'Cost–Benefit Analysis', pp. 119–23.

165 N.A.M. Rodger, 'The Law and Language of Private Naval Warfare', *The Mariner's Mirror*, 100 (2014), p. 7.

166 T. Twiss (ed.), *Monumenta Juridica: The Black Book of the Admiralty*, Rolls Series (London, 1871–6), vol. i, pp. 20–23.

167 L.D. Benson (ed.), *The Riverside Chaucer*, 3rd edn (Oxford, 1988), p. 30.

168 TNA, E122/158/25; E101/179/10, fo. 51v.

169 TNA, E101/40/19, m. 5; Sumption, *Divided Houses*, pp. 582–3, 594.

170 R. Hakluyt, *The Principal Navigations, Voyages, Traffiques and Discoveries of the English Nation* (Glasgow, 1903), vol. ii, pp. 216–23, 245.

171 *Ibid.*, p. 321 and vol. iii, p. 102. Harwich was used as a staging and victual post by the Muscovy company and by English ambassadors going to Russia.

172 C.R. Markham (ed.), *The Hawkins' Voyages during the Reigns of Queen Elizabeth and James I* (London, 1878), p. iii.

Chapter 7

Military aspects of the Peasants' Revolt of 1381

Herbert Eiden

The title of this essay is deliberately broad because I have included the military approach and tactics of the rebels as well as the suppression of the rising by small royal armies commanded by noblemen. While the military background of the armed royal forces is obvious, the connections between the rebels and the military are more elusive. In the absence of direct proof for the participation in the rising of men experienced in armed conflict, my arguments will rely on circumstantial evidence and well-informed historical 'speculation'. However, the organisation of the rising, even on an *ad hoc* basis, the duration of the unrest and the direction it took reveals some knowledge of military logistics and tactics.

The Peasants' Revolt in the early summer of 1381 confronted the English government with a political and social crisis on a hitherto unknown scale. At least 26 counties were affected by some form of protest or disorder between the end of May and the beginning of July.[1] The causes of discontent were manifold and can be mentioned only briefly here. Long-term factors included demographic change as a result of the Black Death; labour laws; a change in the relationship between town and countryside, together with high social mobility and an increase in trades and services; the proletarianisation of the lower clergy; a loss of confidence in lordship and law; and the effects of the Hundred Years War, especially with regard to the government's need for money.[2] In the short term the rising was triggered by the collection of taxes. Since 1377 three so-called poll taxes had been imposed, the most onerous being passed by parliament in December 1380. Every person aged 15 and over had to pay 1s (3 groats), regardless of income. The result was a 'mysterious' drop in taxpayer numbers compared with those recorded in the 1377 poll tax returns. In order to assess the true numbers of taxpayers, the chancery and the exchequer ordered inquiries to be made in several counties.[3]

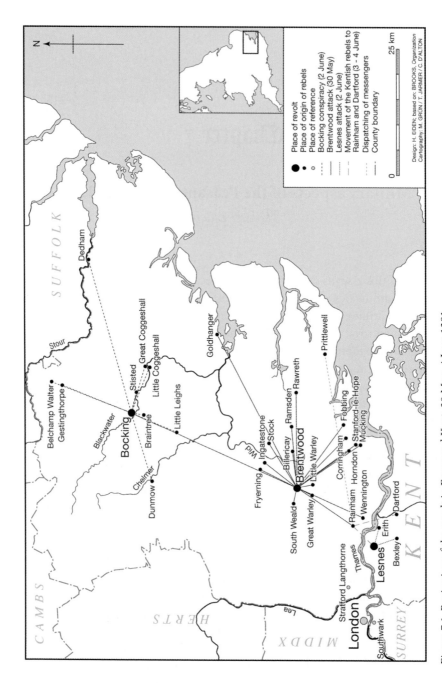

Figure 7.1. Beginning of the revolt in Essex and Kent, 30 May–4 June 1381.

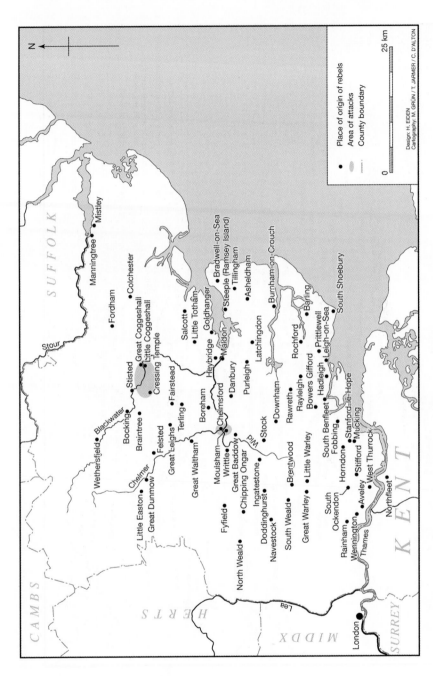

Figure 7.2. Attacks on Cressing Temple, Coggeshall and Chelmsford, 10–11 June 1381.

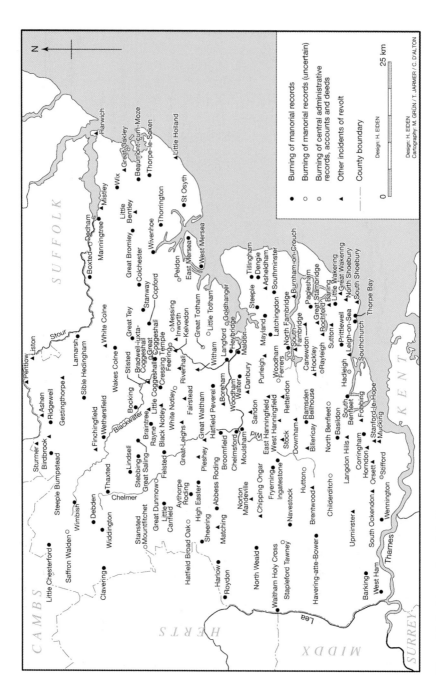

Figure 7.3. Incidents of revolt in Essex.

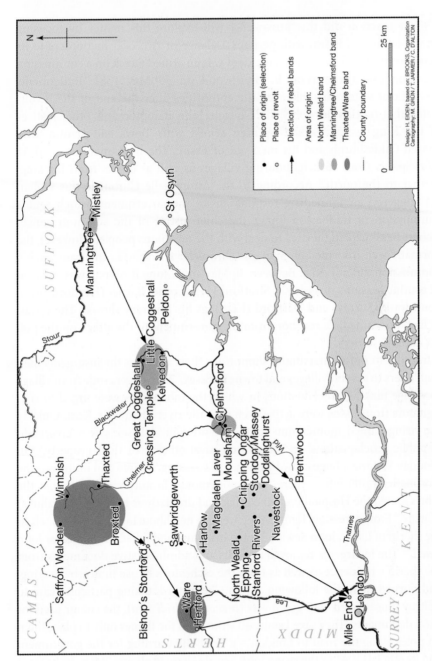

Figure 7.4. Movement of the Essex rebels to London.

What reaction did this provoke? I will explore this matter by focusing on the county of Essex, with perhaps a glance or two over its borders to its neighbours. The first recorded incident was an armed attack on a commission checking poll tax evasion in Brentwood on 30 May 1381. Indictments (i.e. official statements taken by the authorities after the end of the revolt) stated that on this day John Gildesburgh, John Bampton and 'other justices of the King' were attacked by men armed with 'bows and arrows' who chased Gildesburgh and his men out of Essex. The indictments named 31 participants from 16 neighbouring villages as well as others from Bocking, further to the north.[4] According to the Anonimalle Chronicle this violent act triggered an immediate response from the government, which sent a commission of trailbaston under the chief justice of the common bench, Robert Bealknap, to the area to deal with the rebellious people.[5] However, the normally well-informed anonymous chronicler is wrong in this case: such a commission did not exist. Between 30 May and 3 June Bealknap was engaged in routine sessions of assize in Stratford Langthorne, Barnet (Hertfordshire), Southwark (Surrey) and Dartford (Kent), as his itinerary shows.[6] There was, in fact, no immediate reaction from the government to the attack on the poll tax commissioners.

In order to muster maximum support for their activities the insurgents then sent letters to several villages and towns in Essex.[7] Messengers rode from village to village making proclamations in which the inhabitants were urged to rise. Agitators from Essex were active even over the river Thames in Kent. Quickly the rising gained momentum; southern and central Essex saw a 'crescendo of public proclamations' and attacks on royal officials or their property.[8] On Monday 10 June a huge crowd gathered at Cressing Temple and destroyed the Hospitallers' preceptory there. The anonymous chronicler reported that the rebels looted the Hospitallers' wine cellar and drank three barrels (c.90 gallons) of wine.[9] From Cressing Temple they went to neighbouring Coggeshall, seized the sheriff of Essex, John Sewale, looted his house and killed the escheator John Ewell.[10] The insurgents removed all writs and administrative documents from the sheriff's residence as well as from the escheator's house in nearby Feering, and burned them the following day in Chelmsford, taking particular care to destroy those sealed with green wax (*brevia de viridi cera*), the colour used for fiscal documents. They saved some 40 writs from the flames only to place them on poles along the road to London – a symbolic warning for the government and its officials.[11] After the rising John Sewale charged almost 200 persons from 67 places in Essex for the attack on him and his property.[12]

While the majority of the Essex insurgents stayed in their county, attacking manor houses and burning manorial court rolls,[13] numerous rebels moved on to London and took part in the incidents there.[14] At least 112 insurgents from 46 places in Essex were named in indictments and private prosecutions initiated by victims of the rising, such as John of Gaunt, duke of Lancaster, and John Butterwick, under-sheriff of Middlesex, to gain compensation. On this basis it can be assumed that the real number of Essex rebels in London was much higher, probably in the several hundreds.[15]

By grouping together the named rebels according to both their place of origin and the attacks in which they were involved, it is possible to trace three groups of the insurgents marching to the capital. One band recruited its followers from the Manningtree/Mistley area in the north-east of the county and united with the insurgents in Chelmsford before going on to London. A second group gathered in the south-west, in the North Weald/Harlow area. By far the biggest group of Essex insurgents in London, however, consisted of people from Thaxted and the surrounding area. On their advance to London this group joined forces with insurgents from Hertfordshire. All three groups of Essex rebels converged at Mile End, just outside London, on the evening of 12 June, the day before the feast of Corpus Christi. The date was significant, because the life of people in the Middle Ages was structured and governed by feast days. Hardly anyone would have understood an order to meet on the 12th day of June, but everyone would have known exactly when the eve of Corpus Christi was, a feast widely celebrated throughout England in the late fourteenth century.[16] At the same time the insurgents across the river Thames reached their assembly point in Blackheath. It is hard to believe that these simultaneous movements were a mere coincidence. In fact, they must have required a great deal of communication and co-ordination.

Let us pause here for a moment in the chronology of the events to consider the potential military character of the rising. While organisation, communication or brandishing weapons to achieve certain objectives may not be military actions as such, to send out messengers on horseback, to assemble hundreds of armed men at a given time and place and to choose specific targets with full knowledge of their identity and connections with local government or national politics has a distinct military feel. And the bows and arrows with which the rebels in Brentwood were armed are certainly a far cry from the pitchforks, flails or scythes one might expect as peasants' weapons of choice. However, England in the fourteenth century was a highly militarised country and there was an obligation impressed on male subjects by the crown to have – according to income – weapons and armour ready at home. Furthermore, Edward III's order of 1363 is evidence that weapons training was expected of his subjects, despite their apparent preference for other pursuits. It stated 'that every able bodied man on feast days when he has leisure shall in his sports use bows and arrows, pellets and bolts and shall learn and practise the art of shooting, forbidding all and singular on pain of imprisonment to attend and meddle with the hurling of stones, loggets or quoits, handball, football, club ball, cambuc, cock fighting and other vain games of no value'.[17]

Returning to the events in 1381: several chroniclers mention the display of flags and banners by the rebels. While the Essex insurgents assembled at Mile End the rebels from Kent, with Wat Tyler as their leader, camped at Blackheath above Greenwich. They carried banners depicting St George and over 60 pennants.[18] This display of military standards was a highly symbolic gesture. By rallying around flags people gained a kind of group identity and solidarity and expressed self-confidence.[19] And by adopting the image of St George the rebels not only hoped for the blessing of the patron saint of Christian knights, soldiers and armourers but also showed their ultimate allegiance to King Richard II, as the veneration of the dragon-slaying saint was closely related to the English monarchy.[20] The trust in the king, only 14 years old, was also mirrored by the watchword the rebels apparently used throughout the rising: 'With whom haldes yow?', to which someone was advised to answer: 'Wyth kynge Richarde and wyth the trew communes'.[21]

On the morning of Corpus Christi day, still outside the city walls, the rebels attacked the property of some leading men in the government, including Archbishop Sudbury's palace at Lambeth and Sir Robert Hales' manor at Highbury. Sudbury, in his position of chancellor of England, and Robert Hales, as treasurer, were held responsible for the bad governance and maladministration of the country. Once the rebel groups from Essex and Kent had gained entry into the city one of their main targets was John of Gaunt's Savoy Palace, which they burned down. Gaunt, uncle of King Richard and effectively in charge of the realm since Edward III's final ailing years, was the most hated man in England in 1381. Luckily for him, he was on a mission to Scotland when the rising broke out.[22] According to some chroniclers, there was during these attacks some sort of military command structure in place which forbade looting under pain of death.[23] As dawn was breaking the rebels incinerated the headquarters of the knights of St John in Clerkenwell, whose prior was none other than the reviled Robert Hales.[24]

The next day the rebels entered the Tower of London, where Simon Sudbury, Robert Hales, the sergeant-at-arms John Legge and William Appleton, a Franciscan friar who was also the physician to John of Gaunt, had taken refuge. The rebels dragged them all outside and beheaded them on Tower Hill.[25] Another person who lost his life at the hands of the rebels in London on this day was the infamous merchant Richard Lyons. He had acquired a reputation for corruption and financial fraud in the years leading to the revolt. Only two days before his murder in London his manor in Liston, on the Essex–Suffolk border, had been destroyed by insurgents from both counties.[26]

After two days during which the rebels controlled London, the government made preparations for striking back against them. At some point in the night of 14/15 June a militia of several hundred men was secretly mobilised – probably by William Walworth, the mayor of London, and Sir Robert Knolles, a seasoned war veteran from the military campaigns in France – to be ready the next day for the final encounter between King Richard and the rebels in Smithfield.[27] The rebels' spokesman at the meeting was Wat Tyler, who is variously described in the sources as from either Maidstone in Kent or Colchester in Essex.[28] Some chroniclers alleged that he was a tiler by profession.[29] Jean Froissart, the French chronicler more famous for his imagination and entertaining style than for his accuracy, related that Tyler had served with Richard Lyons in France and that the animosity which led to the murder of Lyons originated there.[30] A military background based on time served in France could certainly explain Tyler's initial success in organising and leading the rebellion; however, Froissart's story is not corroborated by any other source and is hardly credible.

During the meeting between Wat Tyler and the king at Smithfield on 15 June the rebels' leader was stabbed and fatally wounded by the mayor of London. Quickwittedly, the 14-year-old king rode towards the now leaderless and confused rebels, assumed command and ordered them to leave London.[31]

With Tyler's death in London on 15 June the momentum changed in favour of the authorities and the king, and his government started to counter-attack. Several military commissions to restore law and order and to prevent further unrest, as well as judicial commissions to sentence the rebels, were empowered by royal writs and troops were gathered to enforce the king's peace.[32] Richard II, accompanied by many officials and a small army, took up headquarters at Waltham Holy Cross and from there moved to Havering-atte-Bower, while Thomas of Woodstock, uncle of King Richard and earl of Buckingham, together with his military lieutenant Sir Thomas Percy, advanced to Chelmsford, where they held court sessions on 25 and 26 June.[33] Buckingham and Sir Thomas had just come back from a largely unsuccessful military campaign in Brittany, which had ended with a negotiated withdrawal of the English army for the payment of around £8,500. Part of the money was used to hire ships to bring the expedition's forces back to England. At the beginning of May Buckingham had landed in Cornwall, and he was probably with his nephew the king in the Tower during the critical time of the rising.[34]

When the rebels heard about the advance of Buckingham and his military retinue the energetic John Geoffrey, bailiff of East Hanningfield, tried to organise resistance against them. Geoffrey, originally a serf from Badmondisfield Hall in Wickhambrook (Suffolk), had been transferred by his lord, the earl of Pembroke, to Essex, presumably because of his administrative skills. He became one of the most active local leaders of the rebellion.[35] In order to resist the royal troops Geoffrey sent messengers to the surrounding villages, commanding the inhabitants to meet at Great Baddow church at dawn on the 27 June. Apparently his order was followed and a large group assembled, which later moved to 'Retyngdonwode' (Rettendon wood), close to Billericay, where they fortified their position in the wood.[36] These activities did not pass unnoticed by the royal army in Chelmsford. The St Albans chronicler Thomas Walsingham reported how Buckingham and Percy set out to rout this last pocket of resistance on 28 June. According to Walsingham 500 rebels were slain and 800 horses captured.[37] The numbers should be regarded with a pinch of salt; however, the record of horses is further evidence of the mobility of the rebels and their high level of organisation. Once the last stand by Essex diehards was over, the county of Essex returned to relative calm.[38] By and large, military reprisals by the government were over by the end of June and the judicial commissions, with wide-ranging discretionary powers, took charge of the prosecution of the rebels.

The speed with which the rebellion spread in south and south-eastern England suggests that some preparation and planning must have gone on secretly before the outbreak at the end of May. The dispatch of messengers, the targeting of certain officials and the successful capture of military strongholds further suggests that a command structure existed, that orders were obeyed and that people with military knowledge must have been present. However, in the absence of any proof this has to remain conjecture. It would be pivotal for the understanding of the spread of the rising if links between known rebels and men who had served in the French military campaigns could be established. Although I have direct evidence of only four men in my sample of 1,000 rebels being sailors,[39] Andrew Ayton and Craig Lambert's persuasive plea for an examination of the part mariners played in the rebellion is certainly worth following up.[40]

Likewise, it would be most important for the understanding of the speedy collapse of the rebellion if it could be shown that soldiers from Buckingham's expeditionary army to Brittany took part in the suppression of the rising. It is to be hoped that future research into military indentures will bring such 'missing links' to light.

Notes

1   For detailed narratives of the rising see R.H. Hilton, *Bond Men Made Free: Medieval Peasant Movements and the English Rising of 1381*, 2nd edn with a new introduction by C. Dyer (London, 2003); W.H. Liddell and R.G. Wood (eds), *Essex and the Great Revolt of 1381* (Chelmsford, 1982); A. Prescott, 'The Judicial Records of the Rising of 1381', PhD thesis (London, 1984); H. Eiden, '"In der Knechtschaft werdet ihr verharren ..." Ursachen und Verlauf des englischen Bauernaufstandes von 1381' ['"In bondage you shall remain ..." On the Causes and Development of the English Peasants' Revolt of 1381'] (Trier, 1995); H. Eiden, 'Joint Action against "Bad" Lordship: The

Peasants' Revolt in Essex and Norfolk', *History*, 83 (1998), pp. 5–30; L.R. Poos, *A Rural Society after the Black Death 1350–1525* (Cambridge, 1991), pp. 231–52; S. Justice, *Writing and Rebellion. England in 1381* (Berkeley, CA, 1994); J. Barker, *England, Arise* (London, 2014).

2   Eiden, 'Joint Action', p. 7; cf. C. Dyer, 'The Social and Economic Background to the Revolt of 1381', in R.H. Hilton and T.H. Aston (eds), *The English Rising of 1381* (Cambridge, 1984), pp. 9–42.

3   R.B. Dobson (ed), *The Peasants' Revolt of 1381*, 2nd edn (London, 1983), pp. 119–22; N. Brooks, 'The Organization and Achievements of the Peasants in Kent and Essex in 1381' in H. Mayr-Harting and R.I. Moore (eds), *Studies in Medieval History Presented to R.H.C. Davis* (London, 1985), p. 251. For the appointment of the poll tax commission for Essex see *CFR*, 1377–83, p. 249.

4   '... cum arcibus et saggitis ipsos persequenda ...': TNA, KB9/166/2 m. 4; cf. J. Sparvel-Bayly, 'Essex in Insurrection, 1381', *Transactions of the Essex Archaeological Society*, new series, 1 (1878), p. 218. The accused came from Fobbing, Stanford-le-Hope, Mucking, Horndon, Corringham, Billericay, Rawreth, Ramsden, Warley, Stock, Fryerning, Bocking, Goldhanger, Rainham, South Weald, Wennington and Ingatestone; see Figure 7.1.

5   V.H. Galbraith (ed.), *Anonimalle Chronicle, 1333–1381* (Manchester, 1927), p. 135. A commission of trailbaston was an itinerant judicial commission hearing presentments for felonies and conspiracy. The Anonimalle Chronicle is considered one of the most reliable sources for the rising, but in this case central administrative documents prove the chronicle wrong; for the value of the Anonimalle Chronicle as a source see Dobson, *Peasants' Revolt*, pp. xxxiii–iv, 33.

6   TNA, JUST1/1491, mm. 11, 29, 30, 43d, 44, 45, 48, 49, 50d, 51.

7   '... litteras suas diversis villis miserunt ...': TNA, KB145/3/6/1 (unnumbered membranes).

8   Brooks, 'Organization', p. 255.

9   Galbraith, *Anonimalle Chronicle*, p. 135.

10   TNA, KB9/166/2 mm. 2, 4; TNA, KB145/6/1 (unnumbered membranes); Eiden, 'Joint Action', p. 13. For the attack on the Cistercian monastery of Coggeshall Abbey see *CPR, 1381–5*, p. 79.

11   TNA, KB145/6/1 (unnumbered membranes). For the sealing of exchequer documents with green wax see Brooks, 'Organization', p. 260.

12   TNA, KB27/484 m. 36; KB27/485 m. 25; KB27/489 mm. 19, 19d, 38, 78; Eiden, 'Joint Action', p. 13; see Figure 7.2.

13   See Figure 7.3 for actions of unrest in Essex in 1381.

14   In the course of my research on the Peasants' Revolt I have traced more than 3,500 persons indicted in connection with the rising or named in central administrative records as having been involved; c.1,000 came from Essex; Eiden, 'Joint Action', p. 10 n. 26; Poos, *Rural Society*, p. 234.

15   A. Prescott, 'Essex Rebel Bands in London', in W.H. Liddell and R.G. Wood (eds), *Essex and the Great Revolt of 1381* (Chelmsford, 1982), p. 57, gives the number of 170 Essex rebels, but some names appear more than once and others cannot be identified with sufficient certainty; cf. Eiden, 'Joint Action', p. 13; Prescott, 'Judicial Records', pp. 292–312; see Figure 7.4.

16   For the importance of Corpus Christi for the timing and coordination of the revolt see M. Aston, 'Corpus Christi and Corpus Regni: Heresy and the Peasants' Revolt', *Past and Present*, 143 (1994), pp. 3–47.

17   *CCR*, 1361–4, pp. 534–5.

18   '... et esplayerount deux baners de seint George et lx penouns ...': Galbraith, *Anonimalle Chronicle*, p. 139.

19   Cf. R. Trexler, 'Follow the Flag. The Ciompi Revolt Seen from the Streets', *Bibliothèque d'Humanisme et Renaissance*, 46 (1984), pp. 357–92, here p. 389.

20   The cult of St George in England had become very popular during the crusades. In 1348 Edward III made St George the patron saint of his newly founded order of the garter; cf. N. Denholm-Young, *The Country Gentry in the Fourteenth Century* (Oxford, 1969), pp. 144–7.

21   Galbraith, *Anonimalle Chronicle*, p. 139.

22 Barker, *England, Arise*, pp. 230–31; C.M. Barron, *Revolt in London: 11th to 15th June 1381* (London, 1981), passim.

23 H.T. Riley (ed.), *Thomas Walsingham, Historia Anglicana*, vol. i (London, 1863), p. 456; L.C. Hector and B.E. Harris (eds), *The Westminster Chronicle, 1381–1394* (Oxford, 1982), p. 4; J.R. Lumby (ed.), *Chronicon Henrici Knighton*, vol. ii (London, 1895), p. 135; F.S. Haydon (ed.), *Eulogium Historiarum sive Temporis*, vol. iii (London, 1863), p. 352.

24 Barker, *England, Arise*, pp. 234–5.

25 For a more detailed account see, for example, Barker, *England, Arise*, pp. 261–5.

26 Eiden, 'Joint Action', p. 14; Barker, *England, Arise*, pp. 202–3.

27 J. Sumption, *Divided Houses. The Hundred Years War, vol. iii* (London, 2009), pp. 427–9, relying mainly on Haydon, *Eulogium Historiarum*, iii, pp. 353–4. For Sir Robert see M. Jones, 'Knolles, Sir Robert (d. 1407)', *Oxford Dictionary of National Biography* (Oxford, 2004); online edn, May 2009.

28 Brooks, 'Organization', p. 258; Prescott, 'Judicial Records', pp. 145–6; Barker, *England Arise*, pp. 419–21.

29 Haydon, *Eulogium Historiarum*, iii, p. 352; Eiden, 'Knechtschaft', pp. 428–30.

30 J. Froissart, *Les Chroniques de Sire Jean Froissart*, ed. J.A.C. Buchon, vol. ii (Paris, 1852), p. 156; Dobson, *Peasants' Revolt*, p. 189.

31 Why the rebels did not react to their leader's death is not clear, but the accepted version is that the valiant action of Richard saved the day; Barker, *England, Arise*, pp. 271–4; A. Dunn, *The Peasants' Revolt. England's Failed Revolution of 1381* (Stroud, 2004), pp. 127–36.

32 Prescott, 'Judicial Records', pp. 36–9.

33 TNA, KB145/6/1 (unnumbered membranes).

34 For Buckingham's expedition in Brittany see Sumption, *Divided Houses*, pp. 408–12. According to Galbraith, *Anonimalle Chronicle*, pp. 138–9, on the eve of Corpus Christ the earls of Buckingham, Kent, Arundel, Warwick, Suffolk, Oxford and Salisbury were present in the Tower.

35 Dyer, 'Social and Economic Background', p. 17.

36 '… et dixit eis quod nisi essent ad ecclesiam de magna Badewe circa ortem solis ad eundum cum comitiva iniquita adversus comitie Bukyngham et alios liegos domini Regis essent interfecti et domos eorum combussi essent.' TNA, KB9/166/2, m. 4; Sparvel-Bayly, 'Essex', p. 218.

37 Riley, *Historia Anglicana*, ii, p. 19.

38 A similar fate had befallen the rebels in Norfolk two days earlier when the local leader of the rising Geoffrey Lister and several other insurgents were killed in a final battle with bishop Henry Despencer at North Walsham. Walsingham modelled his report of the showdown between Lister's men and Despencer's troops on Tacitus' account of the final battle of Boadicea in AD 61; Riley, *Historia Anglicana*, ii, pp. 7–8. For the rising in Norfolk, see H. Eiden, 'The Social Ideology of the Rebels in Suffolk and Norfolk in 1381', in M.-L. Heckmann and J. Röhrkasten (eds), *Von Nowgorod bis London. Festschrift Stuart Jenks* (Göttingen, 2008), pp. 425–40.

39 The four men are Robert Knyght from Fobbing, who owned a boat worth 20s (TNA, KB9/166/2 m. 3; E136/77/1); Thomas Gylle, a 'shipman' from Maldon (TNA, KB27/484 m. 36; KB27/485 m. 25), KB145/6/1 (unnumbered membranes); two further 'shipmen', Jacob Treche of unknown origin in Essex and William Porter of Great or Little Wakering (TNA, KB27/489 m. 19; TNA, C67/29 m. 26).

40 Above, this volume, pp. 129–36.

Bibliography

Manuscript sources
British Library, London
Additional MS 7967
Additional MS 37494
Cotton Augustus I.i
Harleian MS 3968
Stowe MS 553

Essex Record Office, Chelmsford
D/DHf M58; D/DHf T90
D/DL/T1/51, 78
D/DRg 1/35
T/A 233/1

The National Archives, London
Chancery Inquisitions Post Mortem
C134/42
Chancery King's Remembrancer
C49/46/13
Chancery Miscellanea
C47/1/2, 5–6; C47/2/3, 11, 30; C47/2/46, nos 6–14, 18; C47/5/10; C47/30/8, no. 14
Chancery Warrants
C76/15
C81/1735, no. 15; 1759, no. 37
Documents concerning debts
C131/45/9, 17; C131/211/16; C241/184/5
Gascon Rolls

C61/36, 88
Patent Rolls (Supplementary)
C67/8, 10–11, 13, 14–16, 29
Scotch Rolls
C71/6
Exchequer: accounts various
E101/4/8; E101/5/23; E101/6/37; E101/8/23; E101/16/40; E101/17/3; E101/18/3, 31;
    E101/19/16; E101/20/1, 27–8, 34; E101/21/7, 10, 12; E101/23/35; E101/24/9b;
    E101/25/9, 12, 24; E101/26/18, 38; E101/27/22–5, 37; E101/28/23–4;
    E101/29/1, 33, 35, 36, 39; E101/30/13, 15, 21; E101/31/10–12, 14–15, 22–
    3, 27; E101/32/1, 3–4, 6–7, 9–11, 28–9; E101/33/17, 27, 31; E101/34/25;
    E101/35/2; E101/36/14–15, 20; E101/37/3, 7–8, 13–18, 20, 25; E101/38/18–
    19, 30; E101/39/2, 17; E101/40/8–9, 19–21, 36, 40; E101/41/26; E101/42/21–
    2; E101/51/7; E101/78/4a; E101/79/10; E101/92/11–12, 24; E101/93/20;
    E101/173/4; E101/179/10; E101/184/19; E101/378/4; E101/396/11;
    E101/459/24; E101/557/15; E101/602/3; E101/612/40–1, 44, 48; E101/619/15;
    E101/621/3
Customs accounts
E122/7/12; E122/16/14; E122/158/25; E122/159/2
Exchequer: deeds
E43/662
Exchequer: escheator's accounts
E136/77/1
Exchequer: Lay Subsidy rolls
E179/107/12, 13, 14
Exchequer: rolls of foreign accounts
E364/5, rot. 31d
Exchequer: wardrobe and household
E36/204
Court of King's Bench
JUST1/1491
KB9/166/2
KB27/484, 485, 489
KB145/3/5/1; KB145/3/6/1; KB145/6/1
King's Bench Recorda Files, unnumbered
Maps
MPF/1/25
Special Collections: ancient petitions
SC8/194/9654; SC8/299/14911; SC8/303/15124; SC8/306/15282
Special Collections: court rolls
SC2/171/16

Special Collections: ministers' accounts
SC6/849/11; SC6/1110/3, 10, 12, 25
Special Collections: rentals and surveys
SC11/799

Printed primary sources

Bell, A., Brooks, C. and Dryburgh, P. (eds), *Advance Contracts for the Sale of Wool c.1200–c.1327*, List and Index Society 315 (2006).

Benson, L.D. (ed.), *The Riverside Chaucer*, 3rd edn (Oxford, 1988).

Book of Fees, 3 vols (London, 1921–31).

Calendar of Close Rolls preserved in the Public Record Office, 1272–1399, 29 vols (London, 1892–1927).

Calendar of Fine Rolls preserved in the Public Record Office, 1272–1399, 11 vols (London, 1911–29).

Calendar of Inquisitions Miscellaneous preserved in the Public Record Office, 1307–77, 2 vols (London, 1916, 1937).

Calendar of Inquisitions Post Mortem preserved in the Public Record Office, 1216–1399, 17 vols (London, 1904–74).

Calendar of Patent Rolls preserved in the Public Record Office, 1272–1399, 31 vols (London, 1891–1916).

Denholm-Young, N. (ed.), *Vita Edwardi Secundi* (London, 1957).

D'Entrèves, A.P. (ed.) and Dawson, J.G. (trans.), *Aquinas. Selected Political Writings* (Oxford, 1965).

Fenwick, C. (ed.), *The Poll Taxes of 1377, 1379 and 1381*, British Academy Records of Social and Economic History, new series, vol. xxvii, 3 vols (Oxford, 1998–2005).

Froissart, J., *Les Chroniques de Sire Jean Froissart*, ed. J.A.C. Buchon, vol. ii (Paris, 1852).

Froissart, *Chronicles*, ed. G. Brereton (London, 1968).

Furber, E.C. (ed.), *Essex Sessions of the Peace, 1351, 1377–9*, Essex Archaeological Society, Occasional Publication no. 3 (Colchester, 1953).

Galbraith, V.H. (ed.), *The Anonimalle Chronicle, 1333–1381* (Manchester, 1927).

Given-Wilson, C. (ed.), *The Parliament Rolls of Medieval England, 1275–1504*, 16 vols (Woodbridge, 2005).

Given-Wilson, C. and Scott-Stokes, C. (ed. and trans.), *Chronicon Anonymi Cantuariensis: The Chronicle of Anonymous of Canterbury, 1346–1365* (Oxford, 2008).

Glasscock, R.E. (ed.), *The Lay Subsidy of 1334*, British Academy Records of Social and Economic History, new series 2 (Oxford, 1975).

Gough, H. (ed.), *Scotland in 1298: Documents relating to the Campaign of Edward I in that year* (London, 1888).

Hakluyt, R., *The Principal Navigations, Voyages, Traffiques and Discoveries of the*

English Nation, vols ii, iii (Glasgow, 1903).

Haydon, F.S. (ed.), *Eulogium Historiarum sive Temporis Chronicon*, Rolls Series, 3 vols (London, 1858–63).

Hector, L.C. and Harris, B.E. (eds), *The Westminster Chronicle, 1381–1394* (Oxford, 1982).

Hog, T. (ed.), *Adami Murimuthensis Chronica* (London, 1846).

Inquisitions and Assessments relating to Feudal Aids, 1284–1431, 6 vols (London, 1899–1921).

Jones, M. and Walker, S.K. (eds), 'Private Indentures for Life Service in Peace and War 1278–1476', in *Camden Miscellany, Vol. XXXII*, Camden Society, 5th series, vol. 3 (Cambridge, 1994), no. 14, p. 48.

King, A. (ed.), Sir Thomas Gray, *Scalacronica, 1272–1363*, Surtees Society, vol. ccix (Woodbridge, 2005).

Landon, L. (ed.), *The Cartae Antiquae Rolls 1–10*, Pipe Roll Society 17 (London, 1939).

List of Sheriffs of England and Wales from the Earliest Times to 1831, Public Record Office, Lists and Indexes, vol. ix (London, 1898).

Luard, H.R. (ed.), *Flores Historiarum*, 3 vols, Rolls Series, xcv (London, 1890).

Lumby, J.R. (ed.), *Chronicon Henrici Knighton*, Rolls Series, 2 vols (London, 1889–95).

Lyon, M. *et al.* (eds), *The Wardrobe Book of William de Norwell, 12 July 1338 to 27 May 1340* (Brussels, 1983).

Markham, C.R. (ed.), *The Hawkins' Voyages during the Reigns of Queen Elizabeth and James I* (London, 1878).

Martin, G.H. (ed. and trans.), *Knighton's Chronicle, 1337–1396* (Oxford, 1995).

Michel, F., Bémont, C. and Renouard, Y. (eds), *Rôles Gascons, 1242–1307*, 5 vols (Paris, 1885–1962).

Myers, A.R. (ed.), *English Historical Documents: Vol. IV, 1327–1485* (London, 1969).

Palgrave, F. (ed.), *Parliamentary Writs and Writs of Military Summons*, 3 vols, Record Commission (London, 1827–34).

Palgrave, F. (ed.), *Documents and Records Illustrating the History of Scotland and the Transactions between the Crowns of Scotland and England*, Record Commission (London, 1837).

Return, Members of Parliament, part i, Parliaments of England, 1213–1702 (London, 1878).

Riley, H.T. (ed.), *Munimenta Gildhallae Londoniensis*, Rolls Series, 3 vols (London, 1860–62).

Riley, H.T. (ed.), *Thomas Walsingham, Historia Anglicana*, Rolls Series, 2 vols (London, 1863–4).

Riley, H.T. (ed.), *Memorials of London and London Life, 1276–1419* (London, 1868).

Rothwell, H. (ed.), *English Historical Documents: Vol. III, 1189–1327* (London, 1975).

Rotuli Parliamentorum, 6 vols (London, 1783).

Sayles, G.O. (ed.), *Select Cases in the Court of King's Bench, Richard II, Henry IV, Henry V*, Selden Society 88 (London, 1971).

Simpson, G.G. and Galbraith, J.D. (eds), *Calendar of Documents relating to Scotland* (Edinburgh, 1986).

Stubbs, W. (ed.), 'Annales Londonienses', in *Chronicles of the Reigns of Edward I and Edward II*, Rolls Series, lxxvi, 2 vols (London, 1882–3).

Taylor, J., Childs, W.R. and Watkiss, L. (eds), *The St Albans Chronicle. The Chronica Maiora of Thomas Walsingham* (Oxford, 2003).

Treaty Rolls, 1235–1339, 2 vols (London, 1956–72)

Twiss, T. (ed.), *Monumenta Juridica: The Black Book of the Admiralty*, Rolls Series, 4 vols (London, 1871–6).

Ward, J. (ed.), *The Medieval Essex Community. The Lay Subsidy of 1327*, Essex Historical Documents 1, Essex Record Office Publication 88 (Chelmsford, 1983).

Ward, J. (ed.), *Elizabeth de Burgh, Lady of Clare (1295–1360). Household and Other Records*, Suffolk Records Society lvii (Woodbridge, 2014).

Online primary sources

Ayton, A. and Lambert, C. 'Shipping, Mariners and Port Communities in Fourteenth-Century England', *ESRC Data Store*, http://store.dataarchive.ac.uk/store/viewItemPage.jsp?collectionPID=archive%3A665&itemPID=archive%3A772&data=&tabbedContext=collCollection

Gascon Rolls, http://www.gasconrolls.org

Muster Rolls, 1369–1453, http://www.medievalsoldier.org

PROME, The Parliament Rolls of Medieval England, http://www.sd-editions.com/PROME/home.html

www.deremilitari.org/resources/articles/ayton2.htm

Secondary sources

Anon., 'St Osyth Priory', *Essex Review*, 30 (1921), pp. 1–13, 121–7, 205–21.

Alban, J.R., 'English Coastal Defence: Some Fourteenth-Century Modifications within the System', in R.A. Griffiths (ed.), *Patronage, the Crown and the Provinces in Later Medieval England* (Gloucester, 1981), pp. 57–78.

Aston, M., 'Corpus Christi and Corpus Regni: Heresy and the Peasants' Revolt', *Past and Present*, 143 (1994), pp. 3–47.

Ayers, B., Smith, R. and Tillyard, M., 'The Cow Tower, Norwich: A detailed survey and partial interpretation', *Medieval Archaeology*, 32 (1988), pp. 184–207.

Ayton, A., *Knights and Warhorses: Military Service and the English Aristocracy under Edward III* (Woodbridge, 1994).

Ayton, A., 'Edward III and the English Aristocracy at the Beginning of the Hundred Years War', in M. Strickland (ed.), *Armies, Chivalry and Warfare in Medieval*

Britain and France, Harlaxton Medieval Studies, vol. vii (Stamford, 1998), pp. 173–206.

Ayton, A., 'Armies and Military Communities in Fourteenth-Century England', in P. Coss and C. Tyerman (eds), *Soldiers, Nobles and Gentlemen. Essays in Honour of Maurice Keen* (Woodbridge, 2009), pp. 215–39.

Ayton, A., 'Military Service and the Dynamics of Recruitment in Fourteenth-Century England', in A.R. Bell and A. Curry (eds), *The Soldier Experience in the Fourteenth Century* (Woodbridge, 2011), pp. 9–59.

Ayton, A. and Lambert, C., 'A Maritime Community in War and Peace: Kentish Ports, Ships and Mariners, 1320–1400', *Archaeologia Cantiana*, 134 (2014), pp. 67–103.

Ayton, A. and Lambert, C., 'Navies and Maritime Warfare', in A. Curry (ed.), *The Hundred Years War. Problems in Focus Revisited* (London, forthcoming).

Ayton, A. and Preston, P., *The Battle of Crécy, 1346* (Woodbridge, 2005).

Bailey, K., 'Buckinghamshire Poll Tax Records 1377–79', *Records of Buckinghamshire*, 49 (2009), pp. 173–87.

Baker, G., 'Investigating the Socio-Economic Origins of English Archers in the Second Half of the Fourteenth Century', *Journal of Medieval Military History*, 12 (2014), pp. 173–216.

Barker, J., *England, Arise* (London, 2014).

Barron, C.M., *Revolt in London: 11th to 15th June 1381* (London, 1981).

Bartlett, N., *The Lay Poll Tax Returns for the City of York in 1381* (Hull, 1953).

Bellamy, J.G., *Crime and Public Order in England in the Later Middle Ages* (London, 1973).

Bell, A., *War and the Soldier in the Fourteenth Century* (Woodbridge, 2004).

Bell, A., Curry, A., King, A. and Simpkin, D., *The Soldier in Later Medieval England* (Oxford, 2013).

Bennett, M.J., *Community, Class and Careerism: Cheshire and Lancashire Society in the Age of 'Sir Gawain and the Green Knight'* (Cambridge, 1983).

Bettley, J. and Pevsner, N., *The Buildings of England. Essex* (New Haven, CT and London, 2007).

Britnell, R.H., *Growth and Decline in Colchester, 1300–1525* (Cambridge, 1986).

Brooks, N., 'The Organisation and Achievements of the Peasants of Kent and Essex in 1381', in H. Mayr-Harting and R.I. Moore (eds), *Studies in Medieval History presented to R.H.C. Davis* (London and Ronceverte, 1985), pp. 247–70.

Bullock-Davies, C. *Menestrellorum Multitudo: Minstrels at a Royal Feast* (Cardiff, 1978).

Carpenter, C., 'War, Government and Governance in the Later Middle Ages', in L. Clark (ed.), *The Fifteenth Century VII* (Woodbridge, 2007), pp. 1–22.

Carpenter, D., *The Struggle for Mastery. Britain 1066–1284* (London, 2003).

Colvin, H.M. (ed.), *The History of the King's Works. The Middle Ages*, 2 vols (London, 1963).

Cooper, J.C. (ed.), *The Victoria history of the counties of England. A history of the county of Essex. Vol. 9 The borough of Colchester* (London, 1994).

Cooper, J.C., 'Castle', in J.C. Cooper (ed.), *The Victoria history of the counties of England. A history of the county of Essex. Vol. 9 The borough of Colchester* (London, 1994), pp. 241–8.

Cooper, J.C., 'Medieval Colchester', in J.C. Cooper (ed.), *The Victoria history of the counties of England. A history of the county of Essex. Vol. 9 The borough of Colchester* (London, 1994), pp. 19–66.

Cooper, J.C., 'Walls, Gates and Posterns', in J.C. Cooper (ed.), *The Victoria history of the counties of England. A history of the county of Essex. Vol. 9 The borough of Colchester* (London, 1994), pp. 248–50.

Creighton, O. and Higham, R., *Medieval Town Walls. An Archaeology and Social History of Urban Defence* (Stroud, 2005).

Curry, A., *Agincourt: A New History* (Stroud, 2005).

Cushway, G., *Edward III and the War at Sea* (Woodbridge, 2011).

Dasent, A.I., *The Speakers of the House of Commons* (London, 1911).

Davies, R.G. and Denton, J.H. (eds), *The English Parliament in the Middle Ages* (Manchester, 1981).

Davis, P., 'English Licences to Crenellate 1199–1567', *Castle Studies Group Journal*, 20 (2006–7), pp. 226–45.

Denholm-Young, N., *The Country Gentry in the Fourteenth Century* (Oxford, 1969).

Dickin, E.P., *A History of the Town of Brightlingsea, a Member of the Cinque Ports* (Colchester, 1913).

Dobson, R.B. (ed.), *The Peasants' Revolt of 1381*, 2nd edn (London, 1983).

Dove, C., *The Liberty of Brightlingsea* (Brightlingsea, 1996).

Drewett, P.L., 'Excavations at Hadleigh Castle, Essex, 1971–2', *Journal of the British Archaeological Association*, 38 (1975), pp. 90–154.

Dugdale, W., *The History of Imbanking and Draining of Divers Fens and Marshes*, 2nd edn (London, 1722).

Dunn, A., *The Peasants' Revolt. England's Failed Revolution of 1381* (Stroud, 2004).

Dyer, C., 'The Causes of the Revolt in Rural Essex', in W.H. Liddell and R.G. Wood (eds), *Essex and the Great Revolt of 1381*, Essex Record Office Publication 84 (Chelmsford, 1982), pp. 21–36.

Dyer, C., 'The Social and Economic Background to the Revolt of 1381', in R.H. Hilton and T.H. Aston (eds), *The English Rising of 1381* (Cambridge, 1984), pp. 9–42.

Dyer, C., 'The Social and Economic Background to the Rural Revolt of 1381', in C. Dyer, *Everyday Life in Medieval England* (London and New York, 2000), pp. 191–219.

Dyer, C., 'The Rising of 1381 in Suffolk: Its Origins and Participants', in C. Dyer, *Everyday Life in Medieval England* (London and New York, 2000), pp. 221–39.

Eiden, H., '"In der Knechtschaft werdet ihr verharren …" Ursachen und Verlauf des Englischen Bauernaufstandes von 1381' ['"In Bondage you shall remain…" On the Causes and Development of the English Peasants' Revolt of 1381'] (Trier, 1995).

Eiden, H., 'Joint Action against "Bad" Lordship: The Peasants' Revolt in Essex and Norfolk', *History*, 83 (1998), pp. 5–30.

Eiden, H., 'The Social Ideology of the Rebels in Suffolk and Norfolk in 1381', in M.-L. Heckmann and J. Röhrkasten (eds), *Von Nowgorod bis London. Festschrift Stuart Jenks* (Göttingen, 2008), pp. 425–40.

Friel, I., 'How Much Did the Sea Matter in Medieval England (c.1200–c.1500)?', in R. Gorski (ed.), *Roles of the Sea in Medieval England* (Woodbridge, 2012), pp. 167–85.

Gibbs, S. and Bell, A., 'Fighting Merchants', in M. Allen and M. Davies (eds), *Medieval Merchants and Money: Essays in Honour of James L. Bolton* (London, 2016).

Goldberg, P.J.P., 'Urban Identity and the Poll Taxes of 1377, 1379 and 1380–1', *Economic History Review*, 2nd series, 43 (1990), pp. 104–26.

Gray, H.L., 'Incomes from Land in 1436', *English Historical Review*, 49 (1934), pp. 607–39.

Grieve, H.E.P., 'The Rebellion and the County Town', in W.H. Liddell and R.G. Wood (eds), *Essex and the Great Revolt of 1381*, Essex Record Office Publication 84 (Chelmsford, 1982), p. 50.

Grieve, H., *The Sleepers and the Shadows. Chelmsford: a Town, its People and its Past*, Essex Record Office Publication no. 100 (Chelmsford, 1988).

Harriss, G.L., *Shaping the Nation. England 1360–1461* (Oxford, 2005).

Harriss, G.L., *King, Parliament and Public Finance in Medieval England to 1369* (Oxford, 1975).

Hewitt, H.J., *The Organization of War under Edward III* (Manchester, 1966).

Hicks, M., 'Introduction: What were Inquisitions Post Mortem?', in M. Hicks (ed.), *The Fifteenth-Century Inquisitions Post Mortem: A Companion* (Woodbridge, 2012), pp. 1–24.

Hilton, R.H., *Bond Men Made Free: Medieval Peasant Movements and the English Rising of 1381* (London, 1973), and 2nd edn with introduction by C. Dyer (London, 2003).

Holmes, G.A., *The Estates of the Higher Nobility in Fourteenth-Century England* (Cambridge, 1957).

Holt, J.C., *Magna Carta*, 2nd edn (Cambridge, 1992).

Hope, T.M., 'Essex and the French Campaign of 1346–7', *Essex Review*, 51 (1942), pp. 140–43.

Hughes, M., 'The Fourteenth-Century French Raids on Hampshire and the Isle of Wight', in A. Curry and M. Hughes (eds), *Arms, Armies and Fortifications in the Hundred Years War* (Woodbridge, 1994) pp. 121–43.

Jewell, H.M., *English Local Administration in the Middle Ages* (Newton Abbot and New York, 1972).

Jurkowski, M., Smith, C.L. and Crook, D., *Lay Taxes in England and Wales, 1188–1688*, Public Record Office Handbook 31 (London, 1998).

Justice, S., *Writing and Rebellion. England in 1381* (Berkeley, CA, 1994).

Kaeuper, R.W., 'Law and Order in Fourteenth-Century England – Special Commissions of Oyer and Terminer', *Speculum*, 54 (1979), pp. 734–84.

Keen, M., 'Chivalry and English Kingship in the Later Middle Ages', in C. Given-Wilson, A. Kettle and L. Scales (eds), *War, Government and Aristocracy in the British Isles, c. 1150–1500* (Woodbridge, 2008), pp. 250–65.

Kemble, J., 'Essex Beacons and Look-Outs: A Multi-period Place-Names Study', *Essex Journal*, 42 (1) (Spring 2007), pp. 11–15.

Kenyon, J.R., *Medieval Fortifications* (Leicester, 1990).

Kitchen, F., '"The Ghastly War Flame": The Beacon System in Essex', *Essex Journal*, 23 (2) (Summer 1998), pp. 41–4.

Kowaleski, M., *Local Markets and Regional Trade in Medieval Exeter* (Cambridge, 1995).

Kowaleski, M., 'Port Towns: England and Wales 1300–1540', in D. Palliser (ed.), *The Cambridge Urban History of Britain, vol. i: 600–1540* (Cambridge, 2000), pp. 467–94.

Kowaleski, M., 'Warfare, Shipping and Crown Patronage: The Impact of the Hundred Years War on the Port Towns of England', in L. Armstrong, I. Elbl and M. Elbl (eds), *Money, Markets and Trade in Late Medieval Europe* (Leiden, 2005), pp. 233–54.

Kowaleski, M., 'Working at Sea: Maritime Recruitment and Remuneration in Medieval England', in S. Cavaciocchi (ed.), *Ricchezza del mare, ricchezza dal mare, secoli XIII–XVIII* (Florence, 2006), pp. 907–35.

Kowaleski, M., 'The Demography of Maritime Communities in Late Medieval England', in M. Bailey and S.H. Rigby (eds), *England in the Age of the Black Death. Essays in Honour of John Hatcher* (Turnhout, 2012), pp. 74–97.

Lack, W., Stuchfield, H.M. and Whittemore, P., *The Monumental Brasses of Essex*, 2 vols (London, 2003).

Lambert, C.L., *Shipping the Medieval Military: English Maritime Logistics in the Fourteenth Century* (Woodbridge, 2011).

Lambert, C.L., 'The Contribution of the Cinque Ports to the Wars of Edward II and Edward III: New Methodologies and Estimates', in R. Gorski (ed.), *Roles of the Sea in Medieval England* (Woodbridge, 2012), pp. 59–78.

Lambert, C.L. and Ayton, A., 'The Mariner in Fourteenth-Century England', in W.M. Ormrod (ed.), *Fourteenth-Century England VII* (Woodbridge, 2012), pp. 153–76.

Letters, S. (ed.), *Gazetteer of Markets and Fairs in England and Wales to 1516*, 2 vols, List and Index Society, Special Series 32–3 (London, 2003).

Liddell, W.H. and Wood, R.G. (eds), *Essex and the Great Revolt of 1381*, Essex Record Office Publication 84 (Chelmsford, 1982).

Liddy, C., *War, Politics and Finance in Late Medieval English Towns. Bristol, York and the Crown, 1359–1400* (Woodbridge, 2005).

Lloyd, S., *English Society and the Crusade 1216–1307* (Oxford, 1988).

Loftus, E.A. and Chettle, H.F., *A History of Barking Abbey* (Barking, 1954).

Maddicott, J.R., *The English Peasantry and the Demands of the Crown 1294–1341*, *Past and Present* Supplement 1 (1975), pp. 1–75.

Maddicott, J.R., 'The County Community and the Making of Public Opinion in Fourteenth-Century England', *Transactions of the Royal Historical Society*, 5th series, 28 (1978), pp. 27–43.

McKisack, M., *The Fourteenth Century 1307–99* (Oxford, 1959).

Moore, T.K., 'The Cost–Benefit Analysis of a Fourteenth-Century Naval Campaign: Margate/Cadzand, 1387', in R. Gorski (ed.), *Roles of the Sea in Medieval England* (Woodbridge, 2012), pp. 103–24.

Morris, M., *A Great and Terrible King: Edward I and the Forging of Britain* (London, 2008).

Musson, A., *Public Order and Law Enforcement. The Local Administration of Criminal Justice, 1294–1350* (Woodbridge, 1996).

Musson, A. and Ormrod, W.M., *The Evolution of English Justice. Law, Politics and Society in the Fourteenth Century* (Basingstoke, 1999).

Nicolas, N.H., *A History of the Royal Navy*, 2 vols (London, 1847).

Oppenheim, M., 'Maritime History', in W. Page and J.H. Round (eds), *The Victoria history of the counties of England. A history of the county of Essex. Vol. 2* (London, 1907), pp. 259–312.

Ormrod, W.M., *The Reign of Edward III. Crown and Political Society in England 1327–1377* (London, 1990).

Ormrod, W.M., 'The Domestic Response to the Hundred Years War', in A. Curry and M. Hughes (eds), *Arms, Armies and Fortifications in the Hundred Years War* (Woodbridge, 1994), pp. 83–101.

Ormrod, W.M., *Edward III* (New Haven, CT and London, 2011).

Osborne, M., *Defending Essex. The Military Landscape from Prehistory to the Present* (Stroud, 2013).

Oxford Dictionary of National Biography, 60 vols (Oxford, 2004) and online.

Page, W. and Round, J.H. (eds), *The Victoria history of the counties of England. A history of the county of Essex. Vol. 2* (London, 1907).

Palmer, J.J.N., *England, France and Christendom, 1377–99* (London, 1972).

Parry, J.H., *The Age of Reconnaissance: Discovery, Exploration and Settlement* (London, 1963).

Penn, S. and Dyer, C., 'Wages and Earnings in Late Medieval England: Evidence from the Enforcement of the Labour Laws', *Economic History Review*, 2nd series, 43 (1990), pp. 356–76.

Phillips, S., *Edward II* (New Haven, CT and London, 2010).

Poos, L.R., *A Rural Society after the Black Death. Essex 1350–1525* (Cambridge, 1991).

Powell, E., 'The Administration of Criminal Justice in Late Medieval England: Peace Sessions and Assizes', in R. Eales and D. Sullivan (eds), *The Political Context of Law* (London, 1987), pp. 49–59.

Powell, W.R., 'Lionel de Bradenham and his Siege of Colchester in 1350', *Essex Archaeology and History*, 3rd series, 22 (1991), pp. 67–75.

Prescott, A., 'Essex Rebel Bands in London', in W.H. Liddell and R.G. Wood (eds), *Essex and the Great Revolt of 1381* (Chelmsford, 1982), pp. 37–54.

Prestwich, M., *The Three Edwards. War and State in England 1272–1377* (London, 1980).

Prestwich, M., *Plantagenet England 1225–1360* (Oxford, 2005).

Prince, A.E., 'The Indenture System under Edward III', in J.G. Edwards, V.H. Galbraith and E.F. Jacob (eds), *Historical Essays in Honour of James Tait* (Manchester, 1933), pp. 283–97.

Pugh, R.B. (ed.), *The Victoria history of the counties of England. A history of the county of Essex. Vol. 5* (London and Oxford, 1966).

Reaney, P.H., 'Earthquake and Inundations at St Osyth', *Transactions of the Essex Archaeological Society*, new series, 21 (1937), pp. 136–7.

Réville, A., *Le soulèvement des travailleurs d'Angleterre en 1381* (Paris, 1898).

Richmond, C., 'The War at Sea', in K. Fowler (ed.), *The Hundred Years War* (London, 1971), pp. 96–121.

Rodger, N.A.M., *The Safeguard of the Sea: A Naval History of Great Britain, vol. i: 600–1649* (London, 1997).

Rodger, N.A.M., 'The Law and Language of Private Naval Warfare', *The Mariner's Mirror*, 100 (2014), pp. 5–16.

Rose, S., 'Maritime Logistics and Edward I's Military Campaigns: What Can be Learnt from Surviving Documents', *The Mariner's Mirror*, 99 (2013), pp. 388–97.

Roskell, J.S., Clark, L. and Rawcliffe, C. (eds), *The History of Parliament: The House of Commons 1386–1421*, 4 vols (Stroud, 1992).

Ross, J., 'Seditious Activities? The Conspiracy of Maud de Vere, Countess of Oxford, 1403–4', in L. Clark (ed.), *The Fifteenth Century, 3: Authority and Subversion* (Woodbridge, 2003), pp. 25–41.

Round, J.H., 'The Landing of Queen Isabella in 1326', *English Historical Review*, 14 (1899), pp. 104–5.

Saul, A., 'Great Yarmouth and the Hundred Years War in the Fourteenth Century', *Bulletin of the Institute of Historical Research*, 52 (1979), pp. 105–15.

Saul, N., 'Conflict and Consensus in English Local Society', in J. Taylor and W. Childs (eds), *Politics and Crisis in Fourteenth-Century England* (Gloucester, 1990), pp. 38–58.

Saul, N., *Art and Memory in Medieval England. The Cobham Family and their Monuments 1300–1500* (Oxford, 2001).

Searle, E. and Burghart, R., 'The Defense of England and the Peasants' Revolt', *Viator*, 3 (1972), pp. 365–88.

Sherborne, J.W., 'The English Navy: Shipping and Manpower, 1369–89', in A. Tuck (ed.), *War, Politics and Culture in Fourteenth-Century England* (London and Rio Grande, 1994), pp. 29–39.

Sherborne, J.W., 'The Battle of La Rochelle and the War at Sea, 1372–5', in A. Tuck (ed.), *War, Politics and Culture in Fourteenth-Century England* (London and Rio Grande, 1994), pp. 41–53.

Sherborne, J.W., 'The Cost of English Warfare with France in the Later Fourteenth Century', in A. Tuck (ed.), *War, Politics and Culture in Fourteenth-Century England* (London and Rio Grande, 1994), pp. 55–70.

Sherborne, J.W., 'English Barges and Balingers of the Late Fourteenth Century', in A. Tuck (ed.), *War, Politics and Culture in Fourteenth-Century England* (London and Rio Grande, 1994), pp. 71–6.

Simpkin, D., *The English Aristocracy at War: From the Welsh Wars of Edward I to the Battle of Bannockburn* (Woodbridge, 2008).

Simpkin, D., 'Robert de Fishlake: Soldier Profile', in *The Soldier in Later Medieval England*, <http://www.medievalsoldier.org/profiles/february2008.html>.

Simpkin, D., 'The Contribution of Essex Gentry to the Wars of Edward I and Edward II', *Essex Journal*, 46 (2011), pp. 7–14.

Sparvel-Bayly, J., 'Essex in Insurrection, 1381', *Transactions of the Essex Archaeological Society*, new series, 1 (1878), pp. 205–19.

Starr, C., *Medieval Mercenary: Sir John Hawkwood of Essex*, Essex Record Office Publication 153 (Chelmsford, 2007).

Starr, C., *Medieval Lawyer. Clement Spice of Essex*, Essex Society for Archaeology and History, Occasional Papers, new series, no. 2 (Colchester, 2014).

Strickland, M. and Hardy, R., *The Great Warbow: From Hastings to the Mary Rose* (Stroud, 2005).

Sumption, J., *Trial by Battle. The Hundred Years War, vol. I* (London, 1990).

Sumption, J., *Trial by Fire. The Hundred Years War, vol. II* (London, 1999).

Sumption, J., *Divided Houses. The Hundred Years War, vol. III* (London, 2009).

Sumption, J., *Cursed Kings. The Hundred Years War, vol. IV* (London, 2015).

Sweetinburgh, S., 'The Social Structure of New Romney as revealed in the 1381 Poll Tax Returns', *Archaeologia Cantiana*, 131 (2011), pp. 1–22.

Terrier de Loray, H. Ph., *Jean de Vienne, amiral de France, 1341–96* (Paris, 1877).

Thornton, C.C., 'St Osyth', in C.C. Thornton (ed.), *The Victoria history of the counties of England. A history of the county of Essex. Vol. 12* (forthcoming 2017/18).

Thrupp, S.L., *The Merchant Class of Medieval London 1300–1500* (Chicago, IL, 1948; reprinted with updated introduction, 1989).

Tipping, C., 'Cargo Handling and the Medieval Cog', *The Mariner's Mirror*, 80 (1994), pp. 3–15.

Tomkinson, A., 'Retinues at the Tournament of Dunstable, 1309', *English Historical Review*, 74 (1959), pp. 70–89.

Trexler, R., 'Follow the Flag. The Ciompi Revolt Seen from the Streets', *Bibliothèque d'Humanisme et Renaissance*, 46 (1984), pp. 357–92.

Tuck, A. (ed.), *War, Politics and Culture in Fourteenth-Century England* (London and Rio Grande, 1994).

Turner, H.L., *Town Defences in England and Wales* (London, 1971).

Wadge, R., *Arrowstorm* (Stroud, 2009).

Walker, S.K., *The Lancastrian Affinity 1361–1399* (Oxford, 1990).

Ward, J., *The De Bohun Charter of Saffron Walden* (Saffron Walden, 1986).

Ward, J., *The Essex Gentry and the County Community in the Fourteenth Century*, Studies in Essex History 2 (Chelmsford and Wivenhoe, 1991).

Ward, J., 'Sir John de Coggeshale: An Essex Knight of the Fourteenth Century', *Essex Archaeology and History*, 3rd series, 22 (1991), pp. 61–6.

Ward, J., 'Elizabeth de Burgh and Great Bardfield in the Fourteenth Century', in K. Neale (ed.), *Essex Heritage* (Oxford, 1992), pp. 47–60.

Ward, J., 'The Wheel of Fortune and the Bohun Family in the Early Fourteenth Century', *Essex Archaeology and History*, 3rd series, 39 (2008), pp. 162–71.

Weaver, L.T., *The Harwich Story* (Harwich, 1975).

Yearsley, I., *Hadleigh Past* (Chichester, 1998).

Theses

Fenwick, C.C., 'The English Poll Taxes of 1377, 1379 and 1381: A Critical Examination of the Returns', PhD thesis (London School of Economics, 1983).

Gibbs, S., 'The Service Patterns and Social-economic Status of English Archers, 1367–1417: The Evidence of the Muster Rolls and Poll Tax Returns', PhD thesis (University of Reading, 2016).

Jones, G., 'The Bohun Earls of Hereford and Essex, 1270–1322', MLitt thesis (University of Oxford, 1984).

Prescott, A.J., 'Judicial Records of the Rising of 1381', PhD thesis (London University, 1984).

Index

References to illustrations and tables are in italics. The name of the county is only given if the place concerned is outside Essex.